Italian Youth in International Context

T0387225

Italy is not a country for young people. Why? This book provides a unique and in-depth collection of empirical and theoretical material providing multiple answers to this question whilst investigating the living conditions of young people in Italy today.

By bringing together a variety of approaches and methods, the authors of this collection analyze Italian youth through the lenses of three dimensions: 'Activism, Participation and Citizenship', 'Work, Employment and Careers' and 'Moves, Transitions and Representations'. These dimensions are the analytical building blocks for challenging stereotypes and unveiling misinterpretations and taken-for-granted assumptions that portray young people in Italy as selfish, 'choosy', and unwilling to make sacrifices, commit and manage an independent life. These prejudices often underplay the role of constraints they are facing in the transition to adulthood.

Studying Italian youth, therefore, not only allows us to capture their peculiar characteristics but also to reflect more broadly on the conceptual toolbox we need in order to understand contemporary youth more generally. By doing so, the volume aims to contribute to international discussion on the youth condition in Europe.

Valentina Cuzzocrea is assistant professor (tenure track) in sociology at the University of Cagliari (Italy). In 2018, she co-edited with B.G. Bello the special issue 'Making space for youth in Contemporary Italian Studies' in *Journal of Modern Italian Studies*.

Barbara Giovanna Bello is postdoc in sociology of law at the University of Milan (Italy). She is a trainer in the area of human rights, lawyer and mediator. Her research interests cover intersectionality, antidiscrimination law, legislative effectiveness and youth. In 2018, she co-edited with Valentina Cuzzocrea the special issue 'Making space for youth in Contemporary Italian Studies' in *Journal of Modern Italian Studies*.

Yuri Kazepov is professor of international urban sociology and compared welfare systems at the University of Vienna (Austria). His fields of interest are urban governance, citizenship and urban quality of life and social policies in comparative perspective.

Youth, Young Adulthood and Society

Tracy Shildrick, *Newcastle University, UK*
John Goodwin, *University of Leicester, UK*
Henrietta O'Connor, *University of Leicester, UK*

The Youth, Young Adulthood and Society series approaches youth as a distinct area, bringing together social scientists from many disciplines to present cutting-edge research monographs and collections on young people in societies around the world today. The books present original, exciting research, with strongly theoretically- and empirically-grounded analysis, advancing the field of youth studies. Originally set up and edited by Andy Furlong, the series presents inter-disciplinary and truly international, comparative research monographs.

Youth in the Digital Age
Paradox, Promise, Predicament
Edited by Kate C. Tilleczek and Valerie M. Campbell

Modernization as Lived Experiences
Three Generations of Young Men and Women in China
Fengshu Liu

Italian Youth in International Context
Belonging, Constraints and Opportunities
Edited by Valentina Cuzzocrea, Barbara Giovanna Bello and Yuri Kazepov

Brazilian Youth
Global Trends, Local Perspectives
Edited by Cláudia Pereira

Complexities of Researching with Young People
Edited by Paulina Billett, Matt Hart and Dona Martin

For more information about this series, please visit https://www.routledge.com/Youth-Young-Adulthood-and-Society/book-series/YYAS

Italian Youth in International Context

Belonging, Constraints and Opportunities

Edited by
Valentina Cuzzocrea
Barbara Giovanna Bello
Yuri Kazepov

Routledge
Taylor & Francis Group

LONDON AND NEW YORK

First published 2020 by Routledge

2 Park Square, Milton Park, Abingdon, Oxon OX14 4RN
605 Third Avenue, New York, NY 10017

Routledge is an imprint of the Taylor & Francis Group, an informa business

First issued in paperback 2021

British Library Cataloguing-in-Publication Data
A catalogue record for this book is available from the British Library

Library of Congress Cataloging-in-Publication Data
Names: Cuzzocrea, Valentina, editor. | Bello, Barbara Giovanna, editor. | Kazepov, Yuri, editor.
Title: Italian youth in international context : belonging, constraints and opportunities / edited by Valentina Cuzzocrea, Barbara Giovanna Bello and Yuri Kazepov.
Description: Milton Park, Abingdon, Oxon ; New York, NY : Routledge, 2020. | Series: Youth, young adulthood and society | Includes bibliographical references and index.
Identifiers: LCCN 2019054833 (print) | LCCN 2019054834 (ebook) | ISBN 9781138488571 (hardback) | ISBN 9781351039949 (ebook)
Subjects: LCSH: Youth--Italy--Social conditions. | Youth--Political activity--Italy.
Classification: LCC HV799.I8 I83 2020 (print) | LCC HV799.I8 (ebook) | DDC 305.2350945--dc23
LC record available at https://lccn.loc.gov/2019054833
LC ebook record available at https://lccn.loc.gov/2019054834

ISBN: 978-1-138-48857-1 (hbk)
ISBN: 978-1-03-217269-9 (pbk)
DOI: 10.4324/9781351039949

Typeset in Times New Roman
by Lumina Datamatics Limited

Contents

Figures

Tables

Contributors

Massimiliano Andretta is associate professor at the Department of Political Science of the University of Pisa. His recent publications include: 'Protest in Italy in Times of Crisis: A Cross-Government Comparison' (in *South European Society and Politics*, 2018), and with D. della Porta *et al.*, *Legacy and Memory in Movements: Justice and Democracy in Southern Europe* (2018).

Cinzia Albanesi is associate professor of Community Psychology at the University of Bologna. She is a member of the Italian team of the project CATCH-EyoU and of the Board of the Italian Community Psychology Society (SPICO). Her research interests include youth active citizenship, participatory action research, community development, health promotion, service learning in higher education and university-community partnership.

Sonia Bertolini is associate professor at the University of Turin, where she teaches Sociology of Work. Her research interests concern youth labour market entry; female labour market participation; labour market flexibilization and transition to adult life; sociology of professions. She has published 'Giovani senza futuro? Insicurezza lavorativa e autonomia oggi in Italia' (2018). She is PI of the Italian team of European project 'Social Exclusion of Youth in Europe: Cumulative Disadvantage, Coping Strategies, Effective Policies and Transfer' (EXCEPT), funded by H2020.

Rossella Bozzon is a member of the ERC Starting Grant project SHARE – 'Seizing the Hybrid Areas of Work by Re-presenting Self-Employment'. Her research interests include welfare state and labour market transformations, non-standard employment relations, demographic dynamics, gender inequalities and quantitative methods.

Alessandro Cavalli taught as full professor in sociology at the University of Pavia. He has directed the journal *Il Mulino* and many research projects for the IARD Institute over several decades. He has been on the board of many national and international journals and published widely on youth in Italy and more recently on Europe and civic education in books and articles, as well as encyclopedia entries and textbooks.

Dalit Contini is associate professor in social statistics at the University of Turin. Her current research interests cover the area of educational inequalities and school systems, higher education choices and academic careers, school guidance, gender inequalities and impact evaluation of social policies. On these issues, she has published extensively in leading international journals like the *European Sociological Review, Social Science Research, Sociological Methods and Research, Economics of Education Review, Journal of Economic Behavior and Organization.*

Elvira Cicognani is professor of social and community psychology at the University of Bologna and coordinator of the CATCH-EyoU project. Her research interests concern the psychosocial factors and processes influencing civic and political engagement and participation, particularly among youth; interventions aimed at enhancing youth engagement and active citizenship; psychosocial factors in health behaviours and community health promotion interventions.

Federica Cugnata is assistant professor in statistics at the Faculty of Psychology (Vita-Salute San Raffaele University) and involved in the research activities at CUSSB (University Centre for Statistics for the Biomedical Sciences). She participated in numerous research projects across different fields, and her main research interests focus on statistical models for ordinal data, linear and nonlinear mixed-effect models and multivariate statistics.

Donatella della Porta is professor of political science, dean of the Institute for Humanities and the Social Sciences and director of the PD program in political science and sociology at the Scuola Normale Superiore in Florence. Recent publications are *Movement Parties in Times of Austerity* (Polity 2017), *Where Did the Revolution Go?* (Cambridge University Press, 2016); and *Social Movements in Times of Austerity* (Polity 2015).

Markieta Domecka is a sociologist and research fellow at the University of Southampton (UK), currently working on the WORKANDHOME project. She specializes in qualitative research methods, and she has worked in numerous projects on youth, gender, migration and (un)employment in UK, Poland and Italy.

Marianna Filandri is assistant professor (tenure track) in economic sociology at the University of Turin. Her research interests comprise social inequality, housing inequality, youth labour market early career and working poor. Her work has been published in the journals *European Societies, Journal of European Social Policy* and *Journal of Youth Studies.*

Anna Lavizzari is a postdoctoral fellow at the Department of Political and Social Sciences of the Scuola Normale Superiore and a research fellow at the Centre on Social Movement Studies (COSMOS). Her research interests include youth political participation, gender, and social movement studies. She is currently part of the EU-funded project EURYKA – Reinventing Democracy in Europe: Youth Doing Politics in Times of Increasing Inequalities.

Carmen Leccardi is professor of cultural sociology and director of the PhD program in Applied Sociology and Methodology of Social Research at the University of Milan-Bicocca. She is a past president of the European Sociological Association and has researched extensively in the field of youth, gender, time experiences and processes of cultural change. Her last book in English is *Youth, Space and Time. Agoras and Chronotopes in the Global City*, 2016 (Brill, edited with C. Feixa and P. Nilan).

Elisa Lello is a research fellow and adjunct professor in political sociology at the University of Urbino Carlo Bo. She has been involved in various research projects and has published mainly on youth and generational change; social movements and emerging forms of political engagement; territorial inequalities and their impact on electoral change; the transformations within political parties and the eruption of neo-populism.

Lara Maestripieri holds a PhD in sociology and social research. She is assistant professor (tenure track) in Economic Sociology at the Laboratory of Social Policies (DASTU/Polytechnic of Milan). She has been Marie Skłodowska-Curie fellow at the Institute of Government and Public Policies (IGOP) at the Universitat Autònoma de Barcelona (2017–2019). Her main interests of research are marginalized groups in labour markets (women and young people), social vulnerability and emerging professions.

Valentina Moiso is postdoctoral researcher in sociology at University of Turin. Her research interests include household finance and social vulnerability, innovation in money circuits, Islamic finance, mafia expansion and collusive relations. She has published in journals as *Stato e Mercato* and *Critique Internationale*, among others. Recently, she has contributed to the volume *The Making of Finance: Conventions, Devices and Regulation* (Routledge, 2018, edited by I. Chambost, M. Lenglet e Y. Tadjeddine).

Annalisa Murgia is associate professor at the Department of Social and Political Sciences of the University of Milan. Her research interests include the role of subjectivity in shaping individual biographies, paying specific attention to precariousness, gender and the emerging forms of collective organizing. She is the PI of the ERC Starting Grant project SHARE – 'Seizing the Hybrid Areas of Work by Re-presenting Self-Employment'.

Tiziana Nazio is tenured senior researcher at the University of Turin, affiliate fellow at Collegio Carlo Alberto and Marie Skłodowska-Curie Research Fellow at the Berlin Social Science Center (WZB), Berlin. Her research examines how family configurations and ties affect individuals' life courses. She published in the journals *European Sociological Review, European Journal of Population, Work, Employment & Society, Demographic Research* and *International Migration Review.*

Caterina Peroni is postdoc researcher at the National Research Council, working in the project 'ViVa – Monitoring, evaluation and analysis of interventions to prevent and combat violence against women'. Among her most recent publication is 'One step up and two steps back? The Italian debate on secularization, heteronormativity and LGBTQ citizenship', in *Social Compass* (2018, with E. Bellè and E. Rapetti).

Ken Roberts is emeritus professor of sociology at the University of Liverpool and has long researched youth, leisure and class. His books include *Surviving Post-Communism: Young People in the Former Soviet Union* (2000), *Youth in Transition: Eastern Europe and in the West* (2009), *Class in Contemporary Britain* (2011), *Sociology: An Introduction* (2012), *The Business of Leisure* (2016) and *Social Theory, Sport, Leisure* (2016).

Monica Santoro is associate professor in sociology at the University of Milan (Italy). Her research interests include family and demographic changes, youth condition and emigration. She is author of 'Conoscere la famiglia e i suoi cambiamenti' (Carocci, 2013) and of articles on family formation in journals such as *Families, Relationships and Societies* and *International Review of Sociology.*

Andrea Scagni is associate professor in statistics at the University of Turin, where he also teaches data analysis and simulation methods. His recent research activities have combined the practical expertise on university performance evaluation with the analysis of social inequalities in schooling careers. In 2018, he published – with Contini and Cugnata – 'Social selection in higher education. Enrolment, dropout and timely degree attainment in Italy' in the journal *Higher Education.*

Antonella Spanò is professor of sociology at the University of Naples Federico II. Her main areas of research are social exclusion, unemployment and migration, with a particular focus on youth, gender and the Italian Southern context. She recently published 'Studiare i giovani in un mondo che cambia. Concetti, temi e prospettive negli Youth Studies' (2018).

Bruna Zani is professor of social and community psychology at the University of Bologna, and member of the Executive Council of EFPA (European Federation of Psychologists Associations). She is a member of the Italian team of the project CATCH-EyoU. Her main research interests are risk behaviours in adolescence, civic engagement and political participation in adolescents and young people, service-learning methodology in higher education and evaluation of community interventions on health promotion, theatre and mental health.

Acknowledgements

We are grateful for collaboration of the authors in this collection and, indirectly, to the research informants who have made possible to substantiate complex arguments throughout the chapters. Dr Emma Hewitt at 'Word bee' and Nina Goergen at the University of Vienna have helped enormously in the editorial process. We would like to thank for extra patience and precious assistance Emily Briggs and Lakshita Joshi at Routledge, as well as the editors of the series Youth and Young Adulthood. We feel ultimately in debt with the late Andy Furlong, for encouragement in pursuing this project when it was in its very early stages.

Introduction

Italian youth in context – an analysis through multiple dimensions

Valentina Cuzzocrea, Barbara Giovanna Bello and Yuri Kazepov

1 Introduction

Italy is not a country for young people. This book provides a unique and in-depth collection of empirical and theoretical material that leads to this preposition, investigating the living conditions of young people in today's Italy. We aim to discuss the categories commonly used to depict youth in Italy, whilst taking into account the multifaceted and complex reality in which they have to cope in the present, as well as imagine and plan their future. In particular, the volume considers the coexistence of specific characteristics of the Italian scenario and more recent trends characterizing late capitalist societies. Amongst others, these include the compelling spread of neoliberal-inspired regulations, the impoverishment of the middle classes and heightening conditions of vulnerability and uncertainty. Through this book, we aim to disentangle the impact of global trends on Italian youth and discuss the specific configurations that are produced within this context.

Within the existing international research on Italian youth, contributions have been published by prominent Italian scholars mostly in articles and edited volumes. The themes that have been addressed relate to specific aspects of youth, from culture (for instance, see Varriale, 2016) to political cultures (Mammone and Veltri, 2010; Cento Bull, 2000; Garau, 2015) or school-to-work transitions (Pastore, 2017) and youth unemployment (Leonardi and Pica, 2015). However, to date there has been no single edited collection targeting Italian youth *per se*. In addition, the Italian case tends to feature extensively within comparative research, in contrast to other countries, perhaps increasingly so due to the more collaborative projects being pursued across Europe in recent years. Yet, we strongly believe that a specific focus on the multiple aspects of the conditions faced by young Italians is an important add-on to the existing international scholarships in the field.

In order to complete such a project, we invited authors to embed debates regarding young people in Italy within the international literature, with the aim of offering a precise account of the internal mechanisms that have so far seldom circulated outside Italy. The result is a composite and unprecedented collection, in terms of issues covered, methods and theories used. To account for our approach, the structure of this introductory chapter is threefold: first, we introduce the rationale of this book project, its ambitions, and whence it derives, discussing the main issues that guided us in composing the collection and in developing the main analytical frame of reference. Second, we describe the book's tri-partite structure. In doing so, we present the structural contexts in which youth in Italy live and act and how they resonate – and differ – from other cases in Europe. Third, we present our overarching interpretations of the youth condition in Italy that emerged through the chapters and propose a debate that goes beyond the national boundaries. Although this interpretation is emerging from an insider's perspective, we are confident that it will link to international debates in a structured way.

2 Framework of reference for this book

Cavalli and Leccardi (2013) described youth studies in Italy as being composed of four seasons. The first season comprises of studies regarding those who were young in the fifties; the second season is concerned with youth up to the mid-sixties, characterized by political militancy; the third season is marked by widespread reflux to private life and a refusal of politics; and finally, the fourth season is concerned with issues relating to the transition to adulthood. More recently, this fourth season seems to have developed into some sort of fragmented – if not polarized – scenario, either accusing young people, infantilizing them or seeing them as victims of a system that structurally excludes them (see Visentin's discussion, 2018). In a recent interview, Leccardi et al. (2018) discussed how this intersects with studies of time in scholarly research. At the substantive and conceptual level, this also includes attention to the position of youth within the life-course as a 'structuring' element. At the level of public opinion, the debate is deeply entrenched and at times distorted by (mis)representations and/or accusations from the media and politicians who offload societal responsibility to individualized caricatures. To these points, sociologists have often answered by emphasizing the resourcefulness of young people, and how in the end they are able to 'surf' contingencies which are adverse to them (Colombo et al., 2018, see also Colombo and Rebughini, 2019; Bertolini et al., 2019; Leccardi, 2005; Cuzzocrea, 2012), or in Domaneschi's words (2019), they are 'sur-reflexive'. This interpretation is not only applicable to the Italian case. It is, in fact, tied to a wider discourse on 'choice biographies' and individualization, which has influenced several strands of social research. At the policy level, this has resulted into an emphasis on so-called activation policies. The idea of the 'entrepreneurial self' (Kelly, 2006) is popular within the international scenario and our concern is to shed light on how Italian youth studies tie in with these debates. In fact, some characteristics have become paradigmatic in the Italian case. For instance, it is not by chance that the famous label of 'young adults' – coined in relation to the findings of a comparative European project (EGRIS, 2001) – has been widely applied in relation in the

Italian case. Now a popular literature genre, as well as the name of an American movie (Reitman, 2011), and despite in fact being an oxymoron, the term is also an established label in youth studies, indicating a specific cohort experiencing an extreme delay in the transition into adulthood. Various other expressions have also been used simultaneously, which not only capture a sense of prolongation of transitions but also a mixture between lifestyles that are characteristic of different life stages, as for instance, 'adultescente' or 'kidadult', grasping the structural characteristics of the *problematique* in Italy and in the south European context. Along this line, there is also a specifically Italian expression 'long family' (Scabini and Donati, 1988), which refers to the prolonged cohabitation of grown-up children with their parents.

Generally, young people are characterized as being unable or unwilling to act independently. In particular, their dependency is depicted as being structured around the family, serving as an all-solving institution, compensating for functions that in other contexts are absorbed by the welfare state. It has been noted that this Italian characteristic is shared by other southern European countries (Andreotti et al., 2001; Naldini, 2003; Martin, 2015). We do not deny the importance that the family role plays elsewhere. For instance, in a 1992 book on the conditions of youth in the UK, Jones and Wallace (1992: 68) assume that despite the youth's problems, they are going to be backed up by their families, and youth itself is defined as 'a process of definition and redefinition, a *negotiation enacted between young people and their families*, their peers and the institutions of the wider societies' (1992: 4, our emphasis). These definitions – made in relation to the context of another country and before the neoliberal agenda spread across Europe – highlight the importance of qualifying the Italian case and embedding it within wider debates, thus pinpointing its specificities.

Whilst young people throughout the rest of Europe are said to become adults by leaving their parents' home, in Italy their transition to adulthood occurs most often *within* the family, that is, while still living within the parents' home (Cicchelli and Galland, 2009). According to this interpretation, therefore, the issue is not that they do not become adults, as it may seem, but that they become adults through *their own modalities* and following *their own paths*. This is obviously a point in which both cultural aspects of the transition and more structural ones converge in determining what is normally referred to as 'the delay of the transition' (for Italy see: Pastore, 2017; Barbieri et al., 2015; Mauceri and Valentini, 2010). This prolongation or postponing of adulthood and the conditions through which it has changed over time have been studied in abundance through quantitative methods. In general, this seems to be a distinctive feature of Italian youth, to be considered in parallel with the above-mentioned capacity to be creative in inventing solutions.

2.1 Doing research on young people in Italy

Over the past decades, the characteristics of Italian youth we have briefly previously described have been in the spotlight mainly thanks to reports by the

IARD Institute, which carried out studies entitled 'Reports on the condition of Italian youth' every four years, throughout six editions. Some of the themes traditionally explored in these reports are friendship, gender dynamics, family formation, access to the labour market and religion. Also aiming to be nationally representative, recent years have seen the *Toniolo Institute*, another research centre based in Milan, taking onboard *the facto* – the production of reports, books and various papers addressing the youth condition in Italy. One of the latest pieces was devoted to 'Generation Z', that is, the current generation of young people (Alfieri et al., 2018). In addition, there are a number of studies that focus on the territorial realities within Italy, often at a regional level. However, given the massive disparity in socio-economic conditions across the country, in addition to the well-known south–north divide, they risk being of little help in attempting to construct a national scenario.

Overall, these reports tend to reproduce and sustain attention on the usual markers of adulthood, including both those that belong to both the private and the public sphere: completing one's educational path, finding a relatively stable job, leaving the parental home and constituting a new family, and eventually having children. There is an underlying consensus that the transition to adulthood is accomplished when all, or the majority, of those markers have been met. Such a conception of youth sees youth as a 'transitional subject', or as a 'subject in process' (Talburt and Lesko, 2012: 3), from a condition of incompleteness and dependency to one of independence. As such, 'transition' is still defended as the 'lead paradigm for the sociology of youth' (see for instance Roberts, 2018).

Within scholarly literature, recent findings have started to pave the way for new interpretations, following the identification of new markers, or, alternatively, the reconsideration of old ones, and yet they still refer to this established framework. For instance, short-term mobility is increasingly seen as an important turning point in youth biographies (Cairns, 2014; Krzaklewska, 2019; Cuzzocrea and Mandich, 2016). It is once such changes have been made that important life decisions finally seem to be enacted, even in a framework of prolongation of youth and generalized delay of transition. This recent, broad attention on critically re-discussing markers is occurring across European countries and has justified a plethora of comparative studies. Scholz and Rennig (2019), for instance, compare and contrast young people belonging to the so-called 'Generation Z' in Europe (the 'latest' generation of young people), with a view to identifying the characteristics that define them. There is still much to be unveiled about this generation lives, including how they live and interpret the world around them. For instance, a comparative effort is of increasing importance with regard to how they experience the world through social media. Young people across various European countries enjoy different structural conditions of life and largely (or in part), on the basis of this, they reach adulthood at different paces and through different means.

Admittedly, in Italy young people suffer from particularly adverse socio-economic conditions. With a rate of 42.7% youth unemployment and 24.6%

of NEETs (Eurostat, 2019; Sergi et al., 2018), Italy ranks first in Europe for these measures, with Greece and Spain closely behind. These countries are all similarly affected by the inadequacy of what Ferrera calls the 'Southern model of welfare system' (Ferrera, 1996), referring to the well-known model of social welfare identified by Esping-Andersen (1990, 1999). This is characterized by low levels of welfare provision, poor redistributive policies and a highly unequal social structure, and relies on the family as one of the main forms of support (Andreotti et al., 2001; Kazepov, 2008). A high number of NEETs could be seen as a proxy of the marginality of young people within the labour market (Quintini and Martin, 2006).

Specifically with regard to youth studies, British sociologist Ken Roberts (2009) used the concept of 'opportunity structure' to refer to the system of interrelationship between family background, education, labour market processes and employers' recruitment practices. His approach balances structure and agency. Considering class influences in constructing a career in the UK, Roberts argues that 'it has always been possible for some individuals, exercising individual agency, to break out from the main career routes, but the numbers able to break into specific destinations have always been governed and limited by the number of the relevant positions that are available' (2009: 356). Raffe (2008) constructed a typology of youth transition regimes, which takes into consideration the educational system as well as the vocational system. In a recent assessment, Roberts (2018) suggests that the transition paradigm continue to be used, but more extensively, expanding from a focus on integration in the labour market only to other spheres of life. We are in favour of this approach and propose that our collection of essays is read in this vein, considering the integration of several domains, which are relevant to young people as constitutive analytical elements of youth opportunity structures.

An effort of this kind could also prevent further distortions. In studying young people in Italy, we see that some issues have become central at the risk of obscuring others that are also very important. For instance, a singular, widespread focus on NEETs, on which there is a wealth of studies (e.g. Sergi et al., 2018; Rosina, 2015), might distract from the troubles that the current generation of young people working in Italy today will likely encounter later in life due to the inadequate nature of retirement benefits that will be available to those who are young today. Therefore, the 'quality' of working conditions and benefits being offered to young people remain important to us, as well as issues pertaining to the high youth unemployment rate.

This structurally adverse situation is contrasted with a public perception that sometimes stresses the unwillingness of young people in Italy to grow up. Such stereotypes construct them as unresponsive to sacrifices and commitment (Bello and Cuzzocrea, 2018) and as 'not mature enough' (Pitti, 2017). These easily turn into prejudices that disregard the constraints to which they are confronted, and do not help their self-esteem or their engagement with public life. Whatever their merits or failings, such negative public representations of youth need to be updated, whilst also making a few changes in the policy scenario. *Strictu sensu,* the scenario of opportunities available to young people, have changed substantially in Italy throughout the last decade due to a series of reforms introduced by various governments. Obviously, we do not have the space here to provide an exhaustive overview of all these changes but will mention just few of the most important ones in relation to young people.

2.2 The recent reform scenario in Italy

Under the leadership of the centre-left government (February 2014–December 2016) led by Matteo Renzi – the youngest prime minister Italy has ever had – several major reforms were approved. Of these, the *Buona Scuola* ('the good school', Law 107/2015) is of note. This is a complex reform which foresees several measures targeting the whole teaching-learning process and its governance. The reform increased schools' autonomy and flexibility, with the headteacher playing a leading (and strongly contested) role in hiring, evaluating, managing and rewarding teachers. Some of the other changes include the introduction of compulsory intervals in the labour market for each upper secondary school pupil, tax relief for those attending private, publicly recognized schools and a scheme that provided stable contracts for about 100,000 teachers, who had worked under precarious conditions that far. Before the bill was approved, fierce debate raged for several months amongst schools, trade unions, associations and politicians. A key point of the discussion was whether the reform was putting too much responsibility on schools without providing the necessary support for teachers and the other professionals involved. Critics also feared that there was a risk of fostering 'Matthew effects' (Merton, 1968), in other words benefitting students that were already well-off and therefore widening the gap between these and less-privileged ones. The law entered into force on 31 May 2017.

Another major reform initiated under the Renzi government was the *Jobs Act*, which was aimed to reduce both unemployment and the mass of short-term and temporary contracts that had proliferated during the preceding decades. In fact, the changing work arrangements can be traced back to the 'Pacchetto Treu' (Law 196/1997) when first elements of flexibilization of labour market regulation were introduced in Italy. Renzi's Jobs Act replaced a plethora of temporary contracts with a single, uniform contract, providing gradually increasing job protection over three years, ultimately leading to a permanent contract. The Jobs Act was presented in 2014 and 2015 as a major reform of the labour market, undermining the core of the Workers' Statute (1970) with its high protection of employment (although only of certain kinds of employment). Critics have argued that such changes have polarized 'old' and 'new' employees, therefore failing to simplify Italy's labour system or address the precarious conditions faced by some sectors of the workforce. Rather, it is argued that recent reforms have actually accentuated the process of the precarization.

Renzi's government also saw through the first steps in implementing the *Youth Guarantee*, a supranational measure launched by the European Council in 2013 and regulated in Italy through a National Implementation Plan (Law Decree of 28 June 2013). The measure has the explicit goal of fostering of an 'active', 'innovative' and 'qualified' workforce. In the Italian case, the Youth Guarantee attempts to address the gap between education and work experience, which is considered the primary cause of the exclusion of youth from employment. The measures and resources that were introduced aimed to reintegrate the young person into either the education system or the labour market, with a view to minimizing the associated 'social risk'. Unfortunately, we do not have the space to discuss the impact and implementation of this measure in detail; however, it is interesting to note that whilst the measure was designed to target young people under the age of 25, in reality it tends to reach young people under the age of 29. This age discrepancy highlights the magnitude of extended precariousness in which young Italians are living.

Similar to the Youth Guarantee, there is also the 'Reddito di Cittadinanza' (Citizens' income), which aims to integrate socially excluded people into the labour market through activation measures. This highly contested measure, introduced for the first time in Italy, guarantees a basic income to all, provided that they sign an 'Agreement for work' and an 'Agreement for social inclusion' (Law 26, 28 March 2019). It is one of the flagship measures of the Five Star Movement, realized under the first Conte Government (June 2018–September 2019) in order to tackle poverty, inequality and social exclusion. Though not specifically designed for young people, it has the potential to affect this group like no other measure before because for the first time access to benefits and services are guaranteed even for those who do not have an employment record.

These reforms define the historical landscape within which the new generation of young people grow up. Despite the intention of expanding young people's inclusion in welfare redistributory measures, the extent to which these reforms will actually impact positively on the life of young people remains to be seen, especially considering the observation that further flexibilization and precariousness are in fact produced. Moreover, the resulting 'opportunity structures' seem to reinforce rather than counteract the social fragmentation and differentiation between privileged and disadvantaged youth. Many research projects have been undertaken to evaluate of the impact of these reforms (Ballarino et al., 2014; Barbieri and Scherer, 2009; Barone and Ruggera, 2015), the findings of which broadly confirm the scenario we have outlined above.

In addition to these, there have been many debates surrounding access to citizenship – definitely a contentious topic. According to Garau (2015), Italy is currently facing the same challenges that traditional receiving countries encountered decades earlier. However, the fact that it was late to join other hosting countries and that the numbers of migrants population remained below the European average for decades have heavily influenced the debate on migration as well as the nature of migration policies put forward by the various governments (Garau, 2015:8). In this regard, the progressive normalization of anti-migrant discourses under the motto 'prima gli italiani' (namely, 'Italians first') has played a huge part throughout the previous governments, in line with extremization and anti-migration policies in other European countries.

In Italy, restrictive measures have been a huge obstacle for many young people belonging to second generations, preventing them for many decades to have a fully-fledged presence on the political scene, the economic life and in civil society at large. In fact, the Italian law on citizenship (Law 5 February 1992, n. 91) is based on the principle of *ius sanguinis*, meaning that newborn children take the citizenship of their parents. It may make a huge difference for those children of migrants who, despite being born and raised in Italy, going to Italian schools and spending their whole life with Italian peers, are not being given access to the same opportunities as siblings of national Italians (e.g. they cannot take part to elections if they do not acquire the Italian citizenship when they turn 18), and in any case they have to wait until they turn 18 to start the procedure of acquisition of citizenship. Only as late as in 2013, during the Letta government, some amendments were passed to ease the way to the acquisition of the Italian citizenship for these young people, mainly by simplifying the requirements to proof legal residence in the country, which used to be a heavy burden on their shoulders (Law 98/2013) (Bello, 2018). Right after, during the Renzi government (2014–2016), an attempt to reverse the importance of the *ius soli* over the *ius sanguinis* was initiated, but the law was not passed in the end.

With an awareness of this potential line of segregation concerning young people of immigrant origin, in this book we refer to all young people living in Italy. The issue of acquiring citizenship has specific traits bounded by Italian legislation and the overall political climate; however, such matters have become a common preoccupation, with increasing intolerance and anti-immigration feelings, reaching a climax (the so-called 'immigrants crisis') in relation to the issue of the Italian southern border as an immediate entrance to the European Union territory for those coming from Africa. This is hardly surprising given that similar tensions are arising throughout Europe, a clear example of which can be seen in relation to Brexit in the UK. Considering the overall conditions, we believe in an integrated view of the different elements that constitute 'opportunity structures' (in Roberts's terms, 2009) that will help us in reading and interpreting young people's conditions.

3 Why this edited volume?

One important factor that motivated us to publish this collection is the state of existing scholarship on youth in contemporary Italy. It is a fragmented field of study, prone to hybridization and cross-disciplinary confrontation. This situation reflects the traditional divisions in theoretical and methodological approaches in the study of the youth condition. From a research point of view, for instance, we have the counterposition between a laic and a confessional (mainly Catholic inspired) tradition. From a methodological point of view, we have the divide between qualitative and quantitative methods, with some mix methods approach, attempting to bridge the divide. On top of this, disciplinary boundaries and the control of intradisciplinary scientific production – which is at the basis of local and national scholarly evaluation in Italy – strongly conflict with the very idea of open debate. As a result, mainstream youth-related policies or measures seldom engage with the findings of research conducted on the very same topics. Consequently, whilst strong research traditions, such as studies on youth and temporalities, have proven to be productive and tackle important issues at length, for instance, the prolongation of the transitions to adulthood (see for instance Leccardi et al., 2018 for a review), the impact of these contributions may have been diminished by a debate collapsed within the national scenario. Moreover, at times, language barriers may also hinder the spread of excellent research conducted within Italy.

Another important factor is the absence of meaningful national discussion of youth policies and of the study of youth. Such a forum for discussion could contribute to the homogenization of terminology, fostering an interest in young people. Indeed, Italy does not have a national youth law. Although youth are protected by the Italian constitution (art. 31), regions have legislative and executive powers on youth matters, resulting in a territorially fragmented and unbalanced landscape of rights and duties. The excellent youth work conducted in some regions is unlikely to produce results in other regions or spread transversally.

Before describing the structure of the volume, it is worth mentioning that this book is the second step in a wider project that started with the publication of the special issue 'Making space for youth in Italian studies' in the international *Journal of Modern Italian Studies*, edited in 2018 by two of the editors of this collection (Bello and Cuzzocrea), and where the third editor of this collection (Kazepov) contributed with a co-authored article. Going deeper into that interdisciplinary investigation, and including more contributors, this collection allows us to unpack three dimensions, which we present in the following section. Authors have engaged with the international debates, resulting in the first collection of its kind specifically about Italian youth, and the book aims also at contributing both to the development of a less fragmented field of youth studies in Italy, and to the international debate on 'youth studies' more generally.

4 Structure of the book: three dimensions as analytical lenses to understand Italian youth

Bringing together a variety of approaches and methods, the authors of this collection analyse Italian youth through the lenses of three dimensions: (1) activism, participation and citizenship; (2) work, employment and careers; and (3) moves, transitions and representations. These dimensions are the analytical building blocks for challenging stereotypes and unveiling misinterpretations and taken-for-granted assumptions that portray young people in Italy as selfish, 'choosy', unwilling to make sacrifices, or to commit and manage an independent life. These prejudices often underplay the role of the constraints they are facing in the transition to adulthood. By unveiling them, we aim to better understand the challenges and resources of young people in Italy (and beyond).

The first section of this volume, entitled 'Activism, participation and citizenship', is devoted to exploring a variety of forms of youth engagement in public life. Given the difficulties young people face in making a living and obtaining decent employment, this dimension is of utmost importance to understanding their living conditions in the country today. It also helps us in framing their potential and willingness for action. By investigating these forms of participation, we can see how young people's low formal participation – which is usually taken as a proxy for disengagement – is counterbalanced by 'other' forms of participation. An interest in non-formal participation is growing across Europe (see for instance Pickard and Bessant, 2015; Fraser, 2010). This section includes debates on factors that can lead young people to exclusion (e.g. lack of Italian citizenship, a specific sexual orientation and gender identity). Bearing in mind that Italy is a country marked by a strong presence of the Catholic Church and the resurgence of control over bodies by some right-oriented politicians, these aspects are worth keeping in mind of as they are likely to affect decisions and choices.

The chapters in this section of the volume discuss the ways in which youth try to organize themselves through conventional and non-conventional patterns of political participation. The multitude of options contributes to challenging the stereotypes that see youth in Italy as disengaged and taking a distance from the political sphere and seeking refuge in the private realm. This mainstream image was called 'reflux' (*riflusso*) – especially in the 80s – and became hard to correct (Galli della Loggia, 1980).

The chapter entitled 'Young people and politics in Italy in a time of populism' by Elisa Lello sheds light on engagement amongst young people in Italy who have withdrawn from mainstream politics. According to Lello's findings, young people react in different ways to their slightly older counterparts (whom the author refers to as the 'in-between cohort') and seem to be in favour of a technocratic kind of politics. This difference is said to be due to the differing political, economic and cultural environments in which they have been socialized. By disentangling these contextual dimensions, this chapter shows how comparing and contrasting two different generations of young people may be an effective way of investigating both changes in certain contexts and generational changes. Massimiliano Andretta and Donatella della Porta, in their chapter 'When Millennials protest: youth activism in Italy' provide a complementary perspective to the one described by Lello. They show that despite the challenges they face, young people do in fact engage in politics through what Nancy Fraser would call 'non-conventional' forms of participation. Drawing on the extensive international expertise of the authors, this chapter offers a snapshot of youth participation and will be useful to readers who need a compass in this field. One interesting aspect is how, though anti-austerity mobilizations in Italy have not originated from young people as they have in other countries (e.g. Spain), they have indeed become engaged in these kinds of protests from a certain point onwards. Drawing on quantitative data, the authors were able to explore how young citizens overcame barriers of marginalization, network and develop collective identities. It would be interesting to see how developments, inside and outside of Italy, are resonating in Italy, especially in the light of the spreading environmental movement inspired by the Swedish activist Greta Thunberg, which has characterized itself from the beginning as a youth movement – acting, for instance, through school strikes.

Albanesi, Cicognani, and Zani's chapter, entitled 'Discourses and practices of citizenship among young people of different ethnic background living in Italy', chimes with all other chapters in the collection in that it delves into the lives of young people of different ethnic backgrounds, expanding on how they construct their representation of citizenship in Italy. Viewed with a social psychology lens, the authors show that the notion of citizenship is not straightforward but embedded within a broader social, cultural, political, economic and historical context, which goes beyond Marshall's conception of it (Marshall, 1964), based on civil, political and social rights. In fact, the five dimensions that are identified (legal or admittance, instrumental, belonging, everyday practices and participatory) mirror concrete strategies that young people use to deal with their marginalized status in the Italian context. Lastly, Anna Lavizzari's chapter 'Strategy, performance and gender: an interactionist understanding of young activists within the Italian LGTB movement and the Catholic countermovement' touches upon the changing Italian religious and sociopolitical context through the lenses of young individual activists within the LGBT movement and the Catholic countermovement. It shows how, through non-conventional political participation, youth in Italy contribute to shaping the current debate on gender equality and sexual citizenship.

In the second section, 'Work, employment and careers', we address the challenges encountered by youth when trying to access the labour market and obtain a relatively stable position, the scarcity of which is said to have effects not only on the short-term, but also on the medium term. In assessing the concept of precarity at the international level, Alberti et al. (2018) disagree with the famous standing by Standing (2011), which assert that a 'class' of precariat can be identified. They state that this perspective is problematic since, focusing on the idea of one particular segment of population, it is not enough to analyse how global transformations transversally pertain post-work society. Indeed, these authors propose developing the concept of 'precarization as a process', in which both objective conditions and subjective experiences are integrated, whilst shedding light on drivers, patterns and forms of precarization. This reframing aims to capture situations of precarization across contexts. The authors explicitly refer to the Italian case, together with the French one, in the context of protest within the urban service sector in the early 2000s

(Alberti et al., 2018: 448). Such arguments can help us better understand the conditions that young adults face today in Italy. The section devoted to the labour market invites a reflection of this kind.

The chapter by Lara Maestripieri deals with the 'social investment challenge', specifically looking at policies affecting young Italians and their impact. The underlying principle is the principle that sustainable economic growth can be achieved through social and educational policies aimed at investing in the younger generations. The chapter deals with an apparent paradox: despite the decreasing number of young people in Italy due to demographic changes – the opportunities available to them to fulfil their aspirations also decrease, putting them in a condition of multilayered marginality – a phenomenon that Caltabiano and Rosina (2018) have called 'dejuvenation'. Moreover, at the same time as they experience growing difficulty in entering the labour market, once they are employed they are more likely to be overqualified and take lower quality jobs, characterized by a higher degree of destandardization. The analysis is conducted by Maestripieri on the basis of two recent policy reforms (apprenticeships in Higher Education and Youth Guarantee) and show the potential impacts that go beyond the immediate implementation of these policies.

In their chapter 'The synchrony of temporary young workers: employment discontinuity, income discontinuity, and new social inequalities in Italy', Bertolini and Moiso discuss young people's first steps into the labour market, focusing on employment and income discontinuity, which tend to overlap in the Italian case. This happens to precarious workers, despite possessing various levels of knowledge and specialization, and in ways that differ from other European countries. The chapter therefore depicts an Italian specificity, determining what the authors call new types of 'social areas at risk'. They discuss the strategies enacted by young people in such circumstances, encompassing the micro and macro level, and discussing housing orientation. In the light of the new policy guaranteeing citizens a basic income, it will be crucial to see if and how this equilibrium will be revisited. We therefore envisage subsequent studies to develop this line of research, in order to see if the measure has had an impact on youth disadvantage.

The chapter by Filandri and Nazio 'Young graduates' access to the labour market: cumulative or trade-off effects between occupational level, contracts and wages' also has precarity at its core, although from a different and more specific perspective, with its focus on the relationship between occupational level, contracts and wages among young graduates in Italy. Of all European countries, Italy is characterized as having one of the highest degrees of uncertainty in terms of career entrance, coupled with high rates of youth unemployment and non-standard jobs and a very low level of state support for the unemployed. Within this institutional framework, starting a career with a job that is in line with one's educational credentials may help offset the risk of entering into the 'bad jobs' trap, where an initial disadvantage in the labour market may have lasting, detrimental effects on long-term employment outcomes, such as employment prospects, wages and upward job mobility. The strategies implemented in these circumstances are at the core of the chapter. Against many studies across the EU investigating similar mechanisms, in the Italian case, it is found that the family background contributes to the stratification of the employment strategies pursued by young people.

The last chapter in this section, entitled 'When age is academically constructed: the endless status of "young researchers" in Italy', identifies the characteristics of constructing an academic career in Italy, in two different areas of study (science technology engineering mathematics [STEM], and social sciences and humanities [SSH]). This chapter takes a different perspective from the preceding chapters, putting a focus on the social construction of 'youth' while constructing a career. These are analysed to discuss how differences are played out in the two scientific domains analysed. The authors of this chapter – Rossella Bozzon, Annalisa Murgia and Caterina Peroni – draw on qualitative material to explain the different meanings attributed to age, both at the institutional level and in the everyday life of two academic departments, taken here as organizational contexts. The broader structural context in which these dynamics develop is the season of reforms in Italian academia, which was launched with the aim of rejuvenating the universities' staff, which have changed profoundly since the Gelmini Reform in 2010. The chapter takes account of these background changes, whilst also giving some insights on the construction of an early career in relation to cultural environments.

Looking at discourses, the notion of youth has a strong potential in regulating social life (Ostrowicka, 2019). Therefore, the third section of the book deals with 'Moves, transitions and representations'. This is a heterogeneous section that tackles the framework of transitions to adulthood in differing ways. In the first chapter of this section, entitled 'Young Italians: individualization, uncertainty and reconquesting the future', Carmen Leccardi talks about how we see a contraction of the temporal horizon and the way in which this affects the experiences of young people. The chapter also examines the concepts of individualization and uncertainty in a context of social acceleration. Young people are expected to devote their energies to construct their own biographies, and the chapter details the kinds of coping strategies that they employ, which are highly complex – thus suggesting high competences and reflexivity. Leccardi suggests that 'migration' should be seen as one such strategy, and indeed this has become a growing area of research within the field of youth transitions. Within this section, the concept of 'moving' refers to both the geographical and representational sense. The two meanings may converge, as youth literature has started to indicate recently: by moving, young people see changes as possible in their lives (Cuzzocrea and Mandich, 2016).

In the chapter 'Pathways toward adulthood in times of crisis: reflexivity, resources and agency among young Neapolitan' by Antonella Spanò and Markieta Domecka, they specifically focus on the case of young Neapolitans. Whilst the theoretical framework used is very similar to Leccardi's, revolving around the concept of reflexivity in planning a biography, the case study taken in this chapter is one that leads us to consider a major divide between the north and south of the country, and in particular the specific conditions of an area, such as Naples. Therefore, it allows us to reflect on specific lines of class inequalities, and the possibility of agency, which is affected by the amount of available resources. As an example, four cases are discussed in depth.

The divide between north and south is taken forward also in the chapter 'From South to North: internal student migration in Italy' by Dalit Contini, Federica Cugnata and Andrea Scagni. The authors provide a comprehensive picture of the students' and graduates' mobility flows in Italy using data of two cross-sectional national-level surveys carried out by the Italian Statistical Institute (ISTAT), the Survey on Upper Secondary Graduates and the Survey on University Graduates. The internal mobility of southern students to northern regions and their migratory behaviour after graduation can be seen as a kind of brain drain. The problem is that internal migration (usually from south to north) does not contemplate returns. There is also the issue of overseas mobility, which has a serious impact on the resources available within Italy in the medium and long term.

In the final chapter 'Becoming an adult in the new millennium: how the transition to adulthood has changed' by Monica Santoro, the transition into adulthood for young Italians is presented through the results of two qualitative studies, carried out in 2003 and 2013, respectively. The chapter highlights how, in 2003, participants generally lived with their parents and were experiencing uncertainty in the labour market. In contrast, the participants in 2013 showed greater capacity to plan for their future and conveyed reasonable confidence in their possibilities. While the two results are not directly comparable, it is striking that the condition of uncertainty did not seem to undermine the projects or decisions of young people in the latter research. In both studies, social and cultural capital were important resources in defining transitional paths. The chapter shows that throughout the decade, youth conditions underwent deep change, providing some hints on the directions of change. The chapter also confirms – as do all of the chapters – that the capacity to adapt is revealed as key in the transition processes.

5 Conclusions

Since the global economic crisis of 2008, researchers interested in youth have begun investigating the effects upon young people, in particular with regard to the austerity measures that were subsequently implemented. It makes sense to ask similar questions specifically in relation to the Italian case. However, we do not provide definitive answers throughout this volume; rather, we offer the tools that can help us to better understand the conditions within which young people develop coping strategies. We think that the Italian specificities are better understood when a number of relevant dimensions are considered together, and that the importance of each cannot be properly understood without considering them within this wider context. Such factors include the role of the family, the position of young people within the labour market and their experiences of work, and wider issues of identity, citizenship and participation. In this sense, we fully agree with the position of Roberts (2018), who suggests a more integrated approach in order to assist us in identifying the 'transition regime' (Raffe, 2008) that characterizes the Italian case.

Reflecting on how conditions have worsened, with opportunities becoming even more limited further still for some young people whilst extending them for others, it may be especially useful to reflect on other 'transition regimes'. From the analyses of the various authors throughout this volume, it becomes evident that further institutional support is needed within Italy in order to increase the chances of young people participating fully in social and economic life. Though the chapters have not introduced new categories with which to interpret youth, they have illustrated how the scenario is becoming increasingly difficult for them. In a similar way, Schoon and Bynner (2017) found that the recession has not so much qualitatively *altered* but rather *intensified* the impact of pre-existing economic and social difficulties on youth in the US, Germany and the UK.

The German historian Reinhard Koselleck (1972–1997) warned that 'crisis' is an inflated concept. He also argued that the very concept refers to the idea that the time to solve issues is shrinking, so that something must be done immediately. Our concern is that if the contextual conditions worsen further still, young people will no longer be masters of change. The transformation can be likened to the metaphor of 'boiling frogs' used by Noam Chomsky (2014). Various commentators have used this metaphor to describe the way in which the adverse labour market conditions and the associated social and economic environment are becoming 'normal' in the perceptions of young people, and the younger they are the more normal they become. By contrasting two (recent) cohorts of young people, the chapters clearly show this trend.

However, the chapters in this collection also contain some positive developments. For instance, observation on recent mobilization show (forthcoming) stress that NEETs in Italy do not have a lower degree of political participation compared to those in the labour market, as would be expected (Andretta and Bracciale, forthcoming). This suggests us that it is perhaps *inside* categories (like the NEETs category) that we have to (re)-imagine new roles for young people in counteracting the crises, austerity and wider social-economic difficulties, questioning established ways of looking at them. The movement *Friday for the Future*, inspired by the young Swedish activist Greta Thunberg, could perhaps lead one to believe that the (relative) marginalization of young people, in Italy and around the globe, may turn into some visible requests of change on behalf of a generation. Clearly, it is the intersection of various dimensions that composes the experience of youth and adulthood and the transition to adulthood: participation and work are amongst these. It is – we hope – within the capacity of young people and in the wider collectivities relevant to them to identify the means to rectify the boiled-frog syndrome.

Acknowledgements

We share the views expressed in this chapter. If deemed necessary, though, the 'Introduction' and the 'Framework of reference for this book' can be attributed to Valentina Cuzzocrea, except for the subsection on 'The Recent reform scenario in Italy', which is attributed to Barbara Giovanna Bello, who also wrote 'Why this edited volume?'; Yuri Kazepov is responsible for sections 'Structure of the Book' and 'Conclusions'.

This chapter was supported by the Open Access Publishing Fund of the University of Cagliari, with the funding of the Regione Autonoma della Sardegna – L.R. n. 7/2007.

References

Alberti, G., Bessa, I., Hardy, K., Trappmann, V. and Umney, C. (2018). Against and beyond precarity: Work in insecure times. *Work, Employment and Society*, 32(3), 447–457.

Alfieri, S., Elena, M. and Bignardi, P. (eds) (2018). *Generazione Z. Guardare il mondo con fiducia e speranza*. Milano: Vita e Pensiero.

Andreotti, A., Garcia, S.M., Gomez, A., Hespanha, P., Kazepov, Y. and Mingione E. (2001). Does a Southern European model exist? *Journal of European Area Studies*, 9(1), 43–62.

Andretta, M. and Bracciale, R. (forthcoming). Young Italians, NEETs and political engagement: Any good news? In: Cuzzocrea, V., Gook, B. and Schiermer, B. (eds) *Forms of Collective Engagement in Youth Transitions: A Global Perspective*. Leiden: Brill.

Ballarino, G., Panichella, N. and Triventi, M. (2014). School expansion and uneven modernization: Comparing educational inequality in Northern and Southern Italy. *Research in Social Stratification and Mobility*, 36, 69–86.

Barbieri, P., Bozzon, R., Scherer, S., Grotti, R. and Lugo, M. (2015). The rise of a Latin model? Family and fertility consequences of employment instability in Italy and Spain. *European Societies*, 17(4), 423–446.

Barbieri, P. and Scherer, S. (2009). Labour market flexibilization and its consequences in Italy. *European Sociological Review*, 25(6), 677–692.

Barone, C. and Ruggera, L. (2015). Le disuguaglianze sociali nell'istruzione in una prospettiva comparativa. Il rompicapo del caso italiano. *Scuola Democratica*, 2, 321–342.

Bello, B.G. (2018). Seconde Generazioni. In L. Barbari and F. De Vanna (a cura di), *Il 'diritto al viaggio'. Abbecedario delle migrazioni*. Torino: Giappichelli, 257–263.

Bello, B.G. and Cuzzocrea, V. (2018). Introducing the need to study young people in contemporary Italy. *Journal of Modern Italian Studies*, 23(1), 1–7.

Bertolini, S., Moiso V. and Unt, M. (2019). Precarious and creative: Youth facing uncertainty in the labour market. In: Colombo, E. and Rebughini, P. (eds) *Youth and the Politics of the Present: Coping with Complexity and Ambivalence*. London: Routledge, 75–87.

Cairns, D. (2014). *Youth Transitions, International Student Mobility and Spatial Reflexivity: Being Mobile?* Basingstoke: Palgrave Macmillan.

Caltabiano, M. and Rosina, A. (2018). The *dejuvenation* of the Italian population. *Journal of Modern Italian Studies*, 23(1), 24–40.

Cavalli, A. and Leccardi, C. (2013). Le quattro stagioni della ricerca sociologica sui giovani. *Quaderni di Sociologia*, 62, 167–169.

Cento Bull, A. (2000). *Social Identities and Political Cultures in Italy: Catholic, Communist, and Leghist Communities between Civicness and Localism*. New York: Berghahn Books.

Chomsky, N. (2014). *Media e Potere*. Milano: Beepress.

Cicchelli, V. and Galland, O. (2009). Le trasformazioni della Gioventù e dei rapporti tra le generazioni, in Processi e trasformazioni sociali. In: Sciolla, L. (ed) *La società Europea dagli anni sessanta a oggi*. Roma: Laterza.

Colombo, E. and Rebughini, P. (2019). *Youth and the Politics of the Present: Coping with Complexity and Ambivalence*. London: Routledge.

Colombo, E., Leonini, L. and Rebughini, P. (2018). A generational attitude: Young adults facing the economic crisis in Milan. *Journal of Modern Italian Studies*, 23(1), 61–74.

Cuzzocrea, V. (2012). Creativity and the 'Art to get by': or, what is old in new practices of work, In: Cuzzocrea, V., Sahu, P. and James, P. (eds) *Valuing Work: Challenges and Opportunities*. Oxford: Inter-Disciplinary Press, 113–120.

Cuzzocrea, V. and Mandich, G. (2016). Narratives of the future: Imagined mobilities as forms of youth agency? *Journal of Youth Studies*, 19(4), 552–567.

Domaneschi, L. (2019). Learning (not) to labour: How middle-class young adults look for creative jobs in a precarious time in Italy. In: Colombo, E. and Rebughini, P. (eds) *Youth and the Politics of the Present. Coping with Complexity and Ambivalence*. London: Routledge, 19–31.

EGRIS. (2001). Misleading trajectories: Transitional dilemmas of young adults in Europe. *Journal of Youth Studies*, 4(1), 101–119.

Esping-Andersen, G. (1990). *Three Worlds of Welfare Capitalism*. Cambridge: Polity.

Esping-Andersen, G. (1999). *Social Foundation of Post-industrial Economies*. Oxford: Oxford University.

Eurostat. (2019). Online database, edat_lfse_20, accessed 23 October 2019.

Ferrera, M. (1996). The Southern model of welfare in Social Europe. *Journal of European Social Policy*, 6(1), 17–37.

Fraser, N. (2010). Injustice at intersecting scales: On social exclusion and the global poor. *European Journal of Social Theory*, 13(3), 363–371.

Galli della Loggia, E. (1980). *Il trionfo del privato*. Roma: Laterza.

Garau, E. (2015). *The Politics of National Identity in Italy: Immigration and Italianità*. London: Routledge.

Jones, G. and Wallace, C. (1992). *Youth, Family and Citizenship*. Buckingham, Philadelphia: Open University Press.

Kazepov, Y. (2008). The subsidiarization of social policies: Actors, processes and impacts. *European Societies*, 10(2), 247–273.

Kelly, P. (2006). The entrepreneurial self and 'youth at-risk': Exploring the horizons of identity in the twenty-first century. *Journal of Youth Studies*, 9(1), 17–32.

Krzaklewska, E. (2019). Youth, mobility and generations – The meanings and impact of migration and mobility experiences on transitions to adulthood. *Studia Migracyjne – Przegląd Polonijny*, 1(171), 41–59.

Leccardi, C. (2005). Facing uncertainty: Temporality and biographies in the new century. *Young*, 13(2), 123–146.

Leccardi, C., Cuzzocrea, V. and Bello, G.B. (2018). Youth as a metaphor: An interview with Carmen Leccardi. *Journal of Modern Italian Studies*, 23(1), 8–23.

Leonardi, M. and Pica, G. (2015). Youth unemployment in Italy. In: Dolado, J.J. (ed.) *No Country for Young People? Youth Labour Market Problems in Europe*. London: CEPR Press, 89–104.

Mammone, A. and Veltri, G.A. (eds) (2010) *The Sick Man of Europe*. London: Routledge.

Marshall, T.H. (1964). *Class, Citizenship, and Social Development*. Garden City: Doubleday & Company.

Martin, C. (2015). Southern welfare states: Configuration of the welfare balance between state and the family. In: Baumeister, M. and Sala, R. (eds) *Southern Europe? Italy, Spain, Portugal, and Greece from the 1950s Until the Present Day*. Frankfurt: Campus, 77–100.

Mauceri, S. and Valentini, A. (2010). The European delay in transition to parenthood: The Italian case. *International Review of Sociology*, 20(1), 111–142.

Merton, R.K. (1968). The Matthew effect in science. *Science*, 159(3810), 56–63.

Naldini, M. (2003). *The Family in the Mediterranean Welfare States*. London: Routledge.

Ostrowicka, H. (2019). *Regulating Social Life Discourses on the Youth and the Dispositif of Age*. London: Palgrave.

Pastore, F. (2017). The school-to-work transition in the Latin Rim: The case of Italy. In: Caroleo, F.E., Demidova, O., Marelli, E. and Signorelli, M. (eds) *Young People and the Labour Market*. London: Routledge, 200–221.

Pickard, S. and Bessant, J. (eds) (2015). *Young People Re-Generating Politics in Times of Crises*. Basingstoke: Palgrave Macmillan.

Pitti, I. (2017). What does being an adult mean? Comparing young people's and adults' representations of adulthood. *Journal of Youth Studies*, 20(9), 1225–1241.

Quintini, G. and Martin, S. (2006). Starting well or losing their way? The position of youth in the labour market of the OECD countries. *OECD Social, Employment and Migration Working Papers*, No. 39, OECD.

Raffe, D. (2008). The concept of transition system. *Journal of Education and Work*, 21, 277–296.

Roberts, K. (2009). Opportunity structures then and now. *Journal of Education and Work*, 22(5), 355–368.

Reitman, I. (2011). Young Adults, distributed by Paramount Pictures.

Roberts, K. (2018). Youth research meets life course terminology: The transition paradigm revisited. In: Irwin, S. and Nilsen, A. (eds) *Transitions to Adulthood Through Recession: Youth and Inequality in a European Comparative Perspective*. London: Routledge.

Rosina, A. (2015). *NEET. Giovani che non studiano e non lavorano*. Milano: Vita e Pensiero.

Scabini, E. and Donati, P. (eds) (1988). *La famiglia 'lunga' del giovane adulto*. Milano: Vita e Pensiero.

Scholz, S. and Rennig, A. (eds) (2019). *Generation Z in Europe*. Bingley: Emerald.

Schoon, I. and Bynner, J. (2017). Entering adulthood in the great recession: A tale of three countries. In: Parke, R. and Elder Jr., G. (eds) *Children in Changing Worlds: Sociocultural and Temporal Perspectives*. Cambridge: Cambridge University Press, 57–83.

Sergi, V., Cefalo, R. and Kazepov, Y. (2018). Young people's disadvantages on the labour market in Italy: Reframing the NEET category. *Journal of Modern Italian Studies*, 23(1), 41–60.

Standing, G. (2011). *The Precariat: The New Dangerous Class*. New York: Bloomsbury Academic.

Talburt, S. and Lesko, N. (2012). An introduction to seven technologies of youth studies. In: Lesko, N. and Talburt, S. (eds) *Keywords in Youth Studies*. New York: Routledge, 1–10.

Varriale, S. (2016). *Globalization, Music and Cultures of Distinction: The Rise of Pop Music Criticism in Italy*. London: Palgrave.

Visentin, M. (2018). Young people's changing conditions from their origins to their David and Goliath season: A critical review of youth studies. *Italian Journal of Sociology of Education*, 10(1), 1–22.

Part I

Activism, participation and citizenship

Chapter 1

Young people and politics in Italy in times of populism

Elisa Lello

1.1 Introduction

In the last 20 years, research about young people's relationship with politics has largely concerned their growing disengagement. Researchers have shown young Italians' change in values, and in particular their shift from universalist priorities (such as solidarity, social equality, freedom and democracy) towards more intimate and familiar relations (Cavalli and de Lillo, 1988, 1993; Buzzi *et al.*, 1997, 2002, 2007) and a move towards values and interests more closely aligned to one's immediate surroundings, such as family, work, friendship, love, career and self-realization (de Lillo, 2002, 2007).

Many scholars have underlined young people's tendency to abandon institutionalized forms of participation and their traditional channels, such as political parties and unions (Norris, 2004; Gauthier, 2003; Cavalli *et al.*, 2008; Genova, 2010). However, according to some, young Italians should not be considered an individualistic or apathetic generation, given that they simply prefer to engage in civic and social activism along with voluntary work within civil society organizations (Diamanti, 1999; Ceccarini, 1999; Marta and Scabini, 2003; Dalton, 2008). Other scholars hold that younger generations are crucial actors in the redefinition of the meaning and nature of political participation, characterized by innovative and unconventional forms, marked by occasional and time-fragmented activism, the use of new technologies and the interpenetration between public engagement and youth-specific lifestyle (Ward and de Vreese, 2011; Stolle *et al.*, 2010). This kind of activism mainly takes the form of fluid, loosely structured collectivities, such as social movements, single-issue campaigns and online activism. It can also take the form of *individualized collective action*, as in the multiple behaviours associated with political (or critical) consumerism (Stolle *et al.*, 2005; de Moor, 2017). This shift towards innovative forms of *creative* engagement is marked by the increasing individual responsibility and by the search for creative ways to compound social and collective goals with personal objectives of self-fulfilment. Such activism tends to flank with more traditional ways of civic engagement (Micheletti and McFarland, 2010; Ceccarini, 2015).

However, looking at an international scenario challenges this kind of interpretation. While confirming young people's declining rates of institutionalized political engagement, recent studies suggest that if in the 1970s young people were effectively more engaged than adults in non-conventional participation, in the first years of the new millennium this gap has closed. Non-conventional participation has increased over time more among mature individuals than among youth (Goerres, 2009; Garcia-Albacete, 2014). Young people are no longer more active than adults in the field of protest and unconventional participation, neither are they more informed, interested in politics or supportive of the basic principles of democracy, which is why Goerres (2009) suggests a 'greying' of Western democracies.

Yet, another interesting contribution comes from those studies that question the meaning of young people's disengagement from institutionalized channels, contending that it should not be read, in an oversimplified way, as apathy. These studies underline the necessity of problematizing the concept of 'apathy' and of developing extensive qualitative research in order to more deeply grasp young people's images and expectations about politics. They also suggest that young people's disengagement may reflect their perception that traditional parties and political actors do not have anything to offer them. From this perspective, rather than *tuning out*, young people may feel *left out* (O'Toole *et al.*, 2003; Henn *et al.*, 2005).

I argue that this perspective represents a promising interpretative line for the understanding of young people's political behaviours and choices, both inside and outside of Italy. More so, given the most recent developments involving Western democracies. Namely, I refer to the growing importance of new, or recently redefined, anti-establishment political subjects who openly challenge mainstream parties (i.e. centre-left and centre-right). These anti-establishment parties have quite different political identities, but they share an explicit opposition to traditional political elites whom they accuse of having pursued particularistic interests instead of those of the people, who have been hit by impoverishment and social degradation (Kriesi and Pappas, 2015; Diamanti and Lazar, 2018). With different inclinations, these parties claim to represent people who are, or who perceive of themselves, as excluded from the benefits brought about by globalization, against the privileged minority. In some countries, and with more evidence in Southern European ones, this dividing line overlaps with criticism towards the European Union and particularly towards austerity policies that dismantled welfare systems and increased social polarization (Morlino and Raniolo, 2017).

If we consider the recent general worsening of young people's economic and social situation (Furlong and Cartmel, 2007; European Commission, 2017), it does not appear coincidental that in many countries the anti-establishment divide tends to overlap with the generational one. This can be observed more distinctly in Southern Europe, where younger generations more precisely coincide with the excluded, from the redistribution of income, from welfare provisions and from protective legislation on work contracts. Whereas, more mature cohorts keep remarkable guarantees and a more favourable distribution of income (Morlino and Raniolo, 2017).

For instance, in Spain, the Podemos Party has gained wide support from young voters, as shown by surveys carried out by CIS (Centre of Sociological Research). Similar processes take place with the Italian Five Stars Movement (5SM) (Itanes, 2013), but also with the French National Front. The same could be observed in Greece with Syriza, at least until it lost its credibility in effectively contrasting the Troika's diktats. The political elites from these parties also evoke a generational cleavage thus far latent, at least within south European countries. In 2013, 56% of the 5SM elected in the Chamber of Deputies belonged to the age cohort ranging from 25 to 34 years, and 44% from 35 to 44 years. The same distribution pattern holds for Podemos. Moreover, in both cases we find a high degree of education, with high percentages of elected representatives who have graduated or hold a postgraduate qualification (Morlino and Raniolo, 2017; Montesanti and Tarditi, 2016).

In other cases, the affirmation of innovative leadership within more consolidated parties has produced a similar effect of attracting young voters and members. The case of Jeremy Corbyn in the UK appears emblematic because he is an 'old' politician, both in age and for his explicit references to ideals and ideologies of the past, in sharp contrast to the modernizing trend of previous Labour leaders, like Tony Blair. Notwithstanding this – and maybe for this very reason – Corbyn has explicitly addressed youth concerns, stimulating a meaningful rejuvenation both among Labour's membership and electorate (as reported by YouGov and Ipsos Mori surveys in June 2017). Interestingly, and as in this case, one can also point to the success of Bernie Sanders amongst American youth in the 2016 Democratic primary elections. A further parallel can be traced to Jean-Luc Mélenchon, the aged leader of La France Insoumise, who evokes ideals and identities thought to be overcome by history, and whose support is clearly marked in a generational key[1] (Diamanti and Lazar, 2018).

These examples underline the growing importance of the generational factor in explaining political dynamics, and they make Italy an interesting laboratory for observing the relationship between young people and politics. Goerres (2009) notes that in those countries where the young are disadvantaged in comparison to adults and older people, and where policy outcomes tend to privilege more mature cohorts' interests, the young tend to be more engaged in order to redress the balance. In Italy, public expenditure has traditionally privileged old-age pensions rather than other sectors that would interest young people (such as education, family and children, housing and unemployment).[2] During the last ten years (2007–2016) the incidence of poverty has multiplied four times for younger cohorts, while decreasing among people aged 65 and over.[3] In broader terms, together with the other Southern European countries, Italy is a country where the crisis has more dramatically hit younger generations (European Commission, 2017).

It is no coincidence then that in more recent years, strong anti-austerity movements have been taking place in Euro-Mediterranean countries, including Portugal, Spain and Greece. Such movements hold a social base marked by the presence of young people, highly educated individuals, unemployed or underemployed, and precarious workers (della Porta, 2015). Conversely, in Italy there has yet to be a movement that effectively represents the anti-austerity protest, and/ or the younger generations' grievances and claims. After the season of the *alter-mondialist* movements at the turn of the millennium,[4] the landscape of social movements looks fragmented into several locally focused campaigns against the construction of infrastructures thought to be dangerous for the environment and for public health (della Porta and Mosca, 2015), or in defence of the employment in some specific cases (Morlino and Raniolo, 2017).

In Italy, the anti-austerity protest seems to have taken a different path, immediately becoming institutionalized into a party (5SM), without passing through the stage of social movement (Morlino and Raniolo, 2017). Indeed, this party has attracted support from a remarkable proportion of youth, contributing to shaping their images and expectations about politics. In order to fully comprehend young Italians' dynamics of participation (and their choices of not being engaged), it is worth further investigating their views about politics. I will focus on these issues through on both quantitative and qualitative data. However, first we need to seriously consider how dramatic social and economic changes have impacted upon the personality formation of young Italians.

1.2 The young and the *in-between* cohort

Most research about young people, both in the Italian case and at an international level, focuses on the cohort who were young during the first years of the new millennium. However, in the meantime, meaningful societal changes have occurred giving rise to a generation with remarkably different traits and features than those of more than 15 years ago. Consequently, it is necessary to bring some order to the data by clearly identifying our cohort time boundaries. To this purpose, a crucial point regards the idea of an 'open future', which has been undermined by the economic crisis. The concept of an 'open' future, that is a future not tied to the predestination of the past anymore but supported by the optimistic idea of 'progress', has indeed been the key pillar of modernity (Benasayag and Schmit, 2004; Jedlowski, 2012, see also chapter 9 in this volume). That very idea, and the optimistic attitude that accompanied it, constituted the indispensable substratum to the May'68 youth activism (Leccardi, 2012) and supported that generation's capacity to undertake innovative struggles in the name of new values and instances (Inglehart, 1977; Dalton, 1996).

However, the idea of an 'open future' has fallen into crisis throughout the Western world, due to a number of factors. Among these, the progress of science and technology that have become sources of new potential threats; the autonomization of finance from the real economy (Harvey, 1990); the processes of reorganization of the Fordist production towards an increasing insecurity of work contracts, and a reduction of opportunities that has mainly hit the middle classes. The idea of the future as a promise of amelioration, compared with the present, has been displaced by its opposite. Namely, a future conceived as a threat, perceived as synonym of potential decline and of loss of acquired benefits (Benasayag and Schmit, 2004).

We are dealing with gradual changes that have occurred over a long period of time. Nevertheless, it is still possible to identify a period when they precipitated in new laws and policies, which allowed them to develop in a more explicit way, resulting in a deep transformation at the level of social representation. For Italy, it appears plausible to place this watershed moment in the mid-nineties. The first law to introduce short-term work contracts in Italian legislation traces back from 1997.[5] In those same years, Zygmunt Bauman (1999) outlined how the deconstruction of any kind of 'security', both in a cognitive and a socio-economic meaning, was leading to a deep transformation of Western societies marked by the spread of 'risk' and 'precariousness' (Beck, 1992; Bourdieu, 1998). Social polarization and growing economic difficulties spread throughout western European countries, but they exerted quite a distinctive impact on Italy, and on other Southern European countries, where their effects combined and intertwined with long-lasting structural aspects, such as weakness for young people in the access to welfare provisions, employment or in salary levels, which are investigated in Part II of this book. This has resulted in the building of a strong generational disadvantage (Ambrosi and Rosina, 2009; Boeri and Galasso, 2007; Livi Bacci and De Santis, 2007), eventually amplified by the economic crises that began to strike European societies in 2007.[6]

It is important to point out that, since the generational gap traces back decades of Italian politics' disinterest towards declining opportunities for young people, those who are young today are not the only cohort who experience this disadvantage. The generational question involves, besides the young, a slightly older cohort too, constituted of those born approximately between 1970 and the early 1980s. But the crucial point we would like to underline here is that growing up surrounded by a social climate marked by endemic insecurity and distrust towards the future constitutes a remarkably different life-experience than discovering, at an (almost) adult age, that the social world has become uncertain and that there are fewer opportunities than one would have thought during one's youth. Hence, basing on the different environment and conditions of their socialization, I propose a distinction between two age cohorts:

- *Young people*, who were born from 1984 until 1999, and in 2017 were aged between 18 and 33 years.
- A cohort that can be defined as *in-between*, because of their condition of suspension, which continues even though they are now at an age that can be considered adult. I consider people who were born (approximately) between 1972 and 1983 as part of this cohort, meaning that in 2017 they were between the ages of 33 and 45. They are 'suspended' because they were the first generation to experiment with a wide postponement of the

threshold towards adulthood (Modell *et al.*, 1976) because of the generational gap. It is interesting to notice that among them we find the (once) young, described as the 'Kinder der Freiheit' (Beck and Beck-Gernsheim, 2002), who took part in the marches and demonstrations of the so-called *new-global* movement around the turn of the millennium.

My hypothesis is that even though both cohorts share a common perception about their situation and opportunities,[7] we can find relevant differences between them that are connected to the distinctive political, economic, and cultural environments in which they were socialized. In this sense, we are discussing socio-economic cohort effects rather than those of a political generation or specific life cycle, since we underline the impact of socio-economic factors in shaping a cohorts' physiognomy (Inglehart, 1977; Goerres, 2009).

With regard to the *in-between* (or *suspended*) cohort, they have lived the formative phases of their personality during the second part of the 1980s and the early 1990s, a period when the important changes we recalled just above were beginning to take form (Mammone and Veltri, 2010). Yet, social representations and expectations were still aligned with an optimistic cultural climate, where people tended to believe that the model of wellbeing reached within Western societies was a stable acquisition that would indefinitely reproduce itself. So, during their youth they had the chance to cultivate dreams and aspirations, and – for instance – to choose their studies with some freedom to follow their interests and passions without too much pressure from labour market demands. In these respects, they appear closer to previous cohorts. However, they were the first cohort that, at the end of the course of their studies, faced a deeply changed social scenario, marked by instability, unemployment, inadequacy of welfare provisions and a reduction of opportunities. They form the 'lost generation', according to the definition of many, including the former Prime Minister Mario Monti. However, they also represent a 'disappointed generation' since their aspirations and expectations, cultivated within a still optimistic era, have dropped against quite a different reality.

On the contrary, the cohort we define as the *young people* of today, have grown up in the middle of a cultural climate marked by scepticism towards the future – what Bauman (2017) calls *retrotopia*. Moreover, they indirectly experienced the difficulties encountered by the *in-between* cohort in trying to cope with work instability and the obstacles in passing the thresholds of adult life, resulting in biographies often marked by the syndrome of delay. Some observers have also outlined the importance of pedagogical messages. In this respect, it is argued that within this generalized loss of trust towards the future, the educational style has deeply changed so that the exhortations to the young – to make them study and commit themselves – are increasingly based on threats rather than on the promise of what they can conquer in their future (Benasayag and Schmit, 2004). The future has been presented to younger people as a land of hardship and danger, rather than as one of hope and desire.

Growing up in a climate of alerted pragmatism leads to the conviction that one can give importance and value to nothing but concrete, quantifiable things; and that one cannot *afford the luxury* of caring about 'useless' aspects, such as ideals, the pleasure of discovery and knowledge, the joy of sharing, and time freely dedicated to one's interests and relationships, dreams, and projects (Benasayag and Schmit, 2004). This deeply affects what has been called the 'capacity to aspire' (Appadurai, 2013), which can be seen as an individual and cultural capability, but which also involves a collective dimension. Leccardi (2012) has underlined, for instance, young people's tendency to concentrate upon short-time goals. But their range of action seems to be shrinking not only in terms of time, but also regarding the spatial dimension, with a tendency to concentrate on short-range sociability (Birindelli, 2014). Other recent pieces of research underline youth propensity to focus on goals and targets that they may feel within their reach, and appear quite traditional and material (Lello, 2015).[8] So as to avoid possible disappointment later in life, this generation appears to have to downsize their expectations right off the bat. They seem convinced that they must avoid cultivating illusions about their future. If the *in-between* cohort looks like a *disappointed* one, young Italians of today, on the contrary, risk falling into *disillusionment*. The tendency is to downsize the scope of their dreams and aspirations even before verifying if they could withstand the impact of reality, just to avoid the risk of disappointment.

Remarkable consequences can be traced between this habit to disillusionment and young people's relationship to politics.[9] On the one hand, as we will see, their disillusionment tends to translate in the political sphere into a refusal of any ideals. Their idea of politics seems thus deprived of the ideal dimension and based, rather, on the concepts of 'objectivity' and 'technical skills' at the expense of the scope of political action and of its capacity to bring about social change. On the other hand, it affects their capacity to create solidarity linkages, networks and a sense of belonging, also on the intragenerational level. Young people disillusionment, as Jedlowski notes, is not so much about the idea of progress as such, but rather entrenched in the possibility that wealth may be redistributed. Widespread feelings of resentment follow: 'trust in a generalized progress used to include. The perspective of a selective progress divides' (Jedlowski, 2012: 10). The twilight of the idea of future-as-promise also implies the end of collective aspirations (Benasayag and Schmit, 2004) in favour of individualistic ones, which may stand in opposition to those of others. From this perspective, alliances become instrumental and transitory (Bauman, 2003).

1.3 The *in-between* cohort: disappointment goes into politics

We can observe interesting differences between the two cohorts we have identified concerning their relationship with politics. The first interesting evidence involves the feeling of trust (and distrust) towards political institutions: it was not the *young people* that we found to be less trustful. On the contrary, their degree of trust was similar to – and in some cases even somewhat higher than – the older components (Table 1.1). Rather, a loss of confidence seems to involve

Table 1.1 Trust in institutions, political orientation and attitudes towards immigration (%)

	Young (born 1984 to 2002)	In-between cohort (born 1971 to 1983)	Adults and elder (born until 1970)	All
Trust 'much' or 'very much'[a]				
The State	28.2	17.0	26.4	24.5
The President of the Republic	37.5	34.6	55.5	46.1
EU	39.8	22.8	24.3	27.5
Can you tell me what feelings the following words evoke in you?[b]				
Ius Soli (7–10)	28.0	21.0	28.8	26.9
Democracy (7–10)	51.1	43.6	54.8	51.4
Political elections (7–10)	36.0	29.0	33.4	33.0
Democratic Party (7–10)	26.8	11.0	25.8	22.7
Forza Italia (7–10)	19.6	13.1	19.2	18.0
Five-Stars Movement (7–10)	23.5	30.6	15.3	23.5
Grillo (7–10)	13.5	20.7	10.1	13.3
Renzi (7–10)	22.5	12.1	27.4	22.8
Salvini (7–10)	14.5	21.7	22.6	20.4
Trump (7–10)	10	21.6	8.7	11.9
European Union (7–10)	45.7	26.2	41.2	38.9
The politicians (6–10)	19.8	11.4	15.0	15.4
The political parties (6–10)	28.7	19.0	22.3	23.1
Migrants are a danger to public order and to people's safety (much or very much agree)[c]	36.0	46.0	36.4	38.6
According to you, with regard to migrants' and refugees' ships directed towards Italian coasts, it's better to aim above all…[a]				
…for hospitality	55.4	46.4	46.6	48.6
…for refusal of entry	41.3	49.2	42.3	43.8

Notes
a Demos & Pi and Osservatorio di Pavia for Fondazione Unipolis, *Rapporto sulla sicurezza e l'insicurezza sociale in Italia e in Europa,* January 2017, n. 1619.
b The interviewee was asked to express a vote from 1 (very negative) to 10 (very positive). Demos & Pi, *55° Osservatorio sul Capitale Sociale,* June 2017, n. 1409.
c Demos & Pi and Coop for 'la Repubblica', *Osservatorio sul Capitale Sociale,* October 2017, n. 1309.

the *in-between* cohort: they look with more distrust towards main national political institutions and towards the EU. They expressed considerably less positive feelings towards elections and, in broad terms, democracy, when compared both with young and with more mature components.

Moreover, the *in-between* cohort was the most frightened about immigration. They perceived, more than any other age cohort, immigrants' presence as a danger, so their attitude tended to be defensive and repressive. It was this group that expressed the strongest opposition to the proposal of the 'ius soli', that is the law about granting Italian citizenship to children born from migrant parents on Italian territory (albeit with some additional restrictions). And regarding the arrivals of migrants and refugees towards Italian coasts,[10] it is only among this cohort that a repressive response (refuse entry) prevailed on hospitality.

Here the data is significant, especially in relation to the impact of the 'life cycle' on attitudes towards immigration. Data in the existing literature usually identifies the elderly as the most frightened by the issue, and therefore as the most inclined towards defensive and closed responses. This is partly because as they become older, people gradually become more diffident towards what may appear to be new and different. Above all, due to the infrequent direct contact with migrants in real life, for example at work or for study, friendship and leisure. This is coupled with the elderly's greater exposure to mass media, and particularly to television (Demos and Osservatorio di Pavia, 2017). Thus, it seems plausible that behind this data – which shows that fears and 'closed-shop' approaches are more widespread amongst the socially and economically active individuals of the *in-between* cohort – there may be effects at work other than those linked to the life cycle: namely, cohort effects. Their broader feelings of resentment and dissatisfaction (if not frustration) related to their personal economic situation and the opportunities one perceives to have (had) tend to reflect themselves in closure and refusal towards the newly arrived.

After all, we are dealing with a generation within which we can find, even today, high levels of unemployment (the highest for long-term unemployment), underemployment and inactivity (according to Istat data, dati.istat.it). Moreover, while there are various specific measures directed towards younger cohorts and even older ones, this single cohort remains lacking in any form of political attention. It is not surprising, then, that a portion of this cohort may feel excluded, and thus decide to support protest actors who advocate the necessity of radical change, as confirmed by the analysis on the most recent general elections (Bordignon *et al.*, 2018). Indeed, our data locates in this cohort the main protagonists of the revolt against traditional political elites. Mainstream parties, both centre-right (Forza Italia) and centre-left (Democratic Party), evoke remarkably better feelings amongst young and older components, whilst the *in-between* cohort seems to flatly reject them. The situation is specular regarding protest actors: both 5SM and its founder Grillo elicit the most positive feelings amongst them. Moreover, in contrast to young people, it is the *in-between* cohort who tends to support Matteo Salvini, the leader of the 'League' and the main promoter of 'law and order' policies and hard line towards migrants. Even more emblematic are the feelings evoked by Donald Trump: positive for 22% within the *in-between* cohort, compared to 10% among the young and 9% amongst more mature components.

1.4 Young Italians: towards technocratic politics

If the *in-between* cohort seems to translate its disappointment through high levels of institutional distrust and scepticism towards mainstream parties, young Italians' attitudes towards politics appear quite different. Their distance from adults' (as well as from the *in-between* cohort's) orientations emerges above all in relation to the preferences on the abstract role of parties and parliaments and on the institutional structure. Younger people, as we can see in Table 1.2, seem to welcome a (hyper) simplified and decision-taking-oriented version of democracy, which most think could work without political parties, and in which parliament has less power than the executive. In this light, consent towards the idea of a strong leadership (but also of a 'Strong Man') seems related to their broader support for a governing structure oriented towards efficacy and decisional fastness, and then deprived of those constraints and procedures that may slow down the decision-making process.

These suggestions find support in qualitative findings, related to a research based on 92 interviews on young people carried out from 2008 to 2016. These interviewees were balanced in terms of gender, geographical origins, social and economic situation and degree of education (which is discussed in some depth in Lello, 2015). The qualitative findings confirm the demand for a marked simplification of the political system and suggest a *fil rouge*, which links this demand to young people's perception of political ideals as being useless. Young people express a preference for a kind of politics that gets rid of ideals and substitutes them with technical competence and honesty. The crucial point again here is a habit of disillusionment, which seems to affect their confidence in their own chances of influencing political decisions (that is, their political efficacy, which is lower than other cohorts, as we have seen in Table 1.2). But, in broader terms, they also appear persuaded that politics *per se* cannot bring about any relevant changes. As the young woman in the following extract reminds us, if the issue is that of young people's work conditions, the imagined solution is minimal. They renounce in advance to consider or even imagine, the possibility of an acute intervention, able to significantly change the situation:

> I: If you could decide on the government programme, what would you want them to do?
> R: First of all, young people's working conditions, I don't know how, but [they ought] to stabilize the situation.
> I: Then against unstable employment?
> R: It's enough that there are job opportunities. It's better to be a precarious worker than having few possibilities in finding a job (female, student, 22 years old).

If politics cannot bring about relevant changes anymore, then talking in terms of ideals loses any meaning. Indeed, one of the most common charges they ascribe to politics is that it is an ideological confrontation. They argue that talking about

Table 1.2 Orientations on the role of the parties, the institutional structure, political efficacy and the government by technicians (%)

	Young (born 1984 to 2002)	In-between cohort (born 1971 to 1983)	Adults and elder (born until 1970)	All
Think that democracy could work without political parties[a]	56.4	42.0	38.2	42.0
Agree with 'There is too much confusion, we need a Strong Man to lead the Country'[a]	64.1	54.8	60.5	60.1
'A strong leader' evokes positive feelings (7–10 on 1 to 10 scale)[b]	33.8	26.6	29.8	30.0
Would like to directly elect the Premier, in order to make him govern better and more effectively[a]	82.5	73.6	68.6	71.8
Think that the Parliament has too much power and influence over the government's choices[a]	47.2	39.2	35.8	38.4
Think that political parties in Italy are important for the functioning of democracy[c]	38.5	41.4	47.6	45.0
People like me have no influence on what the government does (agree or much agree)[c]	63.1	61.3	54.4	57.1
Consumers, by boycotting or buycotting, can push the multinationals to respect the environment, the human and workers' rights (much and very much agree)[d]	56.6	62.8	70.0	67.6
In this moment of crisis, for Italy it's better to have a government made of technicians and experts, without politicians (agree or much agree)[c]	69.0	60.3	48.5	54.0

Sources and notes
a   Demos & Pi for 'la Repubblica', *Gli Italiani e lo Stato*, November 2010, n. 1300.
b   Demos & Pi, *55° Osservatorio sul Capitale Sociale*, June 2017, n. 1409.
c   Demos & Pi, Osservatorio di Pavia and Fondazione Unipolis 2012, n. 2009.
d   LaPolis – Coop Adriatica 2010, *Consum-attori*, n. 1195.

politics in terms of ideals and identities is a waste of time. It looks, from their perspective, like something that makes people resemble children getting into fights:

> Now it's time to do, to put into practice. So, how can you go on discussing ideals? What we need now is to face the issue of the moment and that's all, to face one problem at a time and this is the only way. Ideals come at the end, in my opinion, and never before. They don't help, and it looks like we are children getting into fights when we're talking about ideals. Also, the politicians, all of them, look like kids, when they take part in debates on TV… like kids, it is very laughable to hear them (male, student, 21 years old).

The same issue emerged when young people discussed political parties. They perceived of there being too many, and hence they strongly desired for things to be streamlined, that is a reduction both in number and simplification of their organizational setup. As things stand, the political landscape was perceived as being too complex, and parties were regarded as 'expensive' machines. Moreover, participants wanted the minor parties and those on the extremes to be primarily shut out. That is, those parties devoted to promoting political ideals rather than striving for government were, for this very reason, perceived as 'useless'.

> We have too many parties. Then, what changes? A little, but they have to make a lot of parties. Minor parties are a waste of time (male, student, 19 years old).

> They are too many: in my opinion two parties would be enough in a country. (…) After all, all those parties: (…) their only use is to make us, the citizens, spend more and more money in order to pay for their leisure pursuits, such as cinema, gymnasium … I go to the gym and I pay it myself (male, employer, 24 years old).

Moreover, since ideal differences between parties had little relevance to their perspective, what really mattered were their leaders. Every consideration about parties was translated into one about its leader, who must be knowledgeable and honest – and that seems to be all.

> I: Do you think parties are useful instruments in solving people's troubles?
> R: Mmmh… Maybe not. You have to look at the person: his/her abilities, honesty, sensitivity to certain arguments … (female, housewife, 24 years old).

The kind of politics they perceive then appears deprived from the possibility of bringing about any relevant change. What remains is a minimalist and *technocratic* version of politics, where *politics* tends to translate and reduce itself in *policies*. In the exercise of administration of the status quo, its major ambition being the possibility to propose fragmented and localized responses to discrete problems perceived as the 'objective' urgencies of the moment. In light of this, the fundamental criteria, which are most needed to evaluate political action, are technical competency and honesty, at the expense of scope or capacity to achieve change:

> Politics is a group of people who discuss and find solutions, appointed to solve problems as quickly as possible. Politicians don't think of the country's real problems, and they spend too much time. Politics must be made by capable and quick people (male, employer, 24 years old).

Since differences between ideals and points of view lose meaning, it is not so important that political decisions are the outcome of inclusive processes. What counts most is that decisions can be taken quickly and at minor cost. The complexity of the institutional asset, necessary to guarantee the goal of inclusion and representativeness, leaves room to a demand for a strong simplification of the political system aimed at nurturing governability.

Coherently, the best solution from their perspective would be to set aside different allegiances and put together the most capable and competent politicians from the various parties. Settlements such as the 'große Koalition', and more so the 'government by technicians', sound more like 'wished in advance' solutions than hardly avoidable compromises. These are indeed supported by young people much more than by other cohorts (see Table 1.2).

> I think the era of parties has come to an end. In order to solve the problems we're facing, they should embrace a common guideline; they should fight for the country's sake and solve the emergencies. Conflicts are not useful nowadays... (male, student, 28 years old).

In sum, young people's set of preferences and expectations from politics can be synthetized in a demand for a technocratic kind of politics, based on the following pillars:

1 *Refusal of ideals and ideologies in favour of concreteness;*
2 *Primacy of the goal of governability rather than representation;*
3 *Demand for a marked simplification of politics: decrease in costs and time;*
4 *Personalization: leaders are more important than parties;*
5 *Honesty and professional competence as the main criteria for evaluating political action;* and,
6 *Preference for cross-party agreement rather than division.*

1.5 Conclusions

In Italy, young people, together with the *in-between* cohort, have accumulated a disadvantage that may make them feel more *excluded from* (mainstream) politics rather than *tuning out* because of their alleged apathy. However, due to the different social conditions that have accompanied their socialization, these two cohorts have reacted quite differently to the same perception of marginalization, showing as a consequence remarkably different approaches to politics. While the *in-between* cohort appears more distrustful towards political institutions, the most frightened by immigration, and the most supportive of anti-establishment and populist political subjects, the political identity of the young is, on the contrary, marked by a deeply different feeling: disillusionment.

They appear persuaded that politics, in the end, may bring about only very limited change, and that its complexity no longer appears justified. If politics is reduced to the administration of the status quo, they basically want it to be effective and honest. Other aspects, such as its scope and its capacity to bring about social change, seem to lose importance to their eyes. In evaluating political programs, economic viability definitely counts more in their perspective than any considerations about ideals and tends to inhibit the possibility of imagining different futures or alternative scenarios.

Understandably, this *technocratic* idea of politics is not one able to enflame young people's hearts so to encourage them to search for more information in order to deepen their knowledge about political issues. Nor are they stimulated in that sense by the perception that politicians really care about issues that are most related with their troubles and interests. As a result, while the *in-between* cohort share a more hostile stance towards (traditional) politics, young people tend just to observe the political scene, keeping themselves on the threshold. Also because they often lack information and competencies, which are needed to effectively understand political facts and dynamics.

On the electoral domain, the *in-between* cohort are the most supportive of the 5SM and of Salvini's Lega. Whereas young people appear less angry, so that their orientations result somewhat less definite, more possibilist. The first of these parties has also gained wide support among them, at least until March 2018 general elections, mainly on the grounds of the refusal of ideologies, the demand for simplification and an emphasis on 'honesty'. Because of these processes, both cohorts have distanced themselves from traditional, mainstream parties, albeit for different reasons and attitudes.

In this sense, after decades during which young people's orientations have been aligned with the social mean, so that they were described as 'invisible' (Diamanti, 1999), in most recent years, their choices have instead become more distinctive and recognizable.

To this point, it appears noteworthy that even during the M5S-Lega government in 2019, in a context marked by the radicalization of the political debate around radical right-wing and security issues (mainly due to the Minister of Interior Matteo Salvini's actions) and despite widespread protests against racism and restrictive policies towards migrants and refugees, the young along with the *in-between* cohort go on keeping their distance from the main opposition (and mainstream) party, the Democratic Party. The 'primary' elections held on 3 March 2019, for the election of that party's secretary have indeed registered very low levels of engagement, notably by these two cohorts, as observed by the group CALS (Candidate and Leader Selection, see data on www.cals.it/questioniprimarie/).

Nevertheless, the experience of 5SM in government may have frustrated some of young people's expectations, such as the ones related to technical competence or the necessity to avoid extremism. Moreover, the gaining of the power by the anti-establishment political actors has decidedly not coincided with a new centrality within the government's agenda of younger generations' interests and grievances. Their electoral choices then, but also their images and expectations about politics may be susceptible to change, and even to become less *technocratic*, where – or when, if it ever happens – the protest against traditional policies that have left young people out may be articulated in a different way, with the capacity to propose a political (instead of a moralistic) perspective and give answers directed towards generational redistribution and equity.

Notes

1 More than 50% of young electors (18–24 and 25–34 years old) in the 2017 French presidential elections voted for 'La France Insoumise' or for Marine Le Pen's 'Front National', while only 18% between them voted for traditional centre-right or centre-left parties (led by Fillon and Hamon), as shown, for instance, by BVA data.

2 Eurostat 2015 data show that 77.2% of social expenditure in Italy is devoted to pensions, while only 3% is dedicated to family and children, and 2.4% to unemployment. The quota of social expenditure devoted to pensions is, for instance, 58.1% in Germany, 61.6% in France, 67.2% in Spain (but only 31.8% in Ireland).

3 The incidence of "absolute poverty" measured by Istat passed from 3.1% to 12.5% for people until 17 years old, from 2.7% to 10% for 18–34 years old while dropping from 4.4% to 3.8% for elderly people (65 and over). Source: http://dati.istat.it/

4 We refer to the movements against neoliberal globalization and international organizations' (such as WTO, IMF, G8) summits.

5 Law of June 24, 1997, nr. 196, known as Treu Law.

6 Interesting empirical evidence about this is the spread of the persuasion that young people of today will find in their future harder times than previous generations, and this is more pronounced in Italy than elsewhere. In 2012, in the middle of the economic crisis, 85% of Italians shared such a conviction (10 percentage points more than France and UK and 20 more than Spain and Germany). Source: Demos & Pi., Fondazione Unipolis and Osservatorio di Pavia, *Fifth European Observatory on Security*, March 2012, based on a sample of 1000 cases for each country.

7 49% of young people (and 51% among the *in-between* cohort) thinks their generation enjoys fewer opportunities than their parents, against 33% of mature and old people, according to data by Demos for Coop Adriatica, October 2017, sample: 1,309 cases.

8 It is interesting to notice that a mild return of the youngest generations towards materialist values was already noted by Inglehart (2008: 135–136) starting from the very last years of a long time-series based on some West-European countries (West Germany, France, Britain, Italy, the Netherlands and Belgium) from 1970 to 2006.

9 These aspects have been exposed and more extensively illustrated with the support of both quantitative and qualitative data in Lello (2015).

10 According to UNHCR data, 550.000 people arrived by sea to Italian coasts between June 2014 and the same month in 2017, mostly from Sub-Saharan Africa.

References

Ambrosi, E. and Rosina, A. (2009). *Non è un Paese per giovani*. Roma: Marsilio.

Appadurai, A. (2013). *The future as Cultural Fact: Essays on the Global Condition*. London and New York: Verso Books.

Bauman, Z. (1999). *In search of Politics*. Cambridge: Polity Press.

Bauman, Z. (2003). *La società sotto assedio*. Roma-Bari: Laterza.

Bauman, Z. (2017). *Retrotopia*. Cambridge: Polity Press.

Beck, U. (1992). *Risk Society: Towards a New Modernity*. London: Sage.

Beck, U. and Beck-Gernsheim, E. (2002). *Individualization: Institutionalized Individualism and its Social and Political Consequences*. London: Sage.

Benasayag, M. and Schmit, G. (2004). *L'epoca delle passioni tristi*. Milano: Feltrinelli.

Birindelli, P. (2014). Keeping it in the family: The absence of young Italians from the public piazza. *Società Mutamento Politica*, 5(10), 147–172.

Boeri, T. and Galasso, V. (2007). *Contro i giovani. Come l'Italia sta tradendo le nuove generazioni*. Milano: Mondadori.

Bordignon, F., Ceccarini, L. and Diamanti, I. (2018). *Le divergenze parallele. L'Italia: dal voto liquido al voto devoto*. Roma-Bari: Laterza.

Bourdieu, P. (1998). La précarité est aujourd'hui partout. In: Bourdieu, P. (ed.) *Contre-feux: Propos pour servir à la résistance contre l'invasion néolibérale*. Paris: Liber – Raisons d'Agir.

Buzzi, C., Cavalli, A. and de Lillo, A. (eds) (1997). *Giovani verso il Duemila: Quarto rapporto Iard sulla condizione.giovanile in Italia*. Bologna: il Mulino.

Buzzi, C., Cavalli, A. and de Lillo, A. (eds) (2002). *Giovani del nuovo secolo: Quinto rapporto Iard sulla condizione giovanile in Italia*. Bologna: il Mulino.

Buzzi, C., Cavalli, A. and de Lillo, A. (eds) (2007). *Rapporto giovani: Sesta indagine dell'Istituto Iard sulla condizione giovanile in Italia*. Bologna: il Mulino.

Cavalli, A., Cicchelli, V. and Galland, O. (eds) (2008). *Deux pays, deux jeunesses? La condition juvénile en France et en Italie*. Rennes: Presses Universitaires.

Cavalli, A. and de Lillo, A. (eds) (1988). *Giovani anni '80: Secondo rapporto Iard sulla condizione giovanile in Italia*. Bologna: il Mulino.

Cavalli, A. and de Lillo, A. (eds) (1993). *Giovani anni '90: Terzo rapporto Iard sulla condizione giovanile in Italia*. Bologna: il Mulino.

Ceccarini, L. (1999). Il disincanto e la radicalità. In: Diamanti, I. (ed.) *La generazione invisibile*. Milano: Edizioni Il Sole 24 Ore.

Ceccarini, L. (2015). *La cittadinanza online*. Bologna: il Mulino.

Dalton, R.J. (1996). *Citizen Politics*. New York: Chatham House Publishers.

Dalton, R.J. (2008). *The Good Citizen: How a Younger Generation Is Reshaping American Politics*. Washington, DC: CQ Press.

de Lillo, A. (2002). Il sistema dei valori. In: Buzzi, C., Cavalli, A. and de Lillo, A. (eds) *Giovani del nuovo secolo. Quinto rapporto IARD sulla condizione giovanile in Italia*. Bologna: il Mulino.

de Lillo, A. (2007). I valori e l'atteggiamento verso la vita. In: Buzzi, C., Cavalli, A. and de Lillo, A. (eds) *Rapporto giovani. Sesta indagine dell'Istituto Iard sulla condizione giovanile in Italia*. Bologna: il Mulino.

de Moor, J. (2017). Lifestyle politics and the concept of political participation. *Acta Politica*, 52: 179–197.

della Porta, D. (2015). *Social Movements in Times of Austerity*. Malden and Cambridge: Polity Press.

della Porta, D. and Mosca, L. (2015). Conflitti e proteste locali fra comitati, campagne e movimenti. In: Salvati, M. and Sciolla, L. (eds) *L'Italia e le sue Regioni: L'età Repubblicana*. Roma: Treccani.

Demos and Osservatorio di Pavia (eds) (2017). L'Europa sospesa tra inquietudine e speranza. Il decennio dell'incertezza globale. Available at: http://www.demos.it/2017/pdf/4225rapporto_sulla__sicurezza_e_insicurezza__sociale_2017.pdf.

Diamanti, I. (ed) (1999). *La generazione invisibile*. Milano: Edizioni Il Sole 24 Ore.

Diamanti, I. and Lazar, M. (2018). *Popolocrazia*. Roma-Bari: Laterza.

European Commission. (2017). Employment and Social Developments in Europe 2017. Available at: http://ec.europa.eu.

Furlong, A. and Cartmel, F. (2007). *Young People and Social Change: New Perspectives*. Maidenshead: Open University Press.

Garcia-Albacete, G. (2014). *Young People's Political Participation in Western Europe: Continuity or Generational Change?* Basingstoke: Palgrave Macmillan.

Gauthier, M. (2003). The inadequacy of concepts: The rise of youth interest in civic participation in Quebec. *Journal of Youth Studies*, 6(3), 265–276.

Genova, C. (2010). *Attivamente impolitici. Giovani, politica e partecipazione in Italia*. Roma: Aracne.

Goerres, A. (2009). *The Political Participation of Older People in Europe: The Greying of Our Democracies*. Basingstoke: Palgrave Macmillan.

Harvey, D. (1990). *The Condition of Postmodernity: An Enquiry into the Origins of Cultural Change*. Cambridge, MA and Oxford: Blackwell.

Henn, M., Weinstein, M., and Forrest, S. (2005). Uninterested youth? Young people's attitudes towards party politics in Britain. *Political Studies*, 53(3), 556–578.

Inglehart, R. (1977). *The Silent Revolution. Changing Values and Political Styles among Western Publics*. Princeton, NJ: Princeton University Press.

Inglehart, R. (2008). Changing values among Western Publics from 1970 to 2006. *West European Politics*, 31(1–2), 130–146.

Itanes. (2013). *Voto Amaro: Disincanto e Crisi Economica nelle Elezioni del 2013*. Bologna: Il Mulino.

Jedlowski, P. (2012). Il senso del futuro. I quadri sociali della capacità di aspirare. In: De Leonardis, O. and Deriu, M. (eds) *Il futuro nel quotidiano. Studi sociologici sulla capacità di aspirare*. Milano: Egea.

Kriesi, H. and Pappas, T. (eds) (2015). *European Populism in the Shadow of the Great Recession*. Colchester: ECPR Press.

Leccardi, C. (2012). I giovani di fronte al futuro: tra tempo storico e tempo biografico. In: De Leonardis, O. and Deriu, M. (eds) *Il futuro nel quotidiano. Studi sociologici sulla capacità di aspirare*. Milano: Egea.

Lello, E. (2015). *La triste gioventù. Ritratto politico di una generazione*. Rimini: Maggioli.

Livi Bacci, M. and De Santis, G. (2007). Le prerogative perdute dei *giovani*. *Il Mulino*, 3, 472–481.

Mammone, A. and Veltri, G.A. (2010). *Italy Today: The Sick Man of Europe*. London: Routledge.

Marta, E. and Scabini, E. (2003). *Giovani volontari. Impegnarsi, crescere e fare crescere.* Firenze: Giunti.

Micheletti, M. and McFarland, A.F. (eds) (2010). *Creative Participation. Responsibility-Taking in the Political World.* Boulder, CO: Paradigm Press.

Modell, J., Furstenberg, F.F. and Hershberg, T. (1976). Social change and transition to adulthood in historical perspective. *Journal of Family History*, 1, 7–32.

Montesanti, L., and Tarditi, V. (2016). Nuovi partiti e nuovo ceto politico? I casi di Podemos e del Movimento Cinque Stelle, Conference "La natura del partito e le sue trasformazioni nell'età contemporanea", University of Calabria, May 4–5.

Morlino, L. and Raniolo, F. (eds) (2017). *The Impact of the Economic Crisis on the South European Democracies.* London: Palgrave Macmillan.

Norris, P. (2004). Young People & Political Activism: From the Politics of Loyalties to the Politics of Choice? Report for the Council of Europe Symposium: "Young people and democratic institutions: From disillusionment to participation" Strasbourg, 27–28 November 2003.

O'Toole, T., Lister, M., Marsh, D., Jones, S., and McDonagh, A. (2003). Tuning out or left out? Participation and non-participation among young people. *Contemporary Politics*, 9(1), 45–61.

Stolle, D., Hooghe, M., and Micheletti, M. (2005). Politics in the supermarket: Political consumerism as a form of political participation. *International Political Science Review*, 26(3), 245–269.

Stolle, D., Micheletti, M., and Berlin, D. (2010). Young people and political consumerism (published in Swedish as "Politik, konsumtion och delaktighet"). Report Fokus 10. En analys av ungas inflytande. Swedish National Board for Youth Affairs.

Ward, J., and de Vreese, C. (2011). Political consumerism, young citizens and the Internet. *Media, Culture & Society*, 33(3), 399–413.

Chapter 2

When millennials protest
Youth activism in Italy

Massimiliano Andretta and Donatella della Porta[1]

2.1 Young and anti-austerity protests in Italy: an introduction

Despite the various threats that the Millennial generation faces (from unemployment, to precariousness and uncertainty), many young citizens still engage in politics, though not necessarily through conventional patterns of participation. The economic crisis and the related austerity policies have triggered protest mobilizations in all southern European countries (della Porta *et al.*, 2017). In these, younger generations have played a crucial role. Even though in Italy anti-austerity mobilizations have been led primarily by the old and established trade unions (Andretta, 2018; Andretta and della Porta, 2015), young people have been very much involved in those and in other kinds of protests. This young generation faces markedly different life expectations and/or conditions than the previous ones, and are more seriously threatened by the current economic crisis. In recent research, examining the participation of Millennials in Italy, Poland, Spain and the UK in progressive social movements, the self-identification as a precarious generation was in fact widespread (della Porta, 2019). This makes for a particularly interesting starting point to investigate how these citizens overcome barriers of marginalization, network and develop collective identities.

Despite the fact that young people tend to be overrepresented in unconventional politics, social movement studies have given scant attention to issues of age. There are, however, exceptions, from which we can draw some inspiration for reflecting on the impact of some specific age issues on contentious politics. In this, a first step would be to conceptualize appropriate terms to allow for this reflection. Indeed, youth, cohort and generation are relevant but distinct terms.

First, research on political participation has addressed the role of *youth*, who are considered in general terms as being less prone to conventional action and more, instead, to protest action. Social movement studies also recognize that protesting requires some biographical availability (McAdam, 1986, 1989). Time availability and lack of responsibilities are considered as relevant. Initially, there was indeed an expectation that growing older (namely, getting a job, marrying, having children) implied less flexibility in the use of one's own time as well as increasing responsibility, which makes protest less likely: it becomes more costly and potentially risky for middle-age persons than, for instance, young students. Also, there was an expectation that some material resources could help in buying time flexibility. Research indicates an effect of protesting on those sociobiographical conditions is that individuals may end up delaying the formation of family or pushing towards some types of work rather than others. However, it could not definitively confirm that the taking up of work and family responsibility reduces the commitment to protest. If indeed married life tends to reduce the level of commitment (Corrigall-Brown, 2011), having a full-time job increases participation in voluntary organizations, and even in high-risk forms of participation (Nepstad and Smith, 1999; Wiltfang and McAdam, 1991; Passy and Giugni, 2001). In particular, growing older, getting a job and building a family do not necessarily reduce participation in protest. Recent research noted, however, that some conditions that affect biographical availability can impact the step that precedes the actual choice to participate: the development of positive motivations towards protest seems to decline for married people and full-time or part-time employees (Beyerlein and Hipp, 2006). At the micro-level, student activism has been linked to specific characteristics of younger people, such as the availability of time and limited responsibilities, but also enthusiasm, idealism and exposure to new ideas (Lipset and Altbach, 1967). Students have been presented as spoiled, highly emotional, rebellious, unable to handle ambiguity, devoted to an ethic of absolute ends, irreverent, adventurist or radicalistic (Lipset, 1971).

Issues of age have been addressed in demographic analysis that point at the relevance of the size of the youth *cohort* on the amount and forms of protests. As Goldstone (2015: 148) summarized:

> An age cohort is simply a group of people of roughly the same age, who were born in a particular period. In the United States, it has become common to refer to those born between 1945 and 1960 as the 'baby boomers'; those born from 1960 to 1980 as 'Generation X;' and those born from 1980 to 2000 as 'Millennials'. However, cohorts do not always vary or form systematic groups (Gen X in the United States is known mainly for being very diverse and hard to classify). Rather, their significance has more to do with whether a cohort experienced a major shift in its size, education, or experience relative to other cohorts.

The Arab Spring[2] has, in this sense, been considered as developing in an environment characterized by a large presence of young people. In fact, the socialization of new generations is considered as less challenging as:

> ...when the numbers of people in society are stable or changing slowly enough for growth in the economy and institutions to accommodate the change. However, rapid change in the size of cohorts, or of particular social groups, can easily disrupt this process and place great strains on institutions. (Goldstone, 2015: 150)

Cohorts acquire more of an impact on collective action when they go through some shared, important event that contributes to shaping their norms, values and behaviour in their future lives. In the conceptualization from Mannheim (1952: 292), we are therefore talking of a political *generation*. That is 'a particular kind of identity of location, embracing related "age groups" embedded in a historical-social process'. In particular, the 1968ers were named as a generation that had come of age during a moment of affluence and reduction of inequalities, endowed with 'post-materialist' values (Inglehart, 1977) and broad political interests (Downtown and Wehr, 1997). Student activists of the 1960s were also said to be more likely to be children of left-wing fathers, often intellectuals, with middle-class (or even upper-class) families with permissive and critical education (Lipset, 1971). Expressing the moral dissonance or frustration of a generation, the young activists criticized nevertheless their parents for their unfulfilled promises (Giugni, 2004).

With the aim of contributing to the debate on the impact of age (youth, cohort, generation) on contentious politics, our chapter focuses on the dynamics of the political commitment of young Italians. The particular cohort is defined as those aged between 14 and 40 years, involved in at least one collective mobilization between 2010 and 2011. The selected age cohort is intended to capture a generation facing a very different type of life expectations and/or conditions than the previous ones, and they are more seriously threatened by the ongoing economic crisis. By relying on data from several surveys carried out during protest events on social, economic and labour issues from 2010 to 2011, a period in which the economic crisis spread and deepened in Italy, we single out differences and similarities between younger and older generations on those aspects that social movement studies underline as crucial in explaining individual participation, namely grievance and emotion, collective identity and network embeddedness (della Porta and Diani, 2006).

The article is structured as follows: in the following section, we present the research method undertaken for this study. Following which, in the literature review we elaborate on the dimensions we decided to focus on, dealing respectively with the generational composition of demonstrations selected, the type of grievances and emotions, collective identities, and, finally, network embeddedness. In the conclusion, we summarize the most important findings and suggest some tentative explanations in the Italian case.

2.2 The empirical research

In addressing the previously mentioned questions, we will use data on surveys of protest demonstrations in Italy carried out by Cosmos (Centre on Social Movement Studies) at the European University Institute within an international consortium coordinated by Bert Klandermans and Stefaan Walgrave, on a project named Contextualizing Contestation (see www.protestsurvey.eu).

For this chapter, we restricted the analysis to four types of demonstrations in Italy: the traditional labour day demonstration (Florence 2011), a typical anti-austerity protest (Rome 2012), an anti-neoliberal type of protest (Florence 2012), and finally, a new type of protest directly involving the younger generation (the EuroMayday in Milan 2011). Demonstrators were sampled randomly and given a questionnaire to mail back. About 1,000 questionnaires were distributed at each demonstration, with an average return rate of 20%.[3]

Using the surveys conducted from the selected Italian demonstrations, this article focuses on the analysis of the 'younger generation' involved in them, operationalized by selecting those demonstrators born after 1985, thus, being 25 years old or less at the moment of the selected demonstrations, compared with the 'older generations': those born between 1970 and 1984, (between 40 years and 26 years old), those born between 1955 and 1969 (between 55 and 41 years old), and those born in 1954 or earlier (over 55 years old). Our youngest generation category includes demonstrators being 24 years old on average (the standard deviation is 2.4 years); the second generation, those protestors being on average 34 years old (the standard deviation is 4.3 years); the third generation, on average 50 years old (the standard deviation is 4 years), while in the last and oldest generation those on average 62 years old (with a standard deviation of 5.5 years).

2.3 Presence and social composition of the younger generations in Italian anti-austerity demonstrations

Research on political participation has long suggested that political participation increases with social centrality. The argument is that a higher socio-economic status is predictive of more political participation. The normative problems involved in this selectivity were increased by the non-representativeness of those who participated: in fact, higher levels of participation were observed, *ceteris paribus*, for the better educated, middle class, men, middle-age cohort, married people, city residents, ethnic majority and citizens involved in voluntary associations (Milbrath and Goel, 1977; Lagroye, 1993). Usually, higher social status implies in fact more material resources (but also free-time) to invest in political participation, as well as a higher probability of being successful in their careers (via personal relationships with powerful individuals) and especially a higher sense of personal achievement. Psychological disadvantages overlap with social disadvantages, reducing the perception of one's own 'droit de parole' (Bourdieu, 1979: 180). If participation responds to demands for equality, it tends however to reproduce inequalities since:

> ...any individual participates, at least potentially, with the differential (or unequal) coefficient (if we do not want to use the word 'privilege', that would have an *ancien régime* flavour) that characterizes his/her position in the system of private interests (Pizzorno, 1966: 90).

Social movement studies have challenged this elitist vision by presenting protest as a resource of the powerless (Lipsky, 1970). They noted indeed that those who protest present some different characteristics than those who use conventional forms of political participation: if the middle classes vote more, workers strike more often; and if those in middle age are more present in party-related activities, students occupy their schools and universities (della Porta, 2015). Nevertheless, social movement studies also recognized that protesting requires some biographical availability (McAdam, 1986, 1989). First, time availability and responsibilities are considered as relevant. Initially, there was indeed an expectation that growing older and the sociobiographical conditions that this usually entails (i.e. getting a job, marrying, having children) implied less flexibility in the use of one's own time as well as increasing responsibility, which makes protest less likely. Even though research indicated an effect of those factors on protesting, and, indeed, married life tends to reduce the level of commitment (Corrigall-Brown, 2011), having a full-time job, however, increases participation in voluntary organizations, even in high-risk forms of participation (Nepstad and Smith, 1999; Wiltfang and McAdam, 1991; Passy and Giugni, 2001). In particular, growing older, getting a job and building a family do not necessarily reduce participation in protest.

Our research indicates that the presence of the youngest generation, in the four types of demonstrations that occurred in the period of crisis, was quite strong, accounting for 18% of the full sample, on average. However, if we look at its presence across the types of demonstrations (Table 2.1), we see that the youngest generation were most concentrated in what we called 'youth against the crisis' type of protest marches (27%) and in the anti-neoliberal type (23%). Meanwhile, about 16% demonstrated in the No Monti[4] rally and as few as 2% in the traditional Labour Day demonstration. Both the No Monti day and the Labour Day demonstrations were dominated instead by the two oldest generations, while the second generation showed patterns of presence across demonstrations similar to the youngest one.

Moreover, only 11.5% of marchers belonging to the youngest generation said they had participated in their first demonstration during in the proceeding twelve months, whilst half had participated in more than one and less than five demonstrations, and the rest had protested more than six times. Finally, against the expectation of the social centrality hypothesis, 17% of them had participated at

Table 2.1 Age cohorts across types of demonstrations

Age Cohorts	Euromayday, Milan	Mayday, Florence	No Monti Day, Rome	Florence 10 + 10	Total
Till 26	26.8%	19%	16.3%	23.7%	17.7%
27–40	53.7%	7.6%	19.5%	29.0%	27.1%
41–55	12.2%	42.9%	39.5%	20.6%	29.5%
56 +	7.3%	47.6%	24.7%	26.7%	25.7%
Total	123	105	190	131	549

$N = 549$; Cr.s V: presence across types of demonstrations Italy, 0.29; significant at 0.001 level.

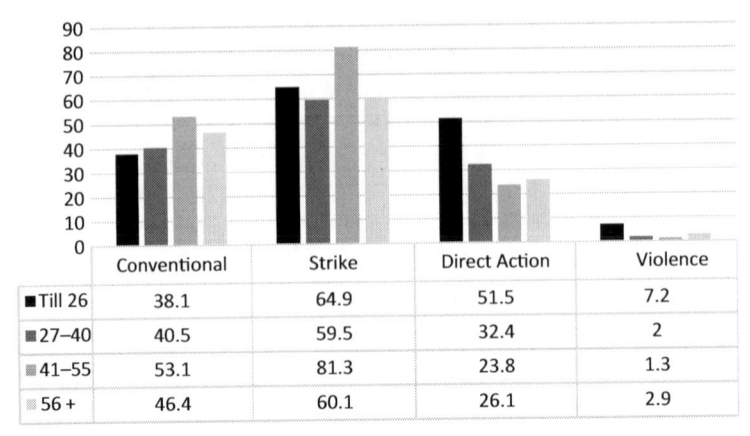

	Conventional	Strike	Direct Action	Violence
■ Till 26	38.1	64.9	51.5	7.2
■ 27–40	40.5	59.5	32.4	2
■ 41–55	53.1	81.3	23.8	1.3
■ 56 +	46.4	60.1	26.1	2.9

■ Till 26 ■ 27–40 ■ 41–55 ■ 56 +

Figure 2.1 Age cohorts by types of protest actions used in the past. (Note: We recoded the forms of action reported in the questionnaire as follows: conventional [contacted politician, government or local government official; signed a petition, donated money to a political organization or group, and worn or displayed a campaign badge or sticker]; strike [joined a strike]; direct action [blockade, occupation, civil disobedience]; and violent [any violent action against things and people]. $N = 543$; Cr.s V: across conventional forms, 0.12, significant at 0.05 level; across strike, 0.20, significant at 0.001 level; across direct actions, 0.21, significant at 0.001 level, across violent forms, 0.12, significant at 0.05 level.)

least 11 times in the last 12 months against about 14% of the central generations and 18% of the oldest one.

Besides participation in protest marches, the youngest generation shows a high degree of commitment to various types of protest actions, and privileges the most radical ones (Figure 2.1).

Gender distribution is more balanced in the youngest generation (53% vs. an average of 47%). As for occupational distribution, those belonging to the youngest generation were most often – but not exclusively – students (47%), 13% were unemployed or between jobs, 21% employed part-time and 8% were full-time. It is not surprising that the youngest generation is the most educated, with about 90% of its members being at least graduates (first stage of tertiary), against an average of 65%.[5]

2.4 Grievances and emotions

Grievances theories have long been challenged by more recent approaches to social movement studies (Klandermans, 1997), suggesting that what is to be analysed is more how grievances are translated into action than grievances per se.

Whilst it is certainly a valid suggestion, it does not mean that we should completely dismiss the analysis of grievances. As van Stekelemburg and Klandermans (2013: 888) have recently argued, 'at the heart of every protest are grievances, be they, experience of illegitimate inequality, feelings of relative deprivation, feelings of injustice, moral indignation about some state of affairs, or a suddenly imposed grievance'. Social psychologists are among the few who continued to pay attention to grievances, by underlining how together with other dimensions, the relations between grievances and emotions is worth analysing to explain collective action. In particular, they point at how grievances trigger a sense of injustice, which often produces indignation, which in turn is transformed in anger (Klandermans *et al.*, 2008).

There has recently been a recognition that social movement politics is passionate politics (Goodwin *et al.*, 2001), as 'participants in rituals communicate whole complexes of ideas and embodied feelings' (Barker, 2001: 188). Social movements are certainly rich in emotion: 'Anger, fear, envy, guilt, pity, shame, awe, passion, and other feelings play a part either in the formation of social movements, in their relations with their targets...and in the life of potential recruits and members' (Kemper, 2001: 58). Different typologies have been built that distinguish emotions that address a specific object from more generic ones, or short-term versus long-term emotions, or reciprocal versus shared emotions (Goodwin *et al.*, 2001). Emotions of trauma (grief, shame, helpless anger) are distinguished from emotions of resistance (pride, happiness, love, safety, confidence, righteous anger) in research on the movement against child sexual abuse (Whittier, 2001: 239). Feelings such as anger, outrage or fear can be particularly relevant in recruitment; indignation, pleasure, and pride can reinforce commitment (Goodwin *et al.*, 2001). Emotions are embedded in a context, where social rules define the proper emotions to feel and the proper way to express them. In fact, emotions are produced in social interactions: rituals produce emotions, and emotions interact with cognition in determining an individual's behaviour.

Social movements as well as protest events tend to transform emotions (e.g. transforming shame into solidarity), or to intensify them (Collins, 2001: 29). Successful rituals produce collective effervescence and group solidarity, strengthening the emotional energy. For example, some protest rituals and language helped transform shame into pride in the gay and lesbian communities (Gould, 2003; see also chapter 4 in this volume). In particular, social movements transform emotions by modifying the everyday relations the 'old' emotions were attached to (Calhoun, 2001: 55). Specific groups or specific environments nurture master emotional paradigms (or habitus) that define appropriate emotions (della Porta and Giugni, 2009).

In order to investigate grievances, we focus on their more political component, by looking at protestors' attitudes toward the political system and main political actors, as well as on their levels of satisfaction with the democracy in their country. Institutional trust is generally very low, showing similarities in the political grievance across generations: only 2.5% of protestors trust quite or very much national governments and 5% the parliament, with no significant differences across age cohorts. But, if only about 6% trust political parties, the percentage rises to 11% amongst the oldest protestors and decline to a mere 3% amongst the two cohorts of young protestors. Trade unions and the EU are more trusted, however, on overage by respectively 24% and 27% of protestors. If trust in EU is similar across generations, trade unions are much more trusted by the two older generations (34% and 25%) than by the young protestors (about 17%).[6]

Satisfaction with democracy is also very low in general with no statistical differences between generations: on a scale from 0 (not satisfied at all) to 10 (very much satisfied), all participants' answers scored only about 2.4, while the average of the youngest generation was 2.2.

Dissatisfaction with democracy calls into question the role of political parties, which were not trusted at all. However, whilst all generations were not trusting of political parties in general, most felt at least quite close to a specific party (about 75%, with no statistical differences across cohorts).

The attitude towards elections did not differ much between generations either: about 58% of the youngest and the following two generations disagreed or strongly disagreed with the statement, 'voting is useless in this country', while the percentage increased to 75% among protestors of the oldest generation.[7] What is more, about 98% of the protestors in our sample voted for one party in the last elections before the demonstrations, mostly for the centre-left and radical-left parties. Therefore, despite the mistrust expressed in relation to political actors and institutions, and the dissatisfaction with the Italian democracy, all protestors seemed to consider elections an important tool to put their claims forward.

As far as emotions are concerned, our questionnaire included a battery of four items, which sought to measure the emotional side of demonstrators' mobilization. Respondents were asked to express how angry, worried, frustrated or fearful they felt when they thought of the problems they were protesting about, using a scale from 1 (not at all) to 5 (very strongly). If we look at the percentages of those feeling each emotion 'very strongly', protestors all felt worried about the current situation (about 70%, with no statistical differences between generations), but a little fearful (only 22% on average, with no statistical differences), the youngest generation felt a bit more frustrated (50% against the average of 42%), but surprisingly, a bit less angry (57% against 63% in average).[8]

On the other hand, even when worried and angry, our protestors had not lost their belief that they could make a difference, and have in impact on the current situation: about 70% on average declared that they have an impact individually, but as many as 80% expressed the belief that 'groups have an impact' and that 'international cooperation among groups has an impact'. Again, no remarkable generational differences could be found on this sense of individual and collective efficacy.

To sum up, the youngest generation protesting in Italy in times of crisis do not differ too much in terms of grievances and emotions from the older generations. They were all indignant towards the political system, a system in which they were probably considered unable to deal with their life problems, and 'deaf' to their voice. The youngest protestors trusted institutions and political actors a bit less, but mistrust was widespread across all generations. The very low trust in political parties and representative institutions is linked to their strong dissatisfaction with democracy. However, if this makes them particularly angry and worried, it had not undermined their confidence on the impact of their voice.

2.5 Is there a generational collective identity in Italy?

Alessandro Pizzorno (1966) noted long ago that the characteristics of political participation are rooted in the systems of solidarity that are at the basis of the very definition of interest: interests can in fact be singled out only with reference to a specific value system, and values push individuals to identify with wider groups in society, providing a sense of belonging to them and the willingness to mobilize for them. From this perspective, participation is an action in solidarity with others that aims at protecting or transforming the dominant values and interest systems. The process of participation requires therefore the construction of solidarity communities within which individuals perceive of themselves and are recognized as equals. Political participation itself aims at this identity construction: before mobilizing as a worker, an individual has to identify herself as a worker and feel that she belongs to a working class. Identification as awareness of being part of a collective *us* facilitates political participation. As Pizzorno (1966: 109) stated, in fact, the latter 'increases (it is more intense, clearer, more precise) when class consciousness is high'. Participation is therefore explained not only by individual resources, but also by collective resources.

In fact, recent research has looked at the shift from individual to group identities, and then the politicization of such identities. In social movement studies, collective identification is expected only if there is awareness of the fact that one's own destiny is in large part linked to material conditions, while the lack of such awareness is defined as false consciousness (Snow and Lessor, 2013).

Identity formation is a complex process, which is difficult to operationalize. As far as our data are concerned, relevant indicators included in the questionnaire are identification with other demonstrators and the organizations staging the demonstrations, as well as various motivations, values and norms that pushed participants into the street. Our research data indicates that the youngest generation of protestors identifies less than the other generations, especially the oldest ones, both with participants (57% identify 'quite', or 'very much' against 67% on average; Cr.s V = 0.21, significant at 0.001 level) and with the organizations staging the demonstration (56% vs. 60%, Cr. V = 0.19, significant at 0.001 level).

With respect to motivations, the youngest generation seemed less motivated to participate in the selected demonstrations 'to express solidarity'; 'to press politicians'; because they 'feel morally obliged'; and because they want 'to raise awareness'

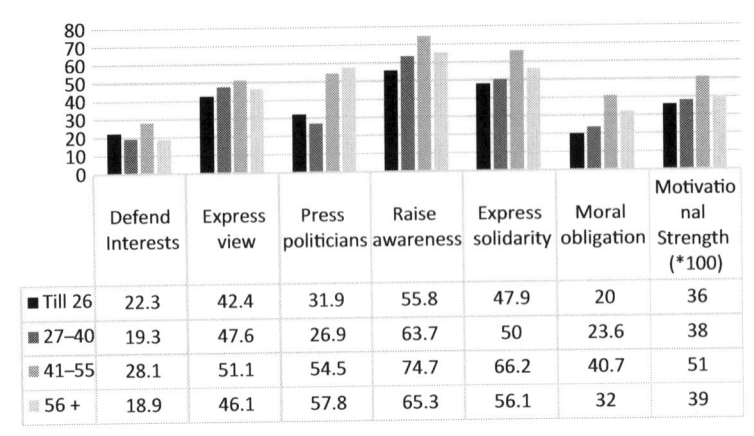

	Defend Interests	Express view	Press politicians	Raise awareness	Express solidarity	Moral obligation	Motivatio nal Strength (*100)
■ Till 26	22.3	42.4	31.9	55.8	47.9	20	36
■ 27–40	19.3	47.6	26.9	63.7	50	23.6	38
▨ 41–55	28.1	51.1	54.5	74.7	66.2	40.7	51
▧ 56 +	18.9	46.1	57.8	65.3	56.1	32	39

■ Till 26   ■ 27–40   ▨ 41–55   ▧ 56 +

Figure 2.2 Age cohorts by motivations for protesting. (Note: N: 469–505. Cr.s V is significant for 'press politicians' [0.28, at 0.001 level]; rise awareness [0.13, at 0.05 level], 'express solidarity' [0.15, at 0.01 level], and 'moral obligation' [0.18, at 0.001 level]. The ETA of the means calculated on the indicator of 'motivational strength' is 0.21, significant at 0.001 level.)

in the public opinion; while no significant differences are found when protestors are motivated 'to express their view' and 'to defend their interests' (Figure 2.2).

If we build an indicator of 'motivation strength', ranging from 0 (no motivation at all) to 1 (strongly motivated),[9] we notice that against a mean of 0.42, the youngest generation scores only 0.36, while the most strongly motivated generation is composed by the protestors who were at least 50 years old at the time of the selected demonstrations, with a score of 0.51 (Figure 2.2).

If we look instead at the self-location of the different generations on a classical left–right scale, we notice that the youngest generation of protestors, together with those of the second youngest generation, are less radical than the others: in the 0–10 left–right scale, in fact, young protestors score on average 1.3 while the two oldest one between 0.7 and 0.8.[10]

Summarizing, it seems that the youngest generation had a weaker collective identity than the other ones, at least as far as identification with other demonstrators (individually or in group) is concerned. The old generations were more radical, identified more with collective identities and were more motivated.

2.6 Networks and embeddedness

A different set of explanations for participation looks at embeddedness in social networks (Diani, 1992; della Porta, 2013). The main assumption is that participation in protests requires supporting networks that provide positive incentives, not only in affective terms but also in cognitive ones. Networks, which are relevant for the explanation of differential political participation, are those that provide information about protest events as well as emotional support. In line with the literature on social capital, these networks are expected to provide norms of reciprocity and reciprocal trust that are relevant for collective action. Embeddedness helps overcome the free-rider phenomenon by providing a sense of commitment as well as social control. So much so, that the single most relevant factor in explaining participation in protests was whether one had been asked to participate (Schussman and Soule, 2005).

The presence of dense but informal networks distinguishes social movements from other collective actors, which instead have clear organizational boundaries. In social movements, individuals and organizations, while keeping their autonomous identities, engage in sustained exchanges of resources oriented to the pursuit of a common goal (della Porta and Diani, 2006: 21).

In a cross-national study on protest participation based on the World Values Survey, Russell Dalton and his colleagues (Dalton *et al.*, 2010) noted that 'involvement in social groups creates networks for recruitment in political life' (ibid.: 59). In fact, 'social group membership are strong and significant predictors of protest' (ibid.: 67). Similarly, in research on immigrants' mobilization, Klandermans *et al.* (2008) observed that participation in associations was very highly correlated with experiences with protest, as well as with other dimensions connected with protest, such as identification with an ethnic group, sense of efficacy and feelings of injustice.

To operationalize network embeddedness, we use three sets of variables: the first set included whomever respondents were protesting with (if alone, with their family, with friends and acquaintances, with colleagues or with other members of the organization they belong to); the second, the most important channels of information through which protesters knew about the demonstration (mainstream or alternative media, family, informal, work or organizational channels); the third, their membership in different types of organizations.

The first set of variables has been aggregated by considering a scale of network embeddedness. This means that if a protesting individual was accompanied by friends and acquaintances, he/she is included in external networks; if he/she was with colleagues, he/she would be put in place of work/study networks; and if he/she was with other members of an organization, he/she would be considered part of an organizational network.

The data presented in Figure 2.3 shows that the youngest generation of protestors were more embedded in informal networks, such as friends, in networks based on the place of work or study, but also in organizational networks. The only relevant difference with the other generations seems to be that they rely more on relations built in their places of study, compared with relations in places of work of the older generations.

As far as the channels of information are concerned, the most important, and indeed interesting, difference refers to the much higher use of online alternative media and informal networks by the youngest generation (Figure 2.4). It is to be

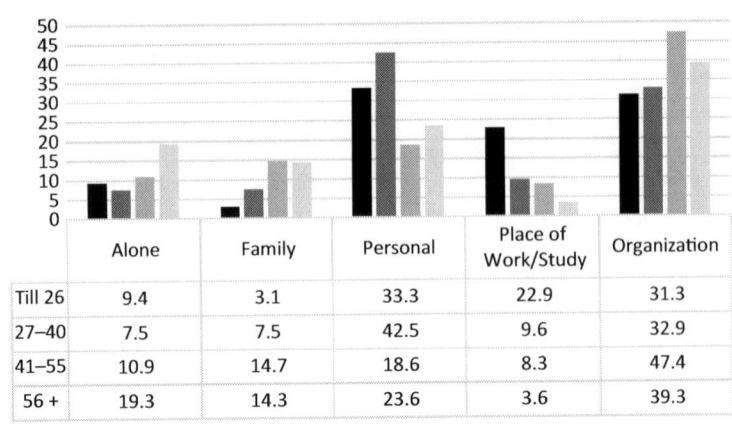

	Alone	Family	Personal	Place of Work/Study	Organization
Till 26	9.4	3.1	33.3	22.9	31.3
27–40	7.5	7.5	42.5	9.6	32.9
41–55	10.9	14.7	18.6	8.3	47.4
56 +	19.3	14.3	23.6	3.6	39.3

■ Till 26   ■ 27–40   ▨ 41–55   ▨ 56 +

Figure 2.3 Network embeddedness of the different generations. (Note: *N*: 538, Cr. s V: 0.20; significant at 0.001 level.)

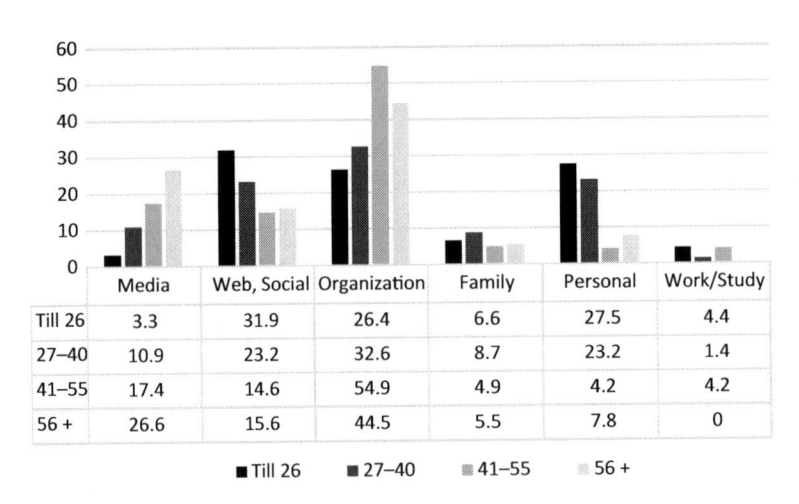

	Media	Web, Social	Organization	Family	Personal	Work/Study
Till 26	3.3	31.9	26.4	6.6	27.5	4.4
27–40	10.9	23.2	32.6	8.7	23.2	1.4
41–55	17.4	14.6	54.9	4.9	4.2	4.2
56 +	26.6	15.6	44.5	5.5	7.8	0

■ Till 26   ■ 27–40   ▨ 41–55   ▨ 56 +

Figure 2.4 Most important channels of information across generations. (Note: *N* = 501; Cr.s V: 0.24, significant at 0.001 level.)

remarked that the youngest protestors were less likely to use traditional media compared with the older ones. Moreover, against an average of 41% of protestors getting informed through organizational channels, only 26% of the youngest ones do so.

Finally, as far as organizational membership is concerned, 25% of the youngest generation participants were members of the organizations staging the demonstrations, against an average of 42%[11]; 37% (vs. 27% on average) were not members of any organization at the time of the demonstration or in the 12 months

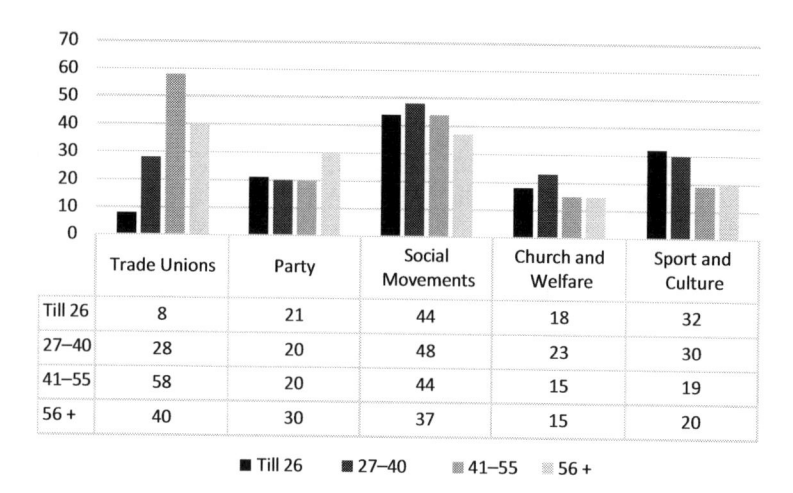

	Trade Unions	Party	Social Movements	Church and Welfare	Sport and Culture
Till 26	8	21	44	18	32
27–40	28	20	48	23	30
41–55	58	20	44	15	19
56 +	40	30	37	15	20

■ Till 26   ■ 27–40   ▨ 41–55   ▨ 56 +

Figure 2.5 Age cohorts by type of organizational membership. (Note: *N*: 549; Cr.s V is significant for membership in trade unions [0.36, at 0.001 level] and in sport and culture organizations [0.13, at 0.05 level].)

previous; 27% (vs. 29% average) were members of a single organization; 26% (vs. 32% average) were members of two or three organizations; and 11% (as on average) were members of more than three.[12]

If we look at the types of organizational membership (Figure 2.5), we notice that the youngest generation were prevalently members of social movement organizations or sports and culture organizations. Surprisingly, 21% of the youngest cohort were members of a political party – only the oldest generation show more party membership – while 18% stated that they were members of church or welfare organizations. Trade unions attracted more of the older generations, and though it comes as no surprise that only 8% of the youngest protestors were among their members, it is of some interest to note the relatively low score in this type of membership of the protestors from the 1970 to 1984 cohort, confirming the decline of unionization among young workers.

To sum up, the different generations were embedded in different types of networks. For the youngest generation of protestors, these were mostly informal and based on new, online, types of communication, whereas the older cohort were more formally embedded in organizations.

2.7 A generational comparison: some conclusions

In conclusion, we have observed that young people have participated in different marches on austerity issues, bringing with them experiences of social groups that are outside of the labour market. While similar to other cohorts in their mistrust for political institutions and trust instead in protest as a form of political participation, the young people we surveyed who had taken part in the anti-austerity protests seemed to have some specific characteristics in terms of a lower degree of collective identification and organizational embeddedness, and instead a higher degree of informal and 'virtual' connectedness.

These results seem, therefore, to resonate with those of recent research on youth mobilization in protest. From the generational point of view, research, in particular in the United States, has often lamented that, in contrast with the generation that came of age during World War II that was highly engaged in a duty-based citizenship (Putnam, 2000; Dalton, 2009), more recent generations have been considered as less engaged in conventional forms of political and civic activities (Fisher, 2012; Caren *et al.*, 2011: 147). As Fisher (2012) noted, however, several recent studies (again, in the United States) observed significant changes in the political participation of young people, who are said to protest at least as much as earlier cohorts, even if alternative forms of commitment, such as consumer activism, are increasingly popular amongst young people (e.g. Nonomura, 2016) and the same is true for petitions (Caren *et al.*, 2011: 147). The social and political engagement of young people is not necessarily declining, but changing form (Earl *et al.*, 2017). So, 'it is not that youth are disengaged, but rather that they do not engage in the same way that "dutiful" generations have' (Earl *et al.*, 2017: 1). In particular, young people's participation has developed towards 'engaged citizenship' in volunteering as well as embedding activism in their everyday life. Moreover, a new generation has been singled out – often called 'Millennials' (Connery, 2008; Dalton, 2009). Referring to this generation, a shift has been observed in terms of, 'an unmistakable expansion of youth interest in politics and public affairs' (Sander and Putnam, 2010: 11), in the forms of volunteering but also of voting. In fact, '2008 provides a baseline from which participation may expand as members of the millennial generation finish their studies, begin a career, purchase a home, and share the other life experiences that foster attention to government and politics' (Dalton, 2009: 196). The so-called Millennials have been characterized as carrying specific values: pluralism and tolerance, even if with low trust in political institutions. Research on political socialization pointed at the tensions between the supply in terms of social movement organizations and the generational taste for horizontal organizing (Earl *et al.*, 2017).

Today, researchers have addressed the Millennials as a generation that faces indeed very different life expectations and/or conditions than the previous ones, and it is more seriously threatened by the current economic crisis. As research in Europe has observed, as young people mobilized en masse in protest campaigns against austerity, for gender rights or territorial concerns, protest repertoires and frames tend to be adapted to a condition described as not only as socially precarious, but also as politically betrayed and civically repressed (della Porta, 2018). This makes it particularly interesting to continue investigating how these citizens overcome barriers of marginalization, network and develop collective identities.

Notes

1 As some assessment process requires formal attribution, we declare that Donatella della Porta is responsible for sections 'Young and anti-austerity protests in Italy: an introduction' and 'A generational comparison: some conclusions', while Massimiliano Andretta for the remaining sections.
2 The sudden and contagious mobilization by young citizens in many North Africa and Middle-East countries in the period between 2010 and 2011 aimed at democratizing their political systems (Abdih, 2011; della Porta, 2017).
3 For detailed information on the sample methodology see van Stekelenburg *et al.* (2012) and Andretta and della Porta (2014).
4 Professor Mario Monti was at the time prime minister of the new take-care government formed after Silvio Berlusconi resignation in 2011.
5 $N = 548$; Cr.s V: across level of education, 0.25, significant at 0.001 level.
6 Cr.s V: only across trust in political parties and trade unions, age cohorts show statistical differences (0.14 and 0.15, respectively, and both significant at 0.01 level).
7 N: 535; CR.s V, 0.13, significant at 0.01 level.
8 N: 431–496; Cr.s V is significant only for 'Angry' – 0.16 at 0.001 level.
9 The indicator is built by dichotomizing each type of motivation getting value '1' if the participant strongly agrees with the relative item, then normalizing the sum of all motivations dummies. The data in Figure 2.2 concerning this indicator are shown by multiplying it by 100.
10 The scale ranges from 0 (left) to 10 (right). Thus, the closer to 0 participants place themselves, the more leftist they are. $N = 529$; ETA: 0.18, significant at 0.001 level. It is worth noticing that young Italian protestors appear to be much less radical than other young protestors from Southern Europe (Andretta and della Porta, 2015; see also della Porta *et al.*, 2017).
11 $N = 515$; Cr.s V: 0.28, significant at 0.001 level.
12 $N = 519$; Cr.s V is not significant.

References

Abdih, Y. (2011). Arab Spring: Closing the Jobs Gap. High youth unemployment contributes to widespread unrest in the Middle East Finance & Development, Finance & Development (International Monetary Fund), June.

Andretta, M. (2018). Protest in Italy in times of crisis: A cross-government comparison. *South European Society and Politics*, 23(1), 97–114.

Andretta, M. and della Porta, D. (2014). Surveying protestors: Why and how. In: della Porta, D. (ed) *Methodological Practices in Social Movement Research*. Oxford: Oxford University Press, 308–334.

Andretta, M. and della Porta, D. (2015). Contentious precarious generation in anti-austerity movements in Spain and Italy. *Revista OBETS*, 10(1), 37–66.

Barker, C. (2001). Fear, laughter, and collective power: The making of solidarity at the Lenin Shipyard in Gdansk, Poland, August 1980. In: Goodwin, J., Jasper, J.M. and Polletta, F. (eds) *Passionate Politics*. Chicago: University of Chicago Press, 175–194.

Beyerlein, K. and Hipp, J.R. (2006). A two-stage model for a two-stage process: How biographical availability matters for social movement mobilisation. *Mobilisation*, 11(3), 299–320.

Bourdieu, P. (1979). *La distinction*. Paris: Minuit.

Calhoun, C. (2001). Putting emotions in their place. In: Goodwin, J., Jasper, J.M. and Polletta, F. (eds) *Passionate Politics*. Chicago: University of Chicago Press, 45–57.

Caren, N., Ghoshal, R.A. and Ribas, V. (2011). A social movement generation: Cohort and period trends in protest attendance and petition signing. *American Sociological Review*, 76, 125–151.

Collins, R. (2001). Social movements and the focus of emotional attention. In: Goodwin, J., Jasper, J.M. and Polletta, F. (eds), *Passionate Politics*. Chicago: University of Chicago Press, 27–44.

Connery, M. (2008). *Youth to Power: How Today's Young Voters Are Building Tomorrow's Progressive Majority*. Brooklyn, NY: Ig Publishing.

Corrigall-Brown, C. (2011). *Patterns of Protest: Trajectories of Participation in Social Movements*. Stanford, CA: Stanford University Press.

Dalton, R., van Sickle, A. and Weldon, S. (2010). The individual-institutional Nexus of protest behaviour. *British Journal of Political Science*, 40(1), 51–73.

Dalton, R.J. (2009). *The Good Citizen: How a Younger Generation Is Reshaping American Politics*. Washington, DC: CQ Press.

della Porta, D. (2013). *Can Democracy Be Saved? Participation, Deliberation and Social Movements*. Cambridge: Polity Press.

della Porta, D. (2015). *Social Movements in Times of Austerity: Bringing Capitalism back into Protest Analysis*. Cambridge: Polity Press.

della Porta, D. (2019). Deconstructing Generations: Concluding Remarks. *American Behavioral Scientist*, 63(11), 1578–1596.

della Porta, D., Andretta, M., Fernandes, T., O'Connor, F., Romanos, E. and Vogiatzoglou, M. (2017). *Late Neoliberalism and Its Discontents in the Economic Crisis*. London: Palgrave.

della Porta, D. and Diani, M. (2006). *Social Movements: An Introduction*. 2nd ed. Oxford: Blackwell Publishing.

della Porta, D. and Giugni, M. (2009). Democracy from below: Activists and institutions. In: della Porta, D. (ed) *Another Europe*. London: Routledge, 86–109.

Diani, M. (1992). The concept of social movement. *The Sociological Review*, 40, 1–25.

Downton, J. Jr. and Wehr, P. (1997). *The Persistent Activist: How Peace Commitment Develops and Survives*. Boulder, CO: Westview.

Earl, J., Maher, T.V., and Elliott, T. (2017), Youth, activism, and social movements. *Sociology Compass*, 11(4), 1–14.

Fisher, D.R. (2012). Youth political participation: Bridging activism and electoral politics. *Annual Review of Sociology*, 38, 119–137.

Giugni, M.G. (2004). Personal and biographical consequences. In: Snow, D.A., Soule, S.A. and Kriesi, H. (eds) *The Blackwell Companion to Social Movements*. Oxford: Blackwell Publishing, 489–507.

Goldstone, J.A. (2015). Demography and social movements. In: della Porta, D. and Diani, M. (eds) *The Oxford Handbook of Social Movements*. Oxford: Oxford University Press, 146–158.

Goodwin, J., Jasper, J.M. and Polletta, F. (eds). (2001). *Passionate Politics: Emotions and Social Movements*. Chicago: University of Chicago Press.

Gould, D.B. (2003). Passionate political processes: Bringing emotions back into the study of social movements. In: Goodwin, J. and Jasper, J. (eds) *Rethinking Social Movements*. Lanham, MD: Rowman & Littlefield, 282–302.

Inglehart, R.F. (1977). *The Silent Revolution*. Princeton: Princeton University Press.

Kemper, T.D. (2001). A structural approach to social movement emotions. In: Goodwin, J., Jasper, J.M. and Polletta, F. (eds) *Passionate Politics*. Chicago: University of Chicago Press, 58–73.

Klandermans, B. (1997). *The Social Psychology of Protest*. Oxford: Blackwell.

Klandermans, B., Van der Toorn, J. and Van Stekelenburg, J. (2008). Embeddedness and grievances: Collective action participation among immigrants. *American Sociological Review*, 73(6), 992–1012.

Lagroye, J. (1993). *Sociologie politique*. Paris: Presse de la Fondation Nationale de Sciences Politiques.

Lipset, S.M. (1971). *Rebellion in the University*. Piscataway, NJ: Transaction Publishers.

Lipset, S.M. and Altbach, P.G. (1967). Student politics and higher education in the United States. In: Lipset, S.M. (ed) *Student Politics*. New York: Basic Books, 199–252.

Lipsky, M. (1970). *Protest in City Politics: Rent Strikes, Housing and the Power of the Poor*. Chicago: Rand Mac Nally.

Mannheim, K. (1952). The problem of generations. In: Paul Kecskemeti, P. (ed) *Essays on the Sociology of Knowledge*. London: Routledge & Kegan, 276–322.

McAdam, D. (1986). Recruitment to high-risk activism: The case of freedom summer. *American of Sociology*, 92(1), 64–90.

McAdam, D. (1989). The biographical consequences of activism. *American Sociological Review*, 54(5), 744–760.

Milbrath, L.W. and Goel, M.L. (1977). *Political Participation*. Chicago: Rand McNally.

Nepstad, S.E. and Smith, C. (1999). Rethinking recruitment high-risk/cost activism: The case of the Nicaragua Exchange. *Mobilisation*, 4(1), 25–40.

Nonomura, R. (2016). Political consumerism and the participation gap: Are boycotting and 'buycotting' youth-based activities? *Journal of Youth Studies*, 20(2), 234–251.

Passy, F. and Giugni, M. (2001). Social networks and individual perceptions: Explaining differential participation in social movements. *Sociological Forum*, 16(1), 123–153.

Pizzorno, A. (1966). Introduzione allo studio della partecipazione politica. *Quaderni di sociologia*, 3–4, 235–286. Now in: Pizzorno, A. (1993). *Le radici della politica assoluta*. Milan: Feltrinelli, 85–128.

Putnam, R.D. (2000). *Bowling Alone: The Collapse and Revival of American Community*. New York: Simon & Schuster.

Sander, T.H. and Putnam, R.D. (2010). Still bowling alone? The post-9/11 split. *Journal of Democracy*, 21, 9–16.

Schussman, A. and Soule, S.A. (2005). Process and protest: Accounting for individual protest participation. *Social Forces*, 84(2), 1083–1108.

Snow, D. and Lessor, R. (2013). Consciousness, conscience, and social movements. In: Snow, D., della Porta, D., Klandermans, B. and McAdam, D. (eds) *Blackwell Encyclopedia on Social and Political Movements*. Oxford: Blackwell, 244–249.

van Stakelemburg, J. and Klandermans, B. (2010). The social psychology of protest. *Current Sociology*, 61(5–6), 886–905.

van Stekelenburg, J., Walgrave, S., Klandermans, B. and Verhulst, J. (2012). Contextualizing contestation: Framework, design and data. *Mobilisation*, 17(3), 249–262.

Whittier, N. (2001). Emotional strategies: The collective reconstruction and display of oppositional emotions in the movement against child sexual abuse. In: Goodwin, J., Jasper, J.M. and Polletta, F. (eds) *Passionate Politics*. Chicago: University of Chicago Press, 233–250.

Wiltfang, G.L. and McAdam, D. (1991). The costs and risks of social movement activism: A study of sanctuary movement activism. *Social Forces*, 69, 987–1010.

Chapter 3

Discourses and practices of citizenship among young people of different ethnic backgrounds living in Italy[1]

Cinzia Albanesi, Elvira Cicognani and Bruna Zani

3.1 Introduction

In this research, we examine the complex ways in which young people of different ethnic backgrounds construct representations of citizenship in Italy. Based on a psychosocial perspective (see Condor, 2011), the chapter describes the various shared representations of citizenship amongst young people and illustrates how they are connected through personal and collective experiences of participation in everyday life, and the need to cope with their marginalized status. The chapter is structured as follows: it begins with a short introduction on the debate about citizenship from a psychosocial perspective and a brief review of the citizenship literature specifically regarding people of immigrant background living in Italy. This provides the theoretical background for the discussion of the empirical research, which is discussed in the subsequent section of this chapter. The research was conducted using focus groups with a total sample of 85 young people of three different ethnic backgrounds (Italian, Moroccan and Albanian). Finally, in the last section of the chapter, the conversations with young people allowed the authors of the paper to clarify the dimensions of representations of citizenship in Italy as they emerged from youth experiences of participation and everyday life.

3.2 The debate about citizenship from a psychosocial perspective

Ever since its classical formulation, provided by Marshall (1964), citizenship in modern Western thought has been closely tied to the nation-state. Citizenship as a legal status determines the configuration of legal rights and duties between individuals and the state. Citizenship regimes serve to define who is entitled to hold the nationality of a given country and are based on either *jus sanguinis* or *jus soli*, or a combination of both. Italy has one of the most restrictive laws in Western Europe concerning citizenship (see also Hasanaj, 2018), based on the principle of *ius sanguinis* according to which, citizenship is not determined by place of birth but by having one or both parents who are citizens of that nation. Children born in Italy from migrant parents can apply for citizenship upon turning 18, and until they turn 19, if they can demonstrate that they have been living in Italy since birth, without interruption. According to the Law in force (L. 91/1992), unless they become Italian citizens, they maintain 'immigrant' status. The derogatory term 'extracomunitari' (literally, those who are out/do not belong to the European community) is used to address their situation, which denies full citizenship rights[2] (e.g. to vote and be elected, Zincone, 2006).

However, citizenship is more than this, and historical analysis of the use of the term in recent decades shows clearly that it contains a cluster of meanings (Heater, 2004). Stewart (1996), for example, proposed that the state-citizenship model (reflective of Marshall's view) can be contrasted with a democratic conception. This gives more weight to the idea that the political community is constructed through common membership in a shared local community. Barnes *et al.* (2004), for instance, called for a shift in focus in the study of citizenship: instead of asking, 'Who is a citizen?', social psychologists should ask, 'How do people claim citizenship?' Thus, citizenship is conceptualized as a political practice, not just in terms of political status. This is particularly relevant in the Italian context where young people, on the one hand, view their access to specific rights (e.g. house, and decent, stable jobs) as being limited, but show a capacity to invent new practices that challenge the status quo (i.e. co-housing, a sharing economy, etc.). Such practices can be seen as increasing their connectivity and mobility. As well as the challenging circumstances faced by many young people in Italy, this resilience and the ability of some to adapt creativity to potentially limiting circumstances is a theme that emerges in several chapters of this book.

These are themes that emerge from the debates among social scientists concerning citizenship, which according to Condor (2011), can be summarized in reference to four key concepts: 'dimensions', 'models', 'membership' and 'boundaries'. The debate around 'dimensions' refers to the question of whether citizenship should be limited to traditional (i.e. civic, political and social) right or should be defined in reference to specific cultural, economic and environmental rights (and responsibilities). 'Models' refer to how political perspectives have shaped citizenship in practice, such as the extent to which they emphasize duties and rights, and formal or substantial citizenship. 'Membership' concerns the legitimate basis upon which claiming citizenship. Finally, the debate around 'boundaries' focuses on two main issues: in particular, the relationship between citizenship and human rights, and whether citizenship borders must match those of the nation.

Citizenship based on the nation state define criteria for marking differences, and these provide the basis for exclusion (Hall, 2000; Yuval Davis, 2006). Such conceptions give an institutional framework for determining membership and 'otherness' in a specific (national) context, which affects the everyday experiences of citizens and non-citizens. As such, nation-based citizenship shapes discursive formations and practices (Andreouli and Dashtipour, 2014), establishing physical and psychological borders and constraints that can marginalize or challenge individuals. This is particularly important in a context such as the Italian one, where there is an increasing number of people (mainly on the basis of the EU legislation) who are entitled to ask for the protection of their individual rights, such as refugees and asylum seekers, without belonging to the nation and/or the political community.

3.3 How migration modifies citizenship

The complexity of migratory experiences affects both members of the host communities, including migrant and non-migrant people. All face the opportunity and challenge of reconstructing their views of citizenship based on different experiences of participation, belonging and recognition. For young people, and adolescents in particular, recognition takes place in very local circumstances bound by home, school and neighbourhood. As Nayak (2003: 177) suggests:

> In a changing world, young people's identities continue to be defined through the material cultures of daily life (including) neighbourhood networks, the institution of schooling, familial relations, local labour markets and place and locality.

Those local circumstances can be the training grounds for the practice of citizenship. Riccio and Russo (2011), in their study of everyday citizenship within migrant associations, show that many immigrants demand recognition in terms of social, economic and political participation. Colombo *et al.* (2011: 335) suggest:

> The presence of migrants leads to the deconstruction of the apparent unit of citizenship, highlighting the fact that the recognition of rights (civil, political and social) and of identity and the willingness to participate to collective life may constitute distinct elements that may also diverge or compete with each other.

In their interviews of more than 100 high school students, all of whom were the children of migrants from different ethnic origins, Colombo *et al.* (2011) found that belonging is multiple and flexible, especially among second-generation immigrants. Moreover, they assert that identity is not necessarily related to the legal dimension of citizenship (see also Colombo *et al.*, 2018). A similar result was also found more recently by Cicognani *et al.* (2018), who identified different identity strategies used in Italy by young people with a Moroccan background to claim recognition and belonging in a context that denies their citizenship as a legal status. However, both studies show that formal citizenship is only recognized as important so far as it gives legal admittance and increases the opportunities to participate in the public sphere. Colombo *et al.* (2011) found that the children of migrants in Italy demanded recognition by formal belonging and by daily enacting their responsibilities as citizens. They tried to make their opinions and preferences heard, to exercise their voice and power in everyday relationships and contexts, thus contributing to collective life. Bloemraad *et al.* (2008) have also shown that for migrants, participation in everyday settings is a way of expressing citizenship and belonging, even in the absence of formal recognition.

Based on these premises, in this research we examine the ways in which young people of different ethnic backgrounds (Italian, Moroccan and Albanian) construct their representations of citizenship in Italy and how these representations are anchored in their experiences of participation and everyday life. To this aim, we invited young people of multiple ethnic origins to join focus-group discussions, where they were encouraged to engage in discussion with their peers on their understandings of citizenship and youth participation. This empirical material is part of an international comparative research project whose findings have been translated into recommendations for national and European institutions and policy makers.

3.4 Methods

The total sample included 85 participants (40 males, 45 females): 28 were native Italians, 28 were Albanians and 29 Moroccans. Five participants had both Italian and Moroccan citizenship (they were included in the Moroccan subsample). The mean age of the sample was 19.50 ($SD = 2.67$; min 14 years, max 26 years). Thirteen focus groups were conducted: two were comprised of Italian young adults ($n = 14$; mixed by gender), and two comprised Italian adolescents ($n = 13$; mixed by gender). The Italians were all students. Two comprised Albanian young adults ($n = 15$; mixed by gender), and two comprised Albanian adolescents ($n = 14$; mixed by gender). Among the Albanian young adults, five participants were employed, and four were looking for a job. None of the Albanian participants had formal Italian citizenship. Among the 29 Moroccan youths, there were 14 males and 15 females (age range 16–23 years). Five focus groups were conducted with the Moroccan participants: two involved young adults ($n = 11$; mixed by gender), and three involved adolescents ($n = 18$; one mixed by gender, one male only, one female only).

Recruitment took place in 2010. At that time, Italy was governed by a rightwing coalition between the party of the prime minister (Forza Italia) and Lega Nord, a regionalist party. Lega Nord was denounced for its xenophobic propaganda by the European Commission against Racism and Intolerance (ECRI) in 2002 and later by other members of the civil society. Actually the Italian goverment is lead by the democratic party (PD) with M5S.

Participants were recruited using a purposive targeted sampling strategy in order to include individuals with varying degrees of civic and political involvement. Key informants and leaders of cultural, ethnic, religious, civic and youth/student groups and associations active in the local community were contacted and sent detailed information about the research project, along with a request for support in the organization of the focus groups. Focus groups took place mainly at groups' and associations' venues in order to facilitate the participation of people living in the community. Concerning levels of civic and political participation and organizational membership, although we explicitly asked to have a balanced number of active and non-active people within civic, political and youth organizations, this balance was not reached. A particular imbalance was especially prevalent amongst adolescents, who reported very low level of organizational membership: only four Albanians belonged to a cultural association, and seven Italians to scout groups. Moroccan adolescents reported no formal experiences of participation. Among young adults, membership in students' associations were common across all groups. Although the sampling was purposive, we still used a convenience sample, which means that the data was drawn from a self-selecting group.

An interview guide was developed in consultation with other members of the research project. The guide included questions concerning a series of predefined issues relating to citizenship, such as understanding of citizenship and of human rights issues, perceptions of young people's participation, opportunities and resources, perceptions of young people's voices, perceptions of young people's information and of themselves as citizens, sources of information on political and social issues and their influence, and personal and group experiences of participation. We did not ask for definitions of citizenship, but we gathered some definitions from the discussions of related themes. The focus groups started with an ice-breaking exercise using photos depicting a series of social problems, a technique called photo elicitation. All the focus groups were conducted in the Italian language; participants with an immigrant background were fluent even if for most of them Italian was their second language. Each focus group lasted between 1 to 2 hours; they were audio recorded and fully transcribed.

The data was analysed following the steps of thematic content analysis (Braun and Clarke, 2006). The focus group transcripts were thoroughly examined; references to experiences and reflections about civic and political participation, social issues, rights and duties were selected and compared across groups with the aim of understanding young people's representations of citizenship and how these were related to ethnicity, age and gender. The analytic process allowed us to progress from descriptions of participatory experiences to the identification of specific patterns of participation that contributed to building young people's views on citizenship. Even where the focus groups were homogeneous according to ethnicity, participants were all aware of living in a multicultural/heterogeneous society and discussed issues of citizenship in light of this awareness.

These specific patterns became the core themes of our analysis and allowed us to identify five dimensions that articulated young people's discourses on citizenship and belonging: the *legal or admittance* dimension, which refers to rights and duties that are recognized as components of citizenship; the *instrumental dimension*, where citizenship does not have a value *per se*, but is seen as a device by which to live 'undisturbed'; the *belonging dimension;* the *everyday performing dimension* and the *participatory* dimension. These dimensions will be discussed in the following sections.

3.5 Results and discussion

3.5.1 Citizenship as legal or admittance

The legal or admittance dimension can be articulated through two subdomains: one deals with rights and opportunities, deriving from legal citizenship; the other deals with duties, and what is expected from good citizens. The most important right was to be able to vote:

> In the end, in what do I participate? I'm under legal age (under 18), I cannot vote, I can't... In my view I do not have any real chance of participating. (FG1, Italian adolescent, female)

The ability to vote is recognized as the premise upon which equality is granted to all citizens (Bloemraad *et al.*, 2008) and a way to formally participate in democratic life. Those who were not eligible to vote, either because they were under the legal age or did not hold citizenship rights, emphasized the symbolic relevance of the right to vote:

> I have been living in Italy for 11 years and I cannot vote because I am not allowed to have citizenship yet. We just had elections, and I wanted to express my opinion. Italy is very far behind in comparison with other EU countries. (FG6, Albanian young adult, female)

This participant expressed the tension between her desire to be recognized as a member of the Italian community (we had elections) and her inability to vote wanted (I) to express my opinion). She was disappointed because Italian laws do not recognize her as full citizen.

Two important rights deriving from holding (Italian) citizenship rights are 'having the opportunity to circulate freely' both in the country and in Europe, and having a public voice:

> Honestly, I would feel ashamed to publicly protest in the street for my rights, as Albanian. I am sure that I would find opposition from most people, they would tell me, 'What are you doing? Go back to your country'. (FG12, Albanian adolescent, female)

The State defines migrants as those who do not belong to the political community. Consequently, this participant did not perceive her presence in the public sphere as feasible because of an anticipated rejection. Further, duties are declined in terms of respect for the nation-state laws, as the following excerpts of a focus-group discussion illustrates:

> Participant 2: Italians could tell you that you choose to come to Italy, so you must respect the Italian rules. That's the point. You must do what you are supposed to do... You cannot come and kill people.

> Participant 3: I agree, but this applies also to Italian people.
> Participant 2: Yes, you are right, but they are at their home.
> Participant 3: In my opinion it is not fair. But law is law and we must respect it, no choice. (FG2, Albanian adolescents, Participant 2 female, Participant 3 male)

> They are at home. Yes. But it does not mean that they are free to break the rules. (FG5, Albanian young adult, male)

> My opinion is that they have hosted us. We need to stay calm and respect their laws. (FG7, Moroccan adolescent, male)

The duty to be respectful of laws applies to everyone, but violations of good, responsible citizen behaviour (e.g. rule-breaking behaviour) are more 'severe' when committed by immigrants. This is not only because they may have dramatic consequences (in particular, in the case of criminal activity, being forced to go back to their country of origin), but also because such behaviour represents a threat to collective efforts towards integration. Participants with an immigrant background distance themselves from those members of their ethnic group that do not follow the rules/laws of Italy, thus contributing, in their view, to jeopardizing their efforts towards integration:

> Even if you do great things, you know what? When they read that some Albanians killed someone, your great deal vanishes. (FG2, Albanian adolescent, male)

A dutiful citizen should also be informed about what goes on, and should increase his/her personal awareness on social issues:

> [It is important] To be informed. It does not mean that everyone has to become an activist, or a volunteer, to establish a party, or become a politician. But one should be aware, should know what global warming is, or what women's rights deal with, or which are the problems relating to immigration. In order to be able to talk about these issues and make reasoned choices when the time to vote comes, or in order to fully participate in democratic life. (FG4, Italian young adult, male)

The final component of the dimension of citizenship relating to duties is caring about the common good and the public domain:

> I am worrying about environmental issues like Italians, because migrants have the same worries of Italians, women's problems, new technologies, welfare, these issues are relevant for all citizens (FG8, Moroccan young adult, male).

Few participants identified this component as being personally relevant to them. When they did, however, the younger participants especially emphasized the burden of responsibility:

> This year I became 18, I voted for the very first time, I really felt the pressure, a very big, big responsibility. (FG9, Italian adolescent, female)

3.5.2 Citizenship as a mere instrument

Those who do not have citizenship status must deal with pervasive and intrusive bureaucracy. For instance, in order to gain a long-term residency permit, they have to bear long waiting times, endless queues and the so-called 'Italian documentation regime' (Tuckett, 2018).

The experience of dealing with police headquarters could be very frustrating, but for some young people it was also considered part of the 'normal' process, or a small thing:

> Participant 2: Some days ago, I went to the police headquarters, for a small thing, concerning my residency permit...It took hours...
> Interviewer: What happened?
> Participant 2: They treat you bad, they are not polite, they answer roughly, there were people with babies waiting for hours. (FG6, Albanian young adults, male)

For others, it was perceived as a clear exclusionary experience and a threat:

> You know the more your future comes closer...the more you feel that if do not get that paper [residency permit], you are not going to have a future...Bureaucracy, this is, a big problem, because it is going to influence our lives. Maybe if we get it, when we have it, having it will be normal and then we will think of other stuff...maybe. (FG3, Moroccan young adult, male)

Under these circumstances, citizenship functions as a sort of guarantee of a 'normal' and legitimate presence in the context of formal delegitimization of one's existence.

There were also young people (in particular, those with an immigrant background) who simply recognized that citizenship was not important *per se*, but for its practical consequences: it is useful because it allows better work opportunities (e.g. in public offices), and it resets the risks of being repatriated to one's own country of origin. They ignored any other related entitlements or obligations, as one Moroccan adolescent pointed out clearly: [Citizenship] is useful. You can stay here forever, that's it.

3.5.3 Citizenship as belonging and identity

Recognition and belonging are crucial dimensions of citizenship and are delineated in different terms that relate to ethnicity, to culture, and to personal experiences of exclusion and inclusion. One delineation of it considers the extraordinary power that comes from multiple belonging (Yuval Davis, 2006), which allowed some participants to define themselves as bridges between cultures, and in a way, between generations (see also Colombo *et al.*, 2018) that become culturally different over time:

> We are not foreigners [who were] born in Italy. We are Italians of foreign origin. Being Italian is not about blood…it is about living and being a citizen of a country. Cultural origins are valued and considered because one has to understand also one's home country: your mother gives you life, your father makes you grow…they are both important, you must be able to talk with both… Italy is the father, your parents are the mother […] We are in a special position in which our role is that of holding the balance of power because most migrants are not capable of approaching the Italian society in a strong a way as we do, so we need to be those ones who stay in-between because we know both our context of origin and the context we live…we can be a sort of bridge…we can understand where we come from, who we are, why our parents are doing these things, and we also need to go into the society. (FG8, Moroccan young adult, male)

Belonging is rooted in culture, social networks and identity. It builds on daily experiences with peers, with local and material cultures and the relevance of those experiences. In fact, young adults with an immigrant background who were born in Italy, or who settled in Italy when they were very young, said they simply felt like children of the nation: Italians. This is shown in the following excerpts:

> Participant 2: I already feel part of this community, we are already members, it is not that someone else should entitle me. The problem is when someone asks me, 'Are you member or not?' This is disappointing, asking me something that I…
> Participant 1: It is the same thing I said before, waking up in the morning and… Why should I think this [being foreign]? (FG8, Moroccan young adults, female)

> We feel Italian. Many of us were born here, we are not so much Albanian anymore… We are not very Albanian; sometimes we speak Albanian at home, but rarely… (FG12, Albanian adolescent, male)

The quote of the Albanian adolescent clarifies that for him, and for many of his friends, being Italian is part of a natural, almost incidental process, relating to the fact that they are more familiar with the Italian culture (i.e. language) than with the one of their parents; for others, feeling Italian has to do with an explicit refusal of their 'ethnicity' and of the culture of their parents (cf. also Frisina, 2007). In the following excerpt, this refusal is expressed in terms of a contrast between 'them' and 'us':

> Participant 5: If they do not want that their children grow up like people here, they should not bring them here.
> Participant 4: Yes, nice saying. If you want to keep your religion, you do it in your home country, you cannot come here and wear the veil, burqa and so...
> Participant 5: I grew up here, I came here when I was four years old, they [my parents] cannot tell me 'You should dress this way', I am used to thinking as Italians do, to dressing as Italians do... I do not wear the veil, absolutely not!
> Participant 5: If I do not agree with what they [my parents]... tell me, I cannot listen to them... Consider marriage. If I had listened to them, by now I would have been at home, with two children, married! (FG10, Moroccan adolescents, all female)

In the above sentence, a refusal of parental religion and culture can be framed in a more general effort of adolescents to affirm their own identity and to engage in developmental separation – the process of individuation from their parents. There is evidence, however, that the ways young Muslim women negotiated religious belonging in a non-Muslim country may vary from refusing to use religious symbols like the veil, or using discursive strategies to defend their religion, to public re-appropriation of Islamic symbols (Cicognani *et al.*, 2018; Frisina and Hawthorne, 2018).

For other participants, material culture and its recognition do not change the reality of ethnicity that cannot be 'removed':

> If one is Italian, he or she is always Italian. The same for us who are Albanians: even if we come here for many years, we speak the language well, we can know everything, but we will never become Italians. I feel Albanian inside and proud of many things... (FG2, Albanian adolescent, female)

For other participants, citizenship was entailed in different layers of identity, which refer to different memberships relating to everyday contexts of experiences (namely, being young, being a student, being a member of an organization etc.). These identities allowed young people to find a place in society and legitimize their choices and participatory behaviour:

> This will be our battle, together with other young people, it is very important, the future that we need to create is a dream. (FG8, Moroccan young adult, male)

But citizenship for some participants represented a right for those who belonged to the wider human community:

> It is not something that one has to choose, to be Moroccan or to be Italian. It would be silly. One should simply be a citizen, a person. (FG8, Moroccan young adult, female)

Their perspective was reminiscent of those scholars who suggest that there is room to conceptualize citizenship as global (Golmohamad, 2008).

Some participants did not perceive of themselves through either a global or national membership sense. Instead, they described their experiences in terms of 'otherness'; a condition of lack of recognition and belonging that is identically dramatic when referred to the country of origin and the country of settlement:

> Participant 1: In my experience, I feel a stranger both here and in Morocco.
> Participant 2: True, when you go to Morocco you feel like a stranger.
> Participant 1: You are born in Italy, when you go to Morocco, they see you as a tourist. This is not probably the case for your family, but other people, they do not welcome you as someone they meet daily, really you are a stranger, here and there.
> Participant 2: So you feel?
> Participant 1: How can you feel? You're in the middle...a foot in two shoes. (FG11, Moroccan adolescents, Participant 1 Female, Participant 2, Male)

3.5.4 Citizenship as participation in civil society

We also found that young people recognized different opportunities to practice citizenship within civil society. One Italian adolescent explained that:

> Young people are more involved in volunteer organizations, parish groups than in politics. They are engaged, but in different ways... (FG1, Italian adolescent, male)

Albanian adolescents mentioned cultural associations as providing opportunities to promote citizenship and intercultural awareness:

> They organized that local event, it was simply great, many different cultures and also many Italians participating to an event where people shared food, culture, music. (FG12, Albanian adolescent, male)

Compared to adolescents, young adults had more experiences of membership within different kinds of organizations (youth forum, students' associations/

union, charity organizations, LGBT organizations, cultural groups, ethnic organizations, political parties):

> Working in that community for disadvantaged women was a relevant experience for me. It fits my ideals, the principle that moves the volunteer organization I worked with is to help other people and promote equality. (FG6, Albanian young adult, female)

> I was a member of the student association in my field (biotechnologies), then I entered the national board in Italy and finally I decided to run for the Left University Student Association, and I was elected. I'm also a member of a Left political party. (FG6, Albanian young adult, male)

Usually, their active experiences within university students' associations or volunteers' organizations were more positive compared to those within political groups and/or the youth sections of political parties, in terms of perceived efficacy and social contribution.

> In my experience, being a member of the student association is great; you develop relationships – because people and social relationship are fundamental – and through these relationships you feel valued and appreciated. You can contribute, you can have a say, discuss social issues, even with faculty members… it is really an opportunity. (FG4, Italian young adult, male)

> In my city, the Left political party pretends to include young people, but it is a fake. They welcome you, but soon after, you are not allowed to write in the newsletter, you are invited to avoid certain discussions or express your authentic opinion… In the end you leave, because power is in the hands of few people, always the same people. (FG13, Italian young adult, male)

Overall, within civil society organizations young people learned to play a role in shaping one's social reality, making one's opinions heard, exercise one's voice and advocate for people's rights.

> You can perform citizenship in youth centres, with associations that are growing… in political parties. (FG8, Moroccan young adults, male)

> The association I belong to deals with immigration issues. We advocate for second generations' rights, we try to help people with practical issues, but we also try to help people develop some awareness. (FG8, Moroccan young adult, male)

3.5.5 Citizenship as an everyday practice

For young people, practicing citizenship in everyday interactions takes the form of having a voice on social, cultural and political issues within their microcontexts of living. Young people, particularly adolescents, rarely spoke out, but they tried to make their voices heard within their own family, in class and at school more generally. One adolescent participant explained how citizenship entered her daily life and the role played by her parents in this process. Her experiences were positive and smooth:

> I have learnt political activism from my father. My mother, she is in politics, she was elected in the local municipality. So, we really have those ideas, regarding politics and vote and participation. We take our vote very seriously. We think and discuss it a lot. And then we vote. And we talk a lot about these issues. (FG1, Italian adolescent, female)

This was not always the case, and intergenerational tensions often emerged when dealing with social and political issues:

> My father, he fights for these things [immigrants' rights], but my mother, she goes from neutral – that's not good – to racist. And I cannot really understand her, given her past experiences. (FG12, Albanian adolescent, female)

> It happens quite often. My parents try to make me change my mind. On immigration issues, they are intolerant. I have an idea and they want me to have their idea. They try hard, but still I do not change my ideas, because they are wrong, and I'm right. (FG1, Italian adolescent, male)

Negotiating with adults about different views relating to social and cultural issues seemed to be a prerequisite skill in order to have voice. Young people, and in particular adolescents, were not always successful and sometimes as a consequence they felt powerless:

> It is impossible to talk about that with parents: if they are really convinced, to try and convince them to change their mind, it is a waste of time...They are full of prejudice. (FG11, Moroccan adolescent, female)

School represented another training ground for citizenship. Citizenship can take the form of group negotiation with adults in order to access some of the benefits, or of a collective protest:

> With our strikes, we finally got the coffee machine. At the beginning with teachers' permission, now without limitations. (FG9, Italian adolescent, female)

It can take also the form of an individual action in order to affirm one's perspective on contrasting social issues. One participant who belonged to a Catholic organization described his sustained efforts to persuade one of his teachers of the illegitimacy of abortion. He engaged in systematic debates to convince his peers as well as his teacher of his perspective, thus revealing a politicized identity (Simon and Klandermans, 2001). Individual actions, however, can also take more 'subtle' forms, where individual agency drives some mentoring efforts. Traditional roles are sometimes reversed so that younger generations take responsibility for educating the adults, sharing their knowledge and experience, to develop adults' understanding of the condition of a young person with a migrant background:

> I wrote a paper on Albanian immigration [she is smiling when she mentions her paper] last year...to get my degree. I wanted to make my teachers understand... I do not say that they are racist, but some look at you in a different way, and I wanted them to understand that I'm like them. (FG12, Albanian adolescent, female)

Another way to practice citizenship is through the arts. This way of performing citizenship is often misrecognized by institution, but young people trusted in the power of the arts to build bridges across cultures. One Italian adolescent explained that music and arts grow through 'contamination', irrespective of minority or majority status. As such, they contribute to intercultural awareness, facilitated by the fact that they speak a universal language. Moroccan adolescents proposed similar consideration with references to rap music: hybridizing cultures allowed them to 'rearticulate' different values and traditions, facilitating the integration processes.

Finally, young people mentioned Internet as a place where they could practice and perform citizenship. Sharing content and commenting on news were perceived by participants as forms of active citizenship, because posting news on the web was considered a form of political activism. Sharing news on the Internet can take the form of protest:

> You do not simply share news, but you comment it and other people react to your comment, and so people can discuss it... (FG4, Italian young adult, male)

3.6 Conclusions

The analysis revealed that young people held multidimensional representations of citizenship that built on ethnic origin, age and experiences of participation and belonging within their everyday contexts. The dimensions that were identified (*legal or admittance, instrumental, belonging, everyday practices, participatory*) expanded on those of Colombo *et al.* (2011) who proposed a recognition of rights, participation and identity as three independent dimensions of citizenship in a previous study based in Italy. The first dimension, *legal or admittance*, deals with rights and duties and entails multiple contradictions. Participants from the three ethnic groups perceived a lack of legal recognition as a condition that hampered conventional forms of political participation. For Italian adolescents, this condition is temporary and unproblematic, while for young people of Moroccan or Albanian origin, it is structural and difficult to deal with. Irrespective of being entitled to citizenship rights, dutiful behaviour (acting as a responsible, good citizen) is required of all people living in the country, even if young people with an immigrant background feel somehow more pressured to adhere to and respect Italian laws and norms. For older participants, this was a consequence of their minority status within their ethnic group; for younger ones, the adherence to Italian norms and values was a way to make explicit their belonging to the (Italian) country, regardless of (lack of) formal recognition.

Many immigrant adolescents had an *'instrumental'* conception of citizenship, where holding legal citizenship status is a guarantee against risks of repatriate, and other annoying situations resulting from lack of formal recognition. This dimension resonates with the notion of 'citizenship as admittance' (Colombo *et al.*, 2011) and is typical of young people who ground their sense of belonging in their ethnic community, and who are somehow sceptical about the idea of multiple belonging.

Between those who refused their ethnic background, because they 'felt' Italian and wanted to be recognized as such, and those who were interested only in the practical consequences of Italian citizenship, there were young people who imagined a more inclusive Italian society, that values and incorporates different ethnic belongings. Even if most of them had an immigrant background, there were also some Italian adolescents who imagined hybrid identities, which benefited from ethnic and cultural contamination. Our results show a variety of creative ways that young people were able to use to negotiate their identity to affirm their multiple belongings (that may or may not include ethnicity, gender, generation etc.) when facing challenges. Hybrid or not, *belonging* appears as a key dimension of citizenship, that is not defined by formal recognition, and that satisfies a fundamental psychological need. Colombo *et al.* (2011) referred to a similar process that was called citizenship as 'identification'.

The data was collected in 2010 and is still relevant because the situation that young people had to deal with in 2018, when this chapter was written, reflects and exacerbates the conditions of that time: an intolerant government that built its consensus on security, restrictive policies against migrants, and scarce (if not totally absent) attention to young people and other minority groups. Now, as then, young people are capable of resilience and of adapting to the challenges they meet, reacting, readapting and reinventing themselves (Colombo *et al.*, 2018), as widely discussed in this book.

Irrespective of their ethnic background, young people highlighted *participation in civil society* activities and associations as an effective way of making one's opinions and preferences heard, thus representing a specific dimension of citizenship. There is evidence also in this sense that many young people are skilled in participatory practices and able to engage in creative acts of contestation, confronting themselves with injustice, power unbalance and their needs' affirmation (Banaji, 2018). In the absence of legal citizen status, civil society organizations continue to provide them with concrete opportunities to participate to political life, both at the local and national level. Italian adolescents and young adults with an immigrant background who are interested in social and political issues recognize membership and participation in civil society organizations as a way of performing political citizenship. This is still true. Even if in 2020 the government in charge in Italy does not have xenophobic policies, and is more concerned with immigrants' well-being, it does not recognize full citizenship to second generation immigrants yet.

However, for adolescents, in particular those with an immigrant background, citizenship is above all an everyday practice based on the affirmation of their right to make their own choices (e.g. clothes, friends, way of life) and to maintain and express their own ideas and perspectives on different social and political issues. Citizenship, as such, is performed at home and at school, where young people need opportunities to practice and learn competences that are critical to participating in an effective and constructive way in their increasingly diverse society. For instance, the ability to communicate, to express and understand different viewpoints, to negotiate, etc. In 2020, adolescents continue to claim real opportunities, to have a say, and to be heard (Malafaia *et al.*, 2018). But more importantly, they claim adults' help to increase and develop critical skills and awareness on societal issues.

In their representations of citizenship, young people saw legal status as a necessity, regardless of their ethnicity. This was the case even for those who were not yet self-sufficient, to avoid institutional discrimination and foster inclusion. Inclusion is, above all, a matter of access and respect of personal, natural and human rights. Young people with immigrant backgrounds, on that basis, contested the Italian model based on *ius sanguinis* and were in favour of a model based on cultural recognition and shared membership in the community. As such, they claimed citizenship on their own terms: a right to presence, autonomy and voice. According to their terms, these were necessary conditions to be protagonists of their own destiny. Unfortunately, their 'claim for citizenship' did not encounter the support of the political parties of the last legislature. The opportunity to change the law and nowadays facilitating the access of the second generation to Italian citizenship seems increasingly remote. In 2011, a reporter from *Euronews*, an online newspaper, commenting on young people's situation in Italy (probably inspired by the title of a famous Cohen brothers movie) defined Italy as, 'No country for young people'. In 10 years' time, the number of NEET (Young People Not in Employment, Education or Training) has increased, reaching a dramatic 25% in 2018, as well as the number of young native Italians who moved abroad to find jobs and live a decent autonomous life. Second generations are not on the political agenda anymore. There are many young people who keep claiming their rights and show resilience, but resilience may not be enough to grant social justice, as it requires structural change and authentic inclusion of marginalized communities (Cattaneo *et al.*, 2014). Italy has already lost (at least) one generation; it would be important not to forget the following ones also.

Notes

1 The research from which this chapter is drawn was supported by a grant received from the European Commission 7th Framework Programme, FP7-SSH-2007-1, Grant Agreement no: 225282, Processes Influencing Democratic Ownership and Participation (PIDOP) awarded to the University of Surrey (UK), University of Liège (Belgium), Masaryk University (Czech Republic), University of Jena (Germany), University of Bologna (Italy), University of Porto (Portugal), Örebro University (Sweden), Ankara University (Turkey) and Queen's University Belfast (UK).

2 In an attempt to reform the law, and to introduce a moderate form of 'ius soli', Rete G2 (a national organization founded in 2005 by heirs of immigrants who were born or grown up in Italy) launched a campaign in 2010 called 'L'Italia sono anch'io (Italy is me too)'. Although the campaign successfully gathered more than 200,000 signatures, the citizenship bill reform supporting second generations' request for citizenship proposed by the Democratic Party finally reached the Italian Parliament only in 2015 and was only approved by the 'Camera' (i.e. one of the two branches of Parliament). When it was proposed to the 'Senato' (i.e. the other branch of Parliament) for approval in 2017, it encountered opposition from the right-wing and centre-right conservative parties (Frisina and Hawthorne, 2018) and therefore was not passed. The Yellow-Green government elected in March 2018 (a coalition of Lega and 5SM-five stars movement) struck down the reform in view of adopting a broader, explicit anti-migration policy. The governement in charge in 2020, lead by the democratic party reloaded the discussion on ius soli.

References

Andreouli, E., and Dashtipour, P. (2014). British citizenship and the 'other': An analysis of the earned citizenship discourse. *Journal of Community & Applied Social Psychology*, 24(2), 100–110.

Banaji, S. (2018). Defining successful citizen action: Practices, politics and motivation in youth citizenship across Europe. CATCH-EyoU Blue papers series. Available at: http://www.catcheyou.eu/the-project/publications/wp8bp/.

Barnes, R., Auburn, T. and Lea, S. (2004). Citizenship in practice. *British Journal of Social Psychology*, 43(2), 187–206.

Bloemraad, I., Korteweg, A. and Yurdakul, G. (2008). Citizenship and immigration: Multiculturalism, assimilation, and challenges to the nation-state. *Annual Review of Sociology*, 34, 153–179.

Braun, V. and Clarke, V. (2006). Using thematic analysis in psychology. *Qualitative Research in Psychology*, 3(2), 77–101.

Cattaneo, L.B., Calton, J.M. and Brodsky, A.E. (2014). Status quo versus status quake: Putting the power back in empowerment. *Journal of Community Psychology*, 42(4), 433–446.

Cicognani, E., Sonn, C.C., Albanesi, C. and Zani, B. (2018). Acculturation, social exclusion and resistance: Experiences of young Moroccans in Italy. *International Journal of Intercultural Relations*, 66, 108–118.

Colombo, E., Domaneschi, L. and Marchetti, C. (2011). Citizenship and multiple belonging: Representations of inclusion, identification and participation among children of immigrants in Italy. *Journal of Modern Italian Studies*, 16(3), 334–347.

Colombo, E., Leonini, L. and Rebughini, P. (2018). A generational attitude: Young adults facing the economic crisis in Milan. *Journal of Modern Italian Studies*, 23(1), 61–74.

Condor, S. (2011). Towards a social psychology of citizenship? Introduction to the special issue. *Journal of Community & Applied Social Psychology*, 21, 193–201.

Frisina, A. (2007). *Giovani musulmani d'Italia*. Roma: Carocci.

Frisina, A. and Hawthorne, C. (2018). Italians with veils and Afros: Gender, beauty, and the everyday anti-racism of the daughters of immigrants in Italy. *Journal of Ethnic and Migration Studies*, 44(5), 718–735.

Golmohamad, M. (2008). Global citizenship: From theory to practice, unlocking hearts and minds. In: Peters, M.A., Britton, A. and Blee, H. (eds) *Global citizenship education: Philosophy, theory and pedagogy*. Rotterdam: Sense Publisher, 521–533.

Hall, S. (2000). Who needs identity? In: du Gay, P., Evans, P. and Redman, P. (eds) *Identity: A Reader*. London: Sage, 15–30.

Hasanaj, S. (2018). Europeanization through migration policies: Legislative comparison between Civil Law Systems and Common Law Systems. *Academic Journal of Interdisciplinary Studies*, 7(2), 73–95.

Heater, D. (2004). *Citizenship: The Civic Ideal in World History, Politics and Education*. Manchester: Manchester University Press.

Malafaia, C., Ferreira, P. and Menezes, I. (2018). Understanding the role of school education in promoting active citizenship. CATCH-EyoU Blue papers series. Available at: http://www.catcheyou.eu/the-project/publications/wp6bp/.

Marshall, T.H. (1964). *Class, Citizenship, and Social Development*. Garden City: Doubleday & Company.

Nayak, A. (2003). *Race, Place and Globalization: Youth Cultures in a Changing World*. Oxford and New York: Berg.

Riccio, B. and Russo, M. (2011). Everyday practiced citizenship and the challenges of representation: Second-generation associations in Bologna. *Journal of Modern Italian Studies*, 16(3), 360–372. doi:10.1080/1354571X.2011.565636.

Simon, B. and Klandermans, B. (2001). Politicized collective identity: A social psychological analysis. *American Psychologist*, 56(4), 319.

Stewart, J. (1996). Innovation in democratic practice in local government. *Policy & Politics*, 24(1), 29–41.

Tuckett, A. (2018). *Rules, Paper, Status: Migrants and Precarious Bureaucracy in Contemporary Italy*. Stanford: Stanford University Press.

Yuval Davis, N. (2006). Belonging and the politics of belonging. *Patterns of Prejudice*, 40(3), 197–214.

Zincone, G. (2006). The making of policies: Immigration and immigrants to Italy. *Journal of Ethnic and Migration Studies*, 32(3), 347–375.

Chapter 4

Strategy, performance and gender

An interactionist understanding of young activists within the Italian LGBT movement and the Catholic countermovement

Anna Lavizzari

4.1 Introduction

As discussed more extensively in Chapter 2, young people are central players in activism in Italy and across Europe. This chapter investigates the linkages among the perceived experience of movement's participants while simultaneously shedding light on the contingencies young protestors are confronted with in the process of negotiating their gender identities.[1]

The LGBT[2] movement and the Catholic countermovement[3] provide a case for the analysis of how young activists perceive gender and sexuality issues in Italy, as they have increasingly and consistently gained saliency in the public arena over the past years. The onset of the mobilization under analysis is part of a political and public debate that has developed around different legislative bills concerning the introduction of the crime of homophobia in the penal code, the recognition of civil unions and the inclusion of gender-oriented educational programs in schools.

However, it is important to point to different factors that single out Italy from other Western countries where similar countermovements exist, and that characterize the Italian context as one of 'slower and softer' secularization. The most noticeable factor is related to the geopolitical position of the Vatican, which grants the Catholic Church a stronger influence, as well as strategic proximity to Italian institutions and the public sphere. More specifically, a distinctive trait of the Italian landscape concerns the direct influence of the Catholic Church in the political activity of all major political parties along the spectrum, preventing a real secularization process (Ozzano and Giorgi, 2015). The Catholic Church calls for politicians and citizens to support its positions, particularly in the realms of family, sexuality and gender equality.

The 'gender issue' is thus diagnosed in Italy through a normative discourse where 'gender theory' and 'gender ideology' are explained by Catholic authorities as a postmodern social problem, a concrete manifestation of rampant individualism and relativism. In this view:

[G]ender represents a homogeneous set of principles, concepts, laws and policies of a new 'ideological dictatorship', whose political program would be the extension of the domain of democracy to the sexual realm. [...] the 'gender ideology' is perceived as a threat through which democratic institutions transgress traditional models based on Catholic values. (Lavizzari and Prearo, 2018)

In this context, both youth LGBT and Catholic claims emerge forcefully, expressing the need not only for political and symbolic recognition, but also for material rights in terms of sexual citizenship. That is, in relation to how rights are granted or denied to different social groups on the basis of sexuality, including but not restricted to rights of sexual expression and identity (Richardson, 2015).

At the same time, social movements are themselves microcosms of the types of gender structures and processes evident in the wider society; activism can therefore be considered a gendered terrain of struggle and negotiation. The main focus of this chapter is on the subjective level and takes into account the 'gendering of consciousness' as an outcome of young activists' practices. The chapter advances the argument that youth activism should be understood as a process of learning and development of critical awareness concerning each individual's rights and interests (Kiecolt, 2000; Kirshner, 2007). This process of learning and development is critical for the formation of gender consciousness. Despite the fact that no linear connection can be drawn between growth in awareness and collective action, we can expect that youth develop forms of activism in which they become aware of gender differences and consequently begin to act with awareness in relation to this difference. Not only does activism provide youth with a space for learning and development through intense socialization processes, but it also provides a context for deep transformation of identities. The transitional dimension of youth constitutes an important aspect in the formation of young people's gender identity.

Scholarship on youth and activism, gender and social movements, remarkably neglected to analyse how gender intervenes in the experience of young activists in Italy. Most current literature has limited its focus to the analysis of gender differences in youth's political participation (Albanesi *et al.*, 2012; Cicognani *et al.*, 2012; Gordon, 2008; Matthews *et al.*, 2010). Yet, the analysis of youth, gender and activism is particularly timely in the Italian context in which, in line with trends in many Western societies, '...sexuality has become a fundamental dimension through which access to and understandings of citizenship are filtered' (Russell *et al.*, 2010: 472).

Indeed, different regulatory practices produce the identity concepts of sex and gender, and more specifically the system of powers that seek to establish and perpetuate a causal and linear connection between biological sex, gender identities and sexuality (Foucault, 1976). In this respect, youth have actively contributed to the current debate on gender and sexuality through different forms of social action and critical civic engagement in the form of activism(s). As we will see, such a relationship of causality and its continuity is central to young Catholic activists' understanding of legitimate, meaning natural, 'human beings'. The practice of a 'substantializing view of gender' is key to Catholic activists, not only in the expression of a naturalistic model but also in the reification of normative gender relations. Conversely, for young LGBT activists, the coherence between gender, sex and desire is put into question through different dynamics of identification – that is the multiple ways in which each individual is able to define their gender identity beyond the male/female binary.

Few scholars have suggested that age categories are useful in order to conceptualize gender in non-polarized ways (Gardiner, 2002). While it is recognized that there is no automatic progression towards womanhood or manhood but rather loosely defined overlapping age categories positioned on a continuum, gender is seen by people in oppositional, unchangeable ways, intrinsic to the individual identity. As Gardiner (2002: 95) puts it:

> [T]hus dissonance between biological age and self-perception is considered normal, though often comic, in comparison with dissonance between biological sex and self-defined gender, which is often tragic.

A useful way to conceptualize gender and age is therefore to think of them not only as socially constructed, but also as performative, as part of each individual's experience and of systems of power relations.

4.2 Methods

The study presents empirical evidence based on 37 in-depth interviews conducted with young Catholic and LGBT activists within the time frame April 2015 to January 2016, disclosing findings on the interplay between identity construction processes, and the social structural context. Overall, the chapter handles data collected from the groups under analysis with a main theoretical premise: the horizontal nature (interactionist) between structural constraints as they are experienced, challenged or reiterated by activists, and the negotiation of gender identities originating from social interaction. The investigation included activists in the 18- to 30-age range and employed the following methods: in-depth interviews with activists from the LGBT and Catholic movements, participant observation at meetings, conventions, organizations' sites and protest events. In addition to collective behaviour, observations were made in relation to individuals' actions, to the concepts of social performance, gender performativity and the symbolic dimensions of protest. In this case, particular attention was given not only to groups' gender composition but also to the ways in which activists and their opponents were performing gender – how gender constituted both the field of contention and a social performance. Both the Catholic and the LGBT movements are formed by actors of different nature, linked by multiple social, political, economic and ideological connections, active in multiple contexts.

For the purpose of this study, the investigation revolves around groups that do not represent the Catholic or the LGBT movement as a whole but rather a subset of players coalescing around the specific issue of gender and LGBT rights.

4.3 Understanding gender: between collectivism and individualism

The notion of gender identity includes the reflexive views and perceptions of social actors derived from processes of interaction with other actors, structures and different social groupings (Wharton, 2005). In particular, it embeds understandings and meanings of femininity and masculinity used to define others, and ourselves, that are usually supported and reinforced by existing social structures and norms. How is being female or male expressed in activists' understandings of gender? These conceptions inform how identities are negotiated through social interactions between individuals, and between the individual and the social structures forming their social environment.

4.3.1 Catholic activists

Even in a context of Catholic matrix, such as the Italian one, where the level of religious activism is traditionally high, we note a tendency of young people to desert religious practices and beliefs. The share of young people aged 18 to 29 who claim to be atheistic or agnostic is now over 30% (Garelli, 2016). Obviously, it is not yet the level of atheism that we find in other countries of Central and Northern Europe, where 45% of young people declare themselves as atheists or agnostics, both in Catholic and in Protestant countries (Garelli, 2016). Italy has always been a country where the level of religious practice is higher than elsewhere, and in which the process of secularization is slower and softer.

Indeed, 70% of young people continue to believe, and a minority of them, increasingly reduced but increasingly qualified (15%), is characterized by a strong commitment to associations; young people who have known relevant religious figures, have a religious past and have remained inside this path of faith (Garelli, 2016).

Questioning gender identity and roles, data on young Catholic activists today shows that one's perceived gender identity cannot be disentangled from the religious structure in which it is embedded. Based on the fundamentals of Catholic discourse and praxis, activists connect questions related to sexual and gender identity to a natural, taken-for-granted, self-evident, commonsensical world. The biological difference between a man and a woman is stated as a governing principle and value for the functioning of society at large. Reflecting on the perceived damage caused by 'gender theory' and the idea that gender identity is a social construction, some activists reacted firmly. The 'data of the flesh', biological sex, gives empirical evidence that cannot be overlooked and must be taken as the only valid fact for the natural construction of one's gender identity, which is a necessary condition for the stability and continuity not only of the individual, but also of society as a whole. Essentialist assumptions – that gender difference is innate, transcultural and historical – therefore constitute the fundamental belief in the real. However, we must ask how what is *natural* is being understood. According to participants' accounts, this is the unquestionable meaning of the act of faith, the absolute truth: sexual identity equates to gender identity, for the sake of procreation. At no point was this assumption questioned by interviewed activists. The conflation of gender with sexual identity is an accepted understanding that does not come from confusion or misunderstanding; rather, it is consciously argued and acted out by activists.

The indisputable character of sexual and gender themes lies at the very heart of Catholic protests. These are issues that are impossible to take a secular standpoint on, young activists claim, and it is precisely around these issues that the need to publicly engage in preventing social change arises. Although understandings of gender identity were consistent in content across different accounts, it is possible to observe variations in participants' reflections on gender roles. While men and women were considered to be born into their respective roles and identities with natural (read, social) masculine or feminine characteristics acquired at birth, some, particularly young, female activists seemed increasingly uncomfortable with gender stereotypes attached to men and women. However, this position is difficult to defend if compared to the overall assumption that women and men are intrinsically different, and that sexuality and gender function in tandem. This duality produced contradictions concerning roles, particularly women's roles. Observations suggest that young Catholic activists are maybe less inclined than earlier generations to emphasize gender polarization. Yet, it is not clear how gender roles develop throughout the life course, as it seems commonly accepted that gender identity is acquired at birth and remains fixed over time. On the one hand, individuals are inscribed into traditional understandings of femininity and masculinity, without being given the agency to change such identities. Men and women are said to hold the status of pairs but not equals. On the other hand, data suggests indecision about the extent to which women and men can choose, in their adulthood, to prioritize identities, whether religious, professional, or, most importantly, as a parent. Although some degree of freedom is granted to women to decide whether to pursue a professional career or a 'maternal career', it is strongly suggested, by both young women and men, that priority should be given to the creation of a family.

However, questions arise concerning the different discourses, knowledge and positioning referred to in participants' narratives. How are these reflections and assumptions intentionally or unintentionally transmitted? While biological sex was cited over and over, and valued at the highest as a distinctive trait of identity and source of identification, *sexuality* as someone's personal experience was constantly subdued in young activists' accounts. It is interesting to note therefore how a certain 'rule of discourse erasure' prevails in narratives about sexuality as in one's sexual identity and experience.

Interestingly, the notion of sexuality was suppressed even when participants were asked about homosexuality. Some seemed to accept the possibility that love could exist between two persons of the same sex. Yet, this love, in order to be accepted, had to be split from sexuality, somehow it must transcend sexual desires and behaviours. Still, the degree of acceptance varied among participants and was notably higher for those who knew or had met homosexual people in their close environment, whether it be friends, fellow students or colleagues.

The overall understanding and representation of homosexuality showed itself to be extremely diverse and relativistic across accounts. However, homosexuality in itself within the context of certain groups remained heavily sanctioned. Very much in practice, some Catholic groups actively participate in the regulation of gender and sexual norms, behaviours and performances. This shows the power of religious structures in shaping *self-monitoring* behaviours and identity management:

> I feel like a completely different person now. Before I converted, my behaviours were more effeminate. Even after the conversion though I wasn't really aware of it, but thanks to a sister in Christ who helped me all along this change, she made me aware of certain behaviours and she helped me feeling more like a man. [...] She pointed to behaviours that for me were maybe 'normal' and she made me notice that a man cannot behave like that, and I started to change [...] She really valued the man that was in me. (Catholic activist)

This observation is in line with studies reporting the radical transformations that individuals often undergo after joining a movement: 'conversion to a cult or a sect often implies more or less radical transformation of one's identity and loyalties, and this is deeper the more demanding membership criteria in the new group are' (della Porta and Diani, 2006: 97).

Maybe unsurprisingly, the most recurrent system of norms and dispositions, in addition and intersecting with religion, through which understandings of gender emerge, is family. It is within the structure of the traditional family that participants formed their own understandings of 'being a man' and 'being a woman' and where first-hand information on gender-appropriate behaviours was learnt. In other words, it is through family relations that a gendered *habitus* is acquired.[4]

Most importantly, data elucidates the ways in which family, as a structure at the intersection with the religious structure, becomes particularly powerful in providing frames of meaning that guide individuals' actions at the individual and collective level. That is, religion plays an important role in reinforcing the gendered structure. However, what emerges from data is not a blatant justification of unequal gender roles between men and women, but rather a peaceful consensus that justifies, once again, for the common good – good of the family, community and society – the differences in roles to be covered by males and females.

Yet, it cannot be taken as a given that young people growing up in a Catholic family will automatically adopt their parents' faith and values (Shepherd, 2010). The process of 'believing and belonging' results from complex life experiences but also, particularly when it is undertaken through active engagement in movement activities, from choice. Indeed, a strong attachment to values and meanings learnt through interactions with family members, which translates into a path-dependent need to *reproduce* the same experiences and practices in the present. The majority of youth thus champion the protection of 'the traditional family' ideal-type from disintegration by the forces of social change. The accounts from Catholic activists overtly synthesize the dominant understanding of the traditional family as a preferred form of organization, giving a representation of 'the family' as an *ideology*, where meanings of gender difference and messages of morality and normality are reinforced. In other words, it is an example of how Catholic activists see their lives (in this case their parents' lives) as experience – a concrete manifestation of principles and a way of living that is 'correct' to be handed down to future generations, with the attitude of 'let me educate my children according to what I believe that is not what I believe, but what I have lived' (Catholic activist). This is consistent with previous studies suggesting that for 'those who grow up in a community of faith being "a Christian" is both a collective identity, a choice and a "youth" lifestyle' (Shepherd, 2010: 151).

Parallel to this, young people might develop resilience at different levels: cognitive, moral and cultural. In a sense, processes of identity work are accelerated through activism, not only in the case of gender. In this, I subscribe to other scholars' argument that 'morality is that dimension of culture which draws implications for judgement and action from the emotions and cognitive understandings that people hold. [...] Protest is pre-eminently about moral vision, for participants make claims about the world should be, but is not' (Jasper, 1997: 135). In a context of distress concerning changes in gender equality and sexual rights, Catholic activists have expressed how their gender identities gained saliency and centrality through their involvement in associational activities. By contrast, a related theme concerns the denial of individual agency in the social construction of one's gender identity, which forms the basis of one of the core values expressed by Catholics: *collectivism*, in contrast to *individualism*, by which Catholic activists attribute importance and meaning to a collective understanding of gender, that is, an understanding of gender related to community and society.

4.3.2 LGBT activists

In their accounts and conceptions of gender identity, LGBT activists reveal a high degree of variation and fluidity with regard to self-perceptions and self-awareness. A common view among participants, in contrast to the ideas expressed by Catholic activists, was a pronounced distinction between one's perceived gender identity, role, expression and the respective sexual identity and orientation. LGBT activists acknowledge the fluid and evolutionary character of their gender identity, which sustains the argument against the fixed and binary notions of identity that Catholic activists support. Moreover, what is clearly evident is the restrictive nature of the distinction between man and woman. This was shown in conversations about personal experience, as well as in discussions concerning the broader understanding of society. In contrast to Catholic activists, LGBT youth all agreed on perceiving and understanding gender identity as being separate from biological sex, as fluid and in constant evolution.

The pattern leading to such understanding often resulted from pressure to socially conform to gender norms in specific social contexts, such as family and work environments. This spurred a quest for identification with traditional/ non-traditional gender models among young LGBT. However, this is not, in turn, necessarily dependent on one's personal acceptance of sexual identity, and/ or orientation. As several activists clearly put it, family members might have tried to impose a certain gender identity on them, particularly during childhood. Similarly, others recounted how, even after having declared their sexual preference, the family environment continued to be particularly oppressive, not only in cases where homosexuality was not accepted, but also in the ones where it had, apparently, been metabolized. The need to adapt, to conform to external expectations in specific social contexts, had pushed some participants to change their behaviours and expressions, consciously and unconsciously, in order to meet those expectations. Moreover, activists mentioned the notions of 'convenience' and 'self-interest' as a basis for gender expression and behaviour, thus alluding to a conscious and strategic use of different performances in different contexts, in order *not* to challenge gender norms and negotiate gender identity. Those participants who felt the need to leave their social environment, in order to be able to live their sexuality and identity freely, have manifestly revealed this pattern. This was a decision that many activists coming from highly Catholic contexts in Southern Italy had made. A strong need for emancipation from the family was expressed in tandem with the need to leave behind a perceived coercive social reality. Unlike the Catholic activists who took part in this project, a lot of LGBT activists had undergone a process of migration, from small provinces to bigger urban centres, and from southern cities to northern ones. For Catholic activists, to have physical proximity to their hometown and family is considered 'normal', or even preferable, while for many LGBT activists, the data suggests the contrary: moving away from the parental home frees them to make their own choices. Engagement in social movement activities coincided in most cases with the change in social setting, namely displacement to a new city. Coming to a new environment went hand in hand with a search for new social ties, networks and the emergence of new socialization processes and feelings of belonging. Identifying with others is an essential way of expressing one's self identity. By adopting a group identity, activists found a source of individual strength and self-expression.

As anticipated, LGBT activists demonstrated an interest in self-expression with regard to gender. That is, an *individual* understanding of their gender identity, and an awareness of the processes of social construction and negotiation of such identities. This attitude must be recognized as contrasting with the *collective* understanding of gender held by Catholic activists. The sense of personal responsibility and personal freedom, and the development of awareness and acceptance, is particularly manifest in younger activists and decreases with time, leaving room for a type of activism that is more engaged in promoting collective social rights of the LGBT community. This process is accompanied by the development of gender consciousness. Age plays an important role in the different practices of activism, including gender awareness. While younger activists are driven by a need for social identification and aggregation, and personal values attached to the self are predominant, in the course of their activist career, they become increasingly oriented towards the promotion of values that take the wider society as the main referent.

4.4 Gender consciousness and moral resilience: a comparison

We have seen so far how social structures and systems of belief – age, family, sexuality and religion – either shape or constrain activists' abilities to produce gender by supplying them with meaning and material practices. Consciousness acquired through different life experiences motivates specific actions. In fact, biographical histories 'may help explain why some individuals fit more easily into expected roles than others do, why some follow the rules more readily or enthusiastically than others' (Jasper, 1997: 67). In the context of protest, these views, in turn, have activated a number of cognitive processes that I refer to as gender consciousness and moral resilience. Categorization of the sexes, for instance, was one of the most important understandings at the basis of Catholic activists' social interactions. It is now important to address how this categorization generates gender differences and inequalities and how, in both cases, gender is activated and becomes central to people's awareness in the context of protest.

4.4.1 Understanding gender difference

Catholic youth actively participate in the legitimation of the dominant gender order, maintaining and implementing the conditions that reproduce gender norms and power relations. In particular, we have seen that sustaining the gender system involves a major process, namely the creation of distinctions among women and men, which simultaneously reproduce gender hierarchies. The first part of this chapter tackled the question of how gender is produced at the individual level, and how participants perceived and projected themselves as gendered beings. In this case, 'sex difference' has been consciously argued and unconsciously experienced by Catholic activists as a governing principle of social relations and interactions. In a way, we can understand motives not only as based on pre-existing beliefs and preference but also as justifications of protestors' activities.

Hence, two major processes are at play in sustaining gender inequality. The legitimation of the natural existence of differences between sex categories (male and female), and the consequent attribution of gender identity and behaviours to these categories; the active institutionalization and reproduction of such categories through social relations and interactions and the fierce defence of models of highly institutionalized gender relationships, such as the ideal type of traditional family and heterosexual marriage (Wharton, 2005; Tilly, 1998). In addition to such processes, activism provides youth with an opportunity to feel more at ease with themselves as a consequence of questioning one's personal history, worthiness and values. One of such processes is the development of *moral resilience*, namely the ability of young Catholic activists to be responsive to moral and ethical challenges in a conscious way – through self-monitoring behaviours – and to revise or adjust their values in view of social change (Masten and Obradovic, 2006). Moral resilience develops during the process of identity negotiation within the diverse, and sometimes conflicting, comprehension and recognition systems available to activists. Taken together, these processes sustain the arguments of Catholic activists with regard to gender. However, while they clearly establish and legitimize the existence of differences between sexes, they do not aim to exaggerate stereotypes about masculinity and femininity as individual traits, but rather to strongly idealize the institutionalization of the traditional family.

The regulation of sexual and gender behaviours according to Christian values, continues to be present in the life course of activists. Through the development of an 'ethics of citizenship' (Clanton, 2005), Catholic activists are guided into the development of critical knowledge and commitment along the lines of the Catholic doctrine. The community becomes the reference, the space of survival, reflection and knowledge production among activists. The moral commitment towards society and the social environment in which someone lives becomes indispensable. Through moral resilience, Catholic activists are able to find meaning in social situations where ethical obligations and moral sensitivity are under threat. Moreover, it allows them to be persistent and consistent in their actions and behaviours despite constraints and pressures coming from outside. That being said, the perception of one's personal involvement and attachment to the movement or group is dependent on individuals' past experiences. Some were somehow 'born in the movement', inheriting parents' affiliations to it. Others indicated that their motivation for joining the movement was a 'need' for belonging and solidarity with a group, to have a space where they could perform their Catholic identity by practicing Christian morals, and above all, to 'live-out' the values mentioned above, which are reflected in a collective understanding of social relations.

As other studies have underlined (Collins-Mayo, 2012), among the possible factors explaining incentives to religious involvement could be a sense of lack of meaning, such as the one expressed in the preceding account, and by other activists who spoke about the 'sense of perdition and loneliness' experienced in their lives. More specifically, some activists alluded to the notion of *individualism*, which they saw as a lack of concern for what is meaningful in life, as a major incentive towards embracing the faith. By providing rules and rituals to develop moral resilience, religion can create a 'safe', and structured social environment to socialize in. In particular, young Catholic activists are directly asked by their spiritual guides to interrogate the surrounding environment, to question social changes, and to critically reflect upon current issues in terms of the ultimate meanings of life. Catholic youth endorse religious tradition with critical awareness, developing a sense of 'believing and belonging' linked to their proximate religious environment and social groupings; in a sense they are distanced from Church hierarchies and are instead ideologically close to the 'spiritual guides' in their immediate context (their neighbourhood, school or university, for example). These communities of 'believing and belonging' are also community of feeling, of the moral and the emotional, and most importantly for young people in search of an authentic faith, of shared solidarity around a particular style of living. Such practices provide activists with a capital to be reflexive and manage social change.

Faith requires a certain gender *habitus* and the group is the place where such *habitus* is reiterated. Faith in God and belonging to the group provide an important source of identity and the ongoing participation in the group is seen as significant in managing the challenges to Christian and traditional gender identities that arise. What distinguishes activists from other believers is that they not only feel Christian because they have been raised as such, but because they have made a conscious choice and are supported by the group. It is important to note that youth choose to involve themselves in political movements and identify with a community which appears from the outside to have a strong emotional hold upon them; belonging as a source of expression and identity is an act of agency. Through moral resilience they are able to navigate and cope with challenges to their moral and ethical positions, particularly their standpoints on gender. However, some activists have stressed the difficulties they faced in defending their understanding of gender roles that were approved by the religious group, to mainstream society:

> On a practical level now things are changing, and we young people, among young people is increasingly rare to see someone who thinks like you, right now I'm the one upstream. So sometimes it's a bit too hard for this. (Catholic activist)

We have also seen how gender polarization is not emphasized as much as might be expected by activists, and it is safe to assume that this is a feature or trend of younger generations. As some female activists expressed, moral resilience towards gender polarization is generated by attempts to integrate different sources of identification: religious and gender based. Sexuality, instead, remains in the realm of the natural, essentialist meaning.

In sum, the ways in which 'gender differences are done and sustained' among young activists is much more diversified and complex than the movement's public images and discourses display. Some activists are more prone to personal reflection, even if directed towards society and the collectivist at large, and are even asked by their spiritual guides to undertake such processes of moral commitment and resilience. In a way, this can be called 'wearing the values' (or equally reading or performing the values) that they are trying to defend, as one activist put it. In actively adopting behaviours and lifestyles consistent with traditional gender expectations, activists express their positions. Others are instead less expressive and more strategic in privileging external, targeted intervention and group action in the public sphere in order to call attention to the issues at stake.

4.4.2 Challenging gender inequality

In contrast to Catholic activists, for many LGBT activists, sexuality is just as political as the personal is political. Challenges to gender norms are displayed through different social practices: the conveyance of gender consciousness, being 'out and proud', and gender performances in the context of drag activism and cross-dressing, among others. Before tackling these questions, it is crucial to understand how movement activities had an impact on the individual transformation of activists, that is, the ways in which activist identities have been transformed over time and came to be gender aware.

Certain expressions of gender and embodiment constitute ways to challenge dominant gender and sexual models. Gender performances that cross boundaries between femininity and masculinity represent a relatively conscious way to challenge gender stereotypes.[5] Although participants might be perfectly conscious of these changes, we cannot infer that individuals have unbounded agency. Rather, it is precisely in these variations that the interplay of structural constraints and participants' actions is most evident. First, social movement activity encourages an awakening of consciousness, affecting activists' gendered *habitus*. Second, alternative ways of being can be articulated in social movements' spaces with the aim of challenging normalized understandings.

It is evident that the LGBT activism environment, as in the case of Catholic activists who felt able to express and practice their religious identity freely and gender identity accordingly, provides a safe space to exercise one's ability to perform gender differently. It is interesting to note, however, that the feeling of belonging to a group that has developed in the LGBT community was established through the 'reverse principle' of Catholic activists' identification strategy. LGBT activists often have a sense of 'being and feeling different' from the majority and so seek shelter in groups where this diversity can be appreciated and respected, as well as fully experienced. Aside from 'born in the movement' activists, Catholic activists often look for a group of belonging in the first place, and then, within this group, they find faith.

In addition, other activists recounted the gradual process of beginning to 'do gender' in different ways within the context of activism, and then progressively taking those performances – now tuned to one's gender and sexual identity – into the 'outside world'. Processes of identity formation do not reflect the advantage of having many different choices available but rather a politicized experience that emphasizes the importance of the expressive and belonging. Although for some it remains difficult or, by choice, not preferable to go through a similar process, for others 'being out and proud' becomes a manifest political stance to express being an LGBT activist in everyday life, a politic of identity. Butler's renowned claim, when she said that since the age of 16 'being a lesbian is what I have been' has important ontological implications in terms of being on the fence between authenticity and innovation. Similarly, activists recognize the process of becoming, or taking up their roles, and the political consequence of performing such roles. Some activists spoke about the ways in which they tried to convey gender awareness to members of their close social environment, such as their family. Many activists also recounted how 'doing activism' has been a positive factor facilitating parents' acceptance of homosexuality. In this sense, activism helped youth acquiring credibility, legitimacy and worthiness in their parents' eyes, particularly in families where there was a tradition of political activism.

We have seen how the gendered *habitus* acquired through different systems of socialization constitutes an obstacle to gender and sexual liberation for many activists, particularly through the mechanism of binding gender performances. Young activists have had to deconstruct a given habitus through their life experiences, and, eventually, then begin a fight to challenge gender norms at the political and social level. Different examples of how this process can take place are seen in the practices of cross-dressing, transvestism and drag activism, which all aim to introduce a different gender than the one that would be commonly expected, but in different ways, with some aspects overlapping among practices. These differences can be traced back to this chapter's assumption that performances can range on a continuum between expressive and strategic.

The heterogeneity of movements is also reflected in the individual modes of participation adopted by single activists. Compared to Catholic activists who act relatively homogenously, it is in fact difficult to find a common pattern of participation for LGBT activists, whose profiles range from drag activists, to militant lesbians, and younger activists who participate 'just for fun', to name but a few. The relationship between individual and collective dimensions of identity in the LGBT movement is therefore much more complex due to the variety of experiences and motivations.

4.5 Conclusion

Throughout this chapter, I have explored how, in constructing their own identities, activists attributed different meanings to their own personal history, including gender and sexual experience and practice. This raised questions about how gender and sexual identities are negotiated at the individual and collective levels and subsequently reproduced/challenged in the context of activism. The first part of the chapter aimed at understanding how gender is produced at the individual level, taking into account the difficulties in pinpointing the exact processes through which this occurs. Nonetheless, differences in how LGBT and Catholic activists perceived themselves as gendered beings were outlined. The analysis continued with findings about the features of the social context in which gender distinctions are produced through social relations and interactions. In addition to social context, evidence showed the influence of age, family, religion and sexuality as gendered social structures and practices that sustain the institutionalization of gender relationships.

Youth representations of gender are constantly confronted by the reactions of social groups, individuals, institutions and public opinion at large in the context of different interactions. Two concepts were revealed to be crucial in this study: moral resilience and gender consciousness. As I have tried to make explicit, 'the story of movements is therefore also the story of their members' ability to impose certain images of themselves, and to counter attempts by dominant groups to denigrate their aspirations to be recognized as different' (della Porta and Diani, 2006: 106). A range of gendered structures impacted activists at the individual and interactional levels, and, overall, have facilitated and influenced the development of gender consciousness and moral resilience in the context of activism. Following from this assertion, we can cite a number of performances and processes that activists engage in, ranging from expressive to strategic, to either contest or reproduce gendered structures. Recalling Giddens (1984), this duality is characteristic of the structure, in which gender practices are, in turn, both structured and structuring.

Notes

1 Here, gender refers to the social and cultural interpretations and expectations that are associated with sex that go beyond biological characteristics.
2 The acronym LGBT (Lesbian, Gay, Bisexual, Transgender) is just one among many – particularly the ones including queer and intersectional identities (LGBTQI), and others (LGBTQI+). Even though the different acronyms share the opposition to sexism as a root of oppression, different values, needs and rights arise depending on which gender/sexual identities are mobilized. I assume that the variety of self-identifications reflects the challenge for inclusivity and visibility confronted by the movement(s), along with the fundamental work carried out by LGBTQI+ organizations on issues of intersectionality. For the purpose of this chapter, I make use of the acronym LGBT, as being the one in which the majority of activists and organizations included in the study self-identify.
3 For the purpose of this chapter, movement and countermovement dynamics refer to the interactional opposition between the originating social movement and the reacting countermovement. Movements are the actors first initiating a campaign for social change, whilst opposing movements are defined as groups mobilized around the issue of contention, responding to the movement's claims.
4 Bourdieu's concept of *habitus* reflects how the social action, representation and practice of agents are dependent on their structural position in the social space, or field, and whose limits are set by the historically and socially situated conditions of its production (Bourdieu, 1977).
5 By 'relatively', I refer to the observation that gender performances can vary greatly depending on their context, particularly whether they take place 'within' or 'outside' the social movement environment.

References

Albanesi, C., Zani, B. and Cicognani, E. (2012). Youth civic and political participation through the lens of gender: The Italian case. *Human Affairs*, 22(3), 360–374.

Bourdieu, P. (1977). *Outline of a Theory of Practice*. Cambridge: Cambridge University Press.

Cicognani, E., Zani, B., Fournier, B., Gravay, C. and Born, M. (2012). Gender differences in youth's political engagement and participation: The role of parents and of adolescents' social and civic participation. *Journal of Adolescence*, 35(3), 561–576.

Clanton, C. (ed) (2005). *The Ethics of Citizenship: Liberal Democracy and Religious Convictions*. Waco: Baylor University Press.

Collins-Mayo, S. (2012). Youth and religion: An international perspective. *Theo-Web. Zeitschrift fuer Religionpaedagogik*, 11(1), 80–94.

della Porta, D. and Diani, M. (2006). *Social Movements: An Introduction*. 2nd ed. London, UK: John Wiley & Sons.

Foucault, M. (1976). *La volonté de savoir*. Paris: Editions Gallimard.

Gardiner, J.K. (ed) (2002). Theorizing age with gender: Bly's boys, feminism, and maturity masculinity. In: *Masculinity Studies and Feminist Theory: New Directions*. New York: Columbia University Press.

Garelli, F. (2016). *Piccoli atei crescono: davvero una generazione senza Dio?* Bologna: il Mulino.

Giddens, A. (1984). *The Constitution of Society: Outline of the Theory of Structuration*. Berkeley and Los Angeles: University of California Press.

Gordon, S.H. (2008). Gendered paths to teenage political participation: Parental power, civic mobility, and youth activism. *Gender & Society*, 22, 31–55.

Jasper, J.M. (1997). *The Art of Moral Protest: Culture, Biography, and Creativity in Social Movements*. Chicago: University of Chicago Press.

Kiecolt, J.K. (2000). Self-change in social movements. In: Stryker, S., Owens, T.J., White, R. (eds) *Self, Identity, and Social Movements*. Minneapolis: University of Minnesota Press.

Kirshner, B. (2007). Introduction: Youth activism as a context for learning and development. *American Behavioral Scientist*, 51(3), 367–379.

Lavizzari, A. and Prearo, M. (2018). The anti-gender movement in Italy: Catholic participation between electoral and protest politics, *European Societies*. Published online: https://doi.org/10.1080/14616696.2018.1536801.

Masten, A.S., and Obradovic, J. (2006). Competence and resilience in development. *Annals of the New York Academy of Sciences*, 1094, 13–27.

Matthews, T.L., Hempel, L.M. and Howell, F.M. (2010). Gender and the transmission of civic engagement: Assessing the influences on youth civic activity. *Sociological Inquiry*, 80(3), 448–474.

Ozzano, L., and Giorgi, A. (2015). *European Culture Wars and the Italian Case: Which Side Are You On?* London and New York: Routledge.

Richardson, D. (2015). Rethinking sexual citizenship. *Sociology*, 51(2), 208–224.

Russell, S.T., Russell, B., Toomey, J.C. and Laub, C. (2010). LGBT politics, youth activism, and civic engagement. In: Sherrod, L.R., Torney-Purta, J. and Flanagan, C. (eds) *Handbook of Research on Civic Engagement in Youth*. Hoboken, NJ and Canada: John Wiley & Sons.

Shepherd, N. (2010). Religious socialisation and a reflexive habitus: Christian youth groups as sites for identity work. In: Collins-Mayo, S. and Dandelion, P. (eds) *Religion and Youth*. Surrey: Ashgate.

Tilly, C. (1998). *Durable Inequality*. Los Angeles: University of California Press.

Wharton, A.S. (2005). *The Sociology of Gender: An Introduction to Theory and Research*. Malden, MA: Blackwell Publishing Ltd.

Part II

Work, employment and careers

Chapter 5

The social investment challenge and young Italians

Lara Maestripieri

5.1 A short introduction to social investment

'Social investment' is one of the most important bywords in contemporary European social policies, as it forms the foundation of the current Europe 2020 strategy (Hemerijck, 2015). This policy approach was established based on the concept of 'the third way', as characterized in the mandates of UK Prime Minister Blair (Morel *et al.*, 2012) and during the Dutch presidency of the European Union in 1997 (Hemerijck, 2015). Rather than regulating the market, the 'third way' seeks to empower individuals to be better equipped to sustain competition, by developing human capital driven by individual success (Esping-Andersen, 2002). Social investment strategy further develops this, by proposing that a certain type of social spending – aimed at fostering human capital – is an investment that characterizes post-industrial societies.

Investment must take place at the societal and the individual level: at the societal level, because contemporary societies have a heightened need for qualified workers, and at the individual level, because highly skilled individuals are more protected from deteriorating labour-market conditions (Nolan, 2013; Kazepov and Ranci, 2017). If welfare states invest in the education of future generations, better-educated workers will be able to create added value for all economic systems. It is argued that they will exploit the human capital of future generations, enabling them to access better working conditions and generating *good jobs* from their increased capabilities. In this sense, social policies should not be considered a passive cost anymore, but as an active investment to create stable and sustainable growth, supported by the state (Morel *et al.*, 2012). As explicitly stated by the European Commission, the goal of a social investment package is *'to "prepare" people to confront life's risks, rather than simply "repairing" the consequences'* (European Commission 2013).

Two main pillars are recognizable in this strategy. The first of which is that the human capital of people can be advanced with education, training and lifelong learning. The other is that participation in the labour market is supported with active labour market policies (Pintelon *et al.*, 2013). The first regards the promotion of the participation of marginal social groups in the labour market, such as

Not in Education, Employment, or Training (NEETs) for instance, with leverage to develop active labour market policies. The second favours improving the average worker's skill level, as a precondition for accessing *'good jobs'*. Such an approach can be seen in the universalization of university education, the growth in lifelong learning and increased investment in basic education. These actions can be associated with an attempt to increase the general level of the human capital of workers, starting from a very early age. Proponents of this theoretical perspective view the Nordic countries as examples of best practice; their equity and economic growth is ascribed to an effective application of labour-market inclusion policies and the state's support for education and lifelong learning (Kazepov and Ranci, 2017).

Empirical applications of social investment policies have been mostly oriented to foster supply-side policies, with the explicit aim of increasing the employability of the workforce, its human capital and its activation. However, employability is an ambiguous term, shifting responsibility for lack or fragile labour market participation on the shoulders of the individual, framing unemployment, precariousness and exclusion as an individual responsibility, forgetting the role of labour demand (Cuzzocrea, 2015). Certainly, there is no guarantee that an increase in human capital *per se* offers sufficient conditions to improve the quality of labour market integration in all contexts. In fact, this assumption can find adequate empirical grounding only in cases where the local economic system is able to offer adequate jobs to those who possess a higher level of human capital (Sánchez-Sánchez and McGuinness, 2015; Maestripieri and Ranci, 2016; Bison *et al.*, 2017).

In the following paragraphs, I discuss why Italy exemplifies *worst practice* for social investment policies (Kazepov and Ranci, 2017), directing special consideration to the condition of young people (aged 18–34) (Rizza and Maestripieri, 2015). Following which, I present data relating to the Italian labour market, highlighting its peculiar performance in terms of young workers' integration. Finally, two policies are analysed in detail. First, the Italian implementation of the Youth Guarantee (*Garanzia Giovani*), a European programme aimed at fostering the labour market participation of NEETs. Second, the Apprenticeship in Higher Education (*Apprendistato in Alta Formazione*), designed to facilitate the transition between university and work. I illustrate how the failure of these two policies arises from a combination of diverse factors, which includes the underestimation of the role of labour demand. In Italy, the problem of youth marginalization in the labour market should be addressed from both the supply and demand side, as the following analysis demonstrates.

5.2 Italian youth faces a segmented labour market[1]

Young people are usually considered outsiders in relation to the labour market, because as a social group they are particularly exposed to social risks relating to the post-industrial transition (Chevalier, 2016). Italy represents one of the most interesting cases, where individuals' integration into the labour market is concerned. Young Italians are a scarce resource in terms of their numbers, yet their position in the labour market is highly precarious, and the quality of work they generally receive is uncertain. The magnitude of their labour market marginalization, and the specific institutional context, that is labour market employment regulations and welfare assets, contribute to producing and reinforcing this situation (Firinu and Maestripieri, 2019). The structure of the opportunities offered to youths in Italy render their transition into adulthood even more difficult, when compared to previous generations (Chauvel and Schroder, 2014). The impact of their precariousness in the labour market on when and how young people in Italy completed their passage to adulthood is explored in detail in Chapter 7 of this book.

As previously stated, the relative proportion of the younger generation in Italy is amongst the lowest in Europe (see Table 5.1). The combined effect of low numbers and the scarce involvement of young people in traditional political containers (Gozzo and Sampugnaro, 2016) make them a less-appealing target for politicians. Italian social expenditure reflects their political irrelevance; undoubtedly, in terms of the distribution of expenditure, young people lose out. Italy spends 13.7% of its gross domestic product (GDP) on old-age protection, compared to 8.2% in Germany (which has a comparable old-age dependency ratio), and 9.5% in Spain (usually aligned with Italy in the welfare regimes debate), while resources devoted to active labour market policies (one of the pillars of social investment strategy) represent barely 0.4% of its total GDP, while France spends 0.9%, and Sweden 1.4%.

The condition of young Italians in the labour market is apparently in contradiction with the traditional assumptions of a neoclassical economy. As shown in Table 5.1, the main barrier to labour market entry is not scarcity in the supply of a younger, more active, more educated and more productive labour force. The majority of under 24 year olds are still not active participants in the labour market. However, the growing participation of young people aged over 25 years of age does not correspond with the capacity of the labour market to absorb this younger, more educated labour force. Younger generations are always less likely to be employed

Table 5.1 Demography and labour market access in Italy by generation, 2017

	Age Class					
	15/24	25/29	30/34	35/39	40/59	60/64
Proportion of total Italian population	9.7	5.4	5.7	6.5	30.8	6.1
Employment rate	17.1	54.2	67.9	72.9	70.2	39.6
Unemployment rate	34.7	21.2	13.5	10.1	8	4.7
Activity rate	26.2	68.8	78.5	81.1	76.3	41.5
Percentages of individuals with ISCED 0–2	51	21.9	28.3	30.9	43	53
Percentages of individuals with ISCED 3–4	44.6	51.3	44.8	44.4	41.3	34.3
Percentages of individuals with ISCED 5–8	4.4	26.8	26.9	24.7	15.7	12.7

Source: Eurostat database, labour market and demographic indicators.

than older generations. This situation is worsened by the fact that the rate at which people under 30 are hired is among the lowest in Europe, at a rate of 1.2 out of every 10, compared to 3 out of 10 in the United Kingdom, and 2.6 out of 10 in Germany (Castellano *et al.*, 2014). Italian employers seem to prefer an older workforce, that does not entail the associated education and training costs (Seghezzi, 2016).

In general, young Italians are disadvantaged by difficult school-to-work transitions. Their high share of destandardized employment and frequent spells of unemployment transform them into 'outsiders' (Sergi *et al.*, 2018). In fact, the deregulation of the Italian labour market (Marques and Salavisa, 2017) has exposed them to deteriorated working conditions, and destandardized forms of work have made their position in the labour market more vulnerable relative to older generations (Schwander and Haussermann, 2013; Firinu and Maestripieri, 2019). When the crisis arrived, older workers with stronger tenure and protected employment proved more resilient to the economic downturn, while the younger generations were more significantly affected. Consequently, the crisis worsened the generational inequality that already characterized the Italian labour market (Rosina, 2013; Reyneri and Pintaldi, 2013; Firinu and Maestripieri, 2019). The highest contraction of standard employment occurred in those aged between 25 and 39 (Reyneri and Pintaldi, 2013; Firinu and Maestripieri, 2019).

Table 5.2 Indicators on labour market integration of youth, percentages by country, 2017

	DE	ES	FR	IT	PL	SE	UK
Tertiary educated 30–34[a]	34	41.2	44.3	26.9	45.7	51.3	48.3
Employment ISCED 3–4 up to 3 years from title 20–34	89.1	58	61	47.1	72.3	84.4	80.1
Employment ISCED 5–8 up to 3 years from title 20–34	92.7	74.7	80.6	58	87.6	91.7	87.4
Unemployment rate – tertiary educated 15–39	2.6	13		6.2	11.2	3.2	4.9	3.3
Early leavers from education/training 18–24[a]	10.1	18.3	8.9	14	5	7.7	10.6
NEET (15–24)	6.3	13.3	11.5	20.1	9.5	6.2	10.3
NEET (25–29)	12	22.1	18.8	31.5	18	7.8	13.1
Long-term unemployment 15–39	31.9	34.7	37.3	56.1	26.2	12.5	20.7
Temporary employee on total employment 25–34	17.5	39.5	20.2	26.7	32.9	20	5.1
Involuntary temporary job 25–34	17.8	82.9	61.9	67	60.9	57.3	31.5
Part-time employee on total employment 15–39	23.9	18.8	17.3	21.8	6.4	27.8	24.1
Involuntary part-time job 15–39	10.3	61.9	45.7	70.4	22.5	31.7	17.4
Young 25–34 living with their parents (%) – 2016	17.9	40.0	13.4	49.1	45.5	6	14.3

Source: Eurostat database, labour market and education indicators.

Note
a Part of the Europe 2020 Baseline Indicators and European Pillars of Social Rights.

Table 5.3 Indicators on productive system, ALMPs and education, by country

	DE	ES	FR	IT	PL	SE	UK
Employed persons in advanced business services (%) – 2017	18.6	18.4	19.2	17.8	13.2	23.6	23.9
Managers and professionals as a % of total employment – 2017	22.5	22.3	25.5	18.7	25.7	34	35.8
Technicians and associate professional employees (%) – 2017	20.4	9.8	18.6	14	11.6	16.8	11.3
Participation in lifelong learning 25–34 (%) – 2017[a]	19.1	18.6	23.5	14.9	7.7	38.8	18
Activation-Support LMP participants per 100 persons wanting to work – 2015	30.3	28.3	41.2	15.1[c]	20.8	42.1	–
Training enterprises as a % of total enterprises – 2010	73.0	75.0	76.0	56.0	22.0	87.0	80.0
Total public expenditure on education (% of GDP) – 2012	4.8	4.3	5.7	4.2	4.9	7.4	6.1
Intramural R&D expenditure – 2016 (euro/inhabitant)[b]	1125	286	732[c]	356	108	1537	619
Expenditure in publicly financed training in GDP % – 2015	0.204	0.115	0.364	0.168	0.012	0.146	0.017[c]
Expenditure in start-up incentives in GDP % – 2015	0.011	0.099	0.031	0.016	0.052	0.006	0.002[c]

Source: Eurostat database.

Notes
a   European Pillars of Social Rights.
b   Europe 2020 Baseline Indicators.
c   2010.

We can confirm the ambivalence of the opportunity structure for young people by consulting the macroindicators portrayed in Tables 5.2 and 5.3. This ambivalence mainly relates to two groups: those who are neither active nor students (the so-called NEET) and those who are highly skilled. Regarding the first group, Italy has the worst performance in Europe in terms of its rate of early school leavers (significantly, it sits above the 10% Europe 2020 target). Differing from Spain (13.3%), in Italy the result of these dynamics is a higher rate of people aged 15–24 neither actively participating in the labour market, nor in the educational system (20.1% in 2017). The NEET rate remains very high around the age of 30 (31.5% vs. 22.1% in Spain), which makes re-entry into the labour market after a long spell of inactivity even more problematic (Rosina, 2013).

Furthermore, disadvantage among young people is not only a problem when accessing the labour market. Indeed, when focusing on the type of work young people get, Italy reveals an overall incapacity in terms of taking advantage of its human capital. A possible indication of this is the high rates of involuntary part-timers and temporary employees among young workers, which can also be interpreted as a form of underemployment (especially in the case of involuntary part-time workers) (Bodnár, 2018). The less educated young people are, the more they struggle to enter the labour market, but even the well-educated are affected (see Table 5.2). In fact, the transition from school to work appears to be especially problematic given the low employment rates for those seeking to achieve at any educational level. Data on employment rates three years after graduation shows that Italian youth employment is among the lowest in Europe: 47.1% for ISCED 3–4 and 58% for ISCED 5–8 in 2017.

Italy seems to be suffering simultaneously from problems in both supply and demand. On the supply side, the percentage of young graduates is half the share in Sweden, United Kingdom and France, far from the EU2020 target (40%). This is not only a problem of quantity but also a result of the composition of graduates: the Italian educational system has failed to develop a network of post-secondary vocational schools, such as those in other countries that offer manufacturing and vocational courses (i.e. Germany). On the demand side, the productive system lacks the capacity to absorb high-skilled workers: the lower percentage of graduates aged 30 to 34 is associated with a greater risk of unemployment among those who have a degree. That is, Italian graduates are typically exposed to unemployment at a rate that is consistently higher than that in other EU countries, with the sole exception of Spain, which has a higher rate of tertiary educated people in their thirties instead (ISCED 5–8).

Young people have reacted to this situation by lowering their expectations. Given the increasing risk of being exposed to inactivity or unemployment, for many this has led them to accept jobs of lesser quality (Rosina, 2013). Bignardi *et al.* (2014) show that young workers are increasingly willing to accept lower salaries. In 47% of cases, they are also willing to accept a job that is not in line with their acquired skills: one graduate in every three affirms that their current job and educational profiles are incoherent (Rosina, 2013). This leads to the risk of entrapment in a situation of overqualification in the medium and long-term (Scherer, 2004). Although the literature confirms that a higher educational level still constitutes an advantage compared to a lower one (Ballarino and Scherer, 2013), in Italy possessing high skills is no longer a sufficient condition to guarantee access to jobs in line with one's qualifications. Unsurprisingly, the result of this is that the share of overqualified workers in Italy is 22.1%, compared to about 13% in France and Germany, and 15.5% in the United Kingdom (source: WISE Dataset, OECD). Workers until their 40s are accustomed to accepting roles for which they are overqualified, as demonstrated in a previous study (Maestripieri and Ranci, 2016).

Scholars have proposed several explanations for the fall of returns of education in Italy (it is lower in Italy than in the rest of Europe) (Beblavý and Veselková, 2015), and its decline in recent years (Ballarino and Scherer, 2013). The trend is not due to an increasing number of graduates being active on the labour market (as this is not the case in Italy) but from a lack of demand of high-skilled workers, arising in part from the below average performance of the advanced business sectors (Bernardi and Ballarino, 2012; Bison *et al.*, 2017). Studies reviewing the characteristics of labour demand reveal that Italian employers prefer to hire those in low-skilled positions (Reyneri and Pintaldi, 2013; Fellini, 2015; Bison *et al.*, 2017). The 2007–2008 financial crisis reinforced pre-existing trends, reducing employment opportunities for young graduates. In the remainder of Europe, the crisis increased the share of knowledge workers in the labour force (Gallie, 2013), but in Italy the opposite occurred, with steady demand remaining only for manual unskilled employment and in the care sector (Reyneri and Pintaldi, 2013; Fellini, 2015).

One of the most accredited explanations for the low demand for high-skilled workers in Italy relates to the extended role that microbusinesses and self-employment plays in the market (representing about one-quarter of the total labour force in Italy). This is a legacy of the absence of a process of concentration, such as that which occurred in other advanced capitalist economies in the 1960s and 1970s. The structure of the Italian productive system is still predominantly family-owned, concentrating on traditional manufacturing activities and characterized by enterprises with an extremely reduced dimension (Colli, 2010), hindering innovation activities and training. The low investment in R&D is paralleled by low shares in enterprises providing training. This picture is striking when compared with countries such as Germany and France (see Table 5.3).

Furthermore, the institutional context seems to be unable to disrupt the trend. The poor performance of the educational system is correlated with reduced public expenditure in education, which is the lowest level among the countries considered. Countries including Germany, the United Kingdom and Sweden seem to be more able to avoid the risk of marginalizing the youth labour force than the Southern European countries, in part due to their better economic performance during the current financial crisis, but also because of the desire for a smoother transition between school and work, as favoured by investment in active labour market policies and training activities. Investment in education and active labour market policies are two of the main pillars of social investment strategy, but they are apparently underfinanced in the context of Italy, at least when the Italian situation is compared with that in concurrent European countries.

In synthesis, a difficult transition takes place between school and work, and the low capacity of the educational system means that it is difficult to sustain students up to university degree level when combined with access to the labour market and characterized by low-quality jobs, reduced opportunities for the highly skilled and involuntary reduced participation in the labour market. One of the causes identified is the substantial incapacity of the Italian productive system to sustain demand for high-skilled jobs (Maestripieri and Ranci, 2016; Bison *et al.*, 2017). The country produces fewer graduates, and high-skilled workers are scarcely requested by the labour market, although their advantage is still sound relative to those with lower educational skills. However, the high share of involuntary part-timers, temporary and overqualified workers among those aged 25–39 years throws into question the capacity of the productive system to benefit from the higher educational attainment of the younger generations. Thus, a context characterized by small and scarcely innovative enterprises, combined with reduced public investment in innovation and training, partially explains the unsatisfactory labour market integration of high-skilled workers. In contrast, the large share of drop-outs and limited investment in active labour market policies determines the higher and more persistent share of NEETs in the country, with over one-third of young people not being in employment, education or training until their thirties.

The Italian context also places many constraints on the beneficial application of social investment policies. Thus, in the next section, the author will investigate the impact of two policies (one targeting NEETs, one targeting high-skilled newly graduated workers), which are usually considered within the scope of a social investment approach, to see how well they perform and what the shortcomings are in relation to their application.

5.3 Tackling the poor integration of youths into the labour market

Despite the evidence, the political debate over the problem of labour-market integration of youths, attributes 'fault' to the education system and young people themselves. Public discourse on the futility of studying for certain degrees (especially those related to soft sciences) has been hegemonic in recent years, and combined with a paternalistic attitude of blaming the young, they are frequently accused by politicians as being lazy, plump and 'choosy'. This rhetoric is partially founded in the fact that young Italians leave the parental home relatively late. 49.1% of Italians aged 25–34 still live with their parent(s), compared to 6% of Swedish, 13.4% of French and 14.3% of British in the same age group (see Table 5.2). This has caused the problematic integration of young Italians to be predominantly framed as a supply-side problem (Cuzzocrea, 2015): an omission of proactivity, linked to the safety net of families and the potential orientation towards soft sciences, hindering the desirability of degrees in the labour market and causing friction to arise, affecting the transition between school and work. The resultant supply-side policies are missing an important component of the equation, that is labour demand.

The following section analyses two relevant policies proposed in recent years: Apprenticeship in Higher Education (*apprendistato in alta formazione*), and the Youth Guarantee scheme (*garanzia giovani*). The analysis will show how those policies resulted in poor performance, given the lack of interest on the policies themselves from the standpoint of prospicient employers. All this, despite these measures having been especially designed to improve the attractiveness of the young on the labour market, and strongly sustained by the state via incentives. A diagnosis based on supply-side arguments, in fact, cannot explain why these two approaches failed in their scope.

5.3.1 Apprenticeship in Higher Education

Apprenticeship in Higher Education is a specific contractual form, combining education and employment. It adopts a dual approach to 'learning by doing' in a firm, whilst acquiring greater competence in the context of high-skilled and knowledge professional training. This kind of contract, as proposed by recent Italian governments, is the main strategy put in place to smooth school-to-work transitions among the newly graduated.

This contractual form was introduced with so-called 'Biagi law' (Law d.lgs. n. 276/2003) in 2003, and then subsequently modified by *Testo unico sull'apprendistato* in 2011 (d.lgs. n. 167/2011), a comprehensive law evaluating all types of apprenticeship. The contract was further modified in reference to ministerial decree in 2013. Its underlying objective was to develop an educational track involving an enterprise, a university and an apprentice; the lectures in class served as a supportive function for the real training, which occurred on-the-job, within the company. The intention was to give greater prominence to *learning by doing* practices, without renouncing the value of a highly skilled workforce. Inspired by the German dual model, its effectiveness is based on the circularity between educational and on-the-job training. It attempts to overcome strictly segregated paths, assuming that *learning-by-doing* practices should be integrated into all types of education at every level. The measure aspires to smooth the transition into the labour market for high-skilled young people, tailoring educational gains to the specific needs of enterprises.

Since its initial inception in 2003, the use of this contract has been limited, involving very few students, far below the legislators' expectations. Even in regions and areas actively promoting the contract, as in Lombardy, Apprenticeship in Higher Education is still a marginal track in the transition from school to work. In the province of Milan, it accounts for fewer than 0.4% of all apprenticeships: during the period 2012/2015 there were 183 contracts of Apprenticeships in Higher Education out of a total 55,000 apprenticeships contracts. The profile of workers employed based on this contract is very consistent: 25–34 year olds with no migration background, mostly employed in the advanced business sector and scientific research, with almost perfect gender parity. Apprenticeship in Higher Education is clearly in line with social investment principles, serving to promote the acquisition of high-skilled competencies by immediately bringing them to the labour market. Yet, this approach is still not attractive to the market, as is clear from the number of contracts signed (Table 5.4).

Table 5.4 Apprentices in higher-education track, Province of Milano – 2012/2015

	Absolute values	Percentages
Construction	9	5%
Manufacturing	18	10%
Traditional services	33	18%
Advanced business services	93	51%
Scientific research	30	16%
	183	100%

Source: Administrative data on employment – Observatory on labour market/ Province of Milano.

This begs the question of why such poor figures have been achieved. Is it a problem of labour supply? From the previous analysis, it seems more appropriate to explain the failure of apprenticeship schemes in higher education from an institutional perspective. The implementation of apprenticeships is fragmented, occurring at the regional level with different requirements and criteria magnifying the institutional weaknesses in the system (Kazepov and Ranci, 2017). There are several possible reasons for this: on the one hand, the dialogue between universities and enterprises is challenging, and on the other, the inherited institutional environment is unable to sustain practices at the local level. The educational system suffers from an incapacity to effectively bridge labour markets (Sergi *et al.*, 2018). However, a crucial role is also played by the reluctance of employers to finance employee training through apprenticeship contracts (Seghezzi, 2016; Kazepov and Ranci, 2017). This problem is not only related to Apprenticeship in Higher Education specifically, but to apprenticeship in general. The most-recent Italian labour reforms have tried to promote apprenticeship contracts by reducing costs and training requirements for prospicient employers. Nevertheless, this deregulation has not led to increased use of this contract. One of the possible explanations for this is that good practice works well in other contexts like Germany and France, but less so in the Italian context, where firms are smaller and less motivated to invest in the education and training of their workers (see Table 5.3). Furthermore, Italy is a favourable context for strategically destandardized contracts, aimed at reducing labour costs without investing in the human capital of workers (Firinu, 2015).

Policies have been designed to subsidize this type of contract, assuming that it constitutes a good strategy for stabilizing young workers engaged in the labour market. Nevertheless, the progressive reduction in the amount of training associated with the contract, especially in the most recent modifications to the measure in 2011 and in 2013, seems to contradict the assumptions of social investment strategy that rely on improved human capital in facilitating the transition from school to work.

5.3.2 Youth Guarantee

The Youth Guarantee is a programme promoted and financed by the European Union, which has been implemented in Italy since December 2013[2] and aims to alleviate the worst consequences of the financial crisis on youth unemployment. Inspired by policies emphasizing active labour market integration carried out in the past year in Austria and Finland, it revolves around the possibility of offering a job, training or educational opportunities to young NEETs within 4 months of their beginning a spell of unemployment. In the official European presentation, the programme has been defined as:

> …social investment which enables young people to put their skills to productive use and to further develop them, as opposed to the skills deterioration and de-motivation which results from protracted unemployment and inactivity.[3]

The belief behind the programme is that young people are in a disadvantaged position because of their personal shortcomings, and thus the programme aims to help them to improve their skills from an explicit social investment perspective.

It works in a very simple way: the young person (15–29 years old) who is unemployed, not in education, nor in training is required to register online at the programmes' portal. Within four months, Public Employment Services (PES) and private agencies get in contact with the person, first measuring their needs using a profiling index, in order to tailor the necessary set of services required to enhance his/her activation on the labour market. Information, orientation, training, internship, social services and support for self-employment exemplify the services offered within the programme. The private and public sector are equally involved in the implementation process: the financial support offered to private partners varies in terms of the occupational outcomes required by the person, with higher contributions for the most problematic cases (Seghezzi, 2016; Lodigiani and Santagati, 2016). The Italian system of integrated e-portals for online use has been indicated by the European Commission as a good model of implementation.[4] The regional portals are connected to a national database that facilitates the verification of fulfilments and the transmission of offers.

One of the most important innovations associated with the programme is the comprehensive system of monitoring, allowing for complete assessment, and it is this that constitutes the empirical basis for the following analysis. According to a recent monitoring report provided by ANPAL (2018), 1,295,609 people were involved in the implementation of the measure, which began in May 2014. About 82.3% were assisted by PES or a private working agency, which resulted in a total of 546,930 young people benefitting from an active labour market measure (53.5% of the total taken in charge by the system). The individuals scored on average 0.67 on the profiling index, which measures the likelihood that the person would become NEET (the index scores 1 when the person is a NEET). Private agencies are the most important actors in the northern regions, while PESs are prevalent in the south (ANPAL, 2018). As shown in Table 5.5, the

Table 5.5 Supported NEET in Youth Guarantee programme, 2014–2017 (update 28 June 2017)

	Absolute Values	Percentages
Low NEET likelihood	110.021	11.5%
Medium-low	65.858	6.9%
Medium-high	382.405	40%
High NEET likelihood	398.104	41.6%
Total	956.388	

Source: Youth Guarantee Monitor.

Note: Although the last report is dated 31/12/2017, the last statistical update on Youth Guarantee is available on the main portal for the 149° week of implementation, dated 28/6/2017.

majority of individuals participating in the Youth Guarantee programme have a medium/high- to high-risk profile of becoming NEET.

However, these figures do not represent the total NEET population because the measure only accounts for those individuals who registered on the system. This presupposed action from the potential beneficiary, although eased by the accessibility of the e-portals, might marginalize the most vulnerable groups who do not have the competencies or necessary digital skills to browse the registration procedure. In fact, the NEET condition is often associated with a series of vulnerabilities, including low education, migration background, disability, difficult family background or structurally weak contextual conditions. This results in a strong disparity among recipients (Cuzzocrea, 2014), which might be at the detriment of an individual initiative when there is insufficient active support for PES in the initial phase (Lodigiani and Santagati, 2016).

The main reason for the incongruity between the registered users and those who had effectively received a support measure (about half of the total) can be found in diverging interests on the programme, which for enterprises have been lukewarm at most. In the last statistical update, in which data about demand was reported,[5] the available job opportunities offered by the programme were 91,847, providing options for fewer than 10% of the total registered young people. Despite several incentives for stabilization being offered to companies (e.g. tax reliefs for hiring young people through apprenticeship contracts or permanent positions), only a residual portion of the jobs were aimed at ensuring effective stabilization. In the last update from ANPAL (2018), of the 624,854 interventions, about 60% resulted in a traineeship being offered, only 23% provided incentives for a labour contract (also temporary contracts, of a minimum six-month duration, are included) and about 12% were educational programs. About 70,000 young people were offered jobs within the frame of the Youth Guarantee measure, representing only 10% of the total. Such disproportion between the number of jobs offered and the number of young people willing to enter the Youth Guarantee programme puts a serious question mark on those who are actually employed via the Youth Guarantee, with an inherent risk to incur in Matthew effect employing only the most employable profiles (Lodigiani and Santagati, 2016).

The persistent high number of internships, which is the main option offered within the programme, is problematic given the precariousness associated with this type of labour market entry, which leads to a permanent position in a residual number of cases only (Seghezzi, 2016). In fact, only 47.9% of young people included in a Youth Guarantee intervention were employed at 31 December 2017 (ANPAL, 2018); denoting about 225,990 of young workers, which is a minority considering the number of young people involved in the programme throughout the three years in which it was active (2014–2017). A positive element can be found amongst those already employed: eight out of ten were in stable contracts, equally divided between apprenticeships and permanent contracts. However, even apprenticeship contracts, which in theory are tenure-track contracts to subsequent stable permanent contracts, are not immune from precariousness, as they are quite likely to be interrupted before their end, or not renovated (Kazepov and Ranci, 2017). Nevertheless, an additional confirmation of the implicit Matthew effect of the Youth Guarantee action is given when looking at occupational performances by level of profiling. Among those with a low likelihood of being NEET, about 61% of people are employed, but only 36.5% of those with a high likelihood of being NEET are employed (ANPAL, 2018).

Seghezzi (2016) identifies the main reasons why the Youth Guarantee is not working in Italy as the joint effect of a general diffidence among Italian enterprises towards public programmes and the fact that they prefer hiring older adults, in order to avoid initial training costs. This partly explains why apprenticeship measures are not as diffused in the Youth Guarantee programme, and also why higher education apprenticeships fail (§ 3.1). The outcome shown in Youth Guarantee is a clear signal of these trends: a reduced number of jobs, mostly concentrated in temporary and precarious profiles, probably integrating only those young workers who can easily find a job even without the programme.

5.4 Conclusions

Italy is a relevant case to assist in understanding the role of contextual conditions when specific policies are developed and implemented, as in the case of social investment (Kazepov and Ranci, 2017). As demonstrated throughout the chapter, the specific Italian productive structure, the dominance of micro and small enterprises, and the strong segmentation across age bands exposes young people to marginalization, non-standard employment and low-quality jobs, despite their higher educational level being higher compared to previous generations. At the same time, activities demanding a high intensity of human capital are weaker in Italy than in the other countries in Europe, reducing the occupational opportunities for highly skilled workers. All these elements are an integral part of a system that is highly dualized in terms of the generations, and extremely unequal in terms of labour market opportunities for young workers within the wealthy north and economically vulnerable south (Sergi *et al.*, 2018). The national averages presented in the chapter do, in fact, cover different situations in terms of youth labour market participation and the economic performances of local productive systems, which must not be forgotten.

Italy effectively represents the overall pattern in southern European countries, which are characterized by a large share of long-term unemployed and discouraged job seekers. However, there is the additional peculiarity of not being a favourable environment for those with higher skills (Maestripieri and Ranci, 2016), unlike, for example, Spain (Ibáñez, 2011). Social investment policies that fail to consider these aspects are unable to attain target outcomes: as demonstrated in the analysis of the two policies investigated in the chapter. The ultimate reason behind their failure is the low level of interest among employers in investing in employee training (Apprenticeship in Higher Education) or in hiring young workers (Youth Guarantee).

Given these characteristics, Italy can be regarded as a very good example of why a social investment perspective could produce negative effects for high-skilled young workers entering an unfavourable labour market. The intersection of the principal characteristics of three systems produces this outcome: first the educational system, which has a high dropout rate and struggles to facilitate a smooth transition towards the labour market for highly skilled individuals; second, the productive system, which offers limited opportunities in the form of high-skilled job positions, due to a combination of low knowledge-intensive production and a low propensity to innovation; finally, the social protection system, which divides outsiders and insiders on the basis of age cleavages. Overall, a definition of *worst practice* is appropriate for Italy, as it does not offer the necessary preconditions for the effective application of social investment policies (Kazepov and Ranci, 2017).

The result of this situation is that young Italians are exposed to both increasingly difficult entry into the labour market, and to lower job quality, given the greater exposure to non-standard jobs and overqualification. The two phenomena that can be considered interlinked in southern Europe (Ortiz, 2010) negatively influence the future careers of young workers, as deteriorating entry positions in the labour market can have long-lasting negative effects (Scherer, 2004). A feeling of uselessness and helplessness is on the rise among young people. If some of them are willing to accept deteriorated labour market conditions, the more active and entrepreneurial are more inclined to leave the country, triggering a *brain drain* from which countries including Germany and the United Kingdom benefit (Balduzzi and Rosina, 2011).

In accordance with the principle of social investment, the most relevant policies have been oriented towards fostering employability, focusing only on a supply-side policy orientation, without considering the relevant dimensions associated with the educational system, the productive system and the protection system on the demand side (Cuzzocrea, 2015). Two emblematic examples of the failure of a merely supply-side approach were presented in this chapter: Apprenticeships in Higher Education and the Youth Guarantee. In the first case, the unwillingness to invest in the education of employees and the low preference of potential employers for high-skilled apprentices has led to a substantial failure of the measure. In the second case, the Youth Guarantee programme has demonstrated a mismatch between supply and demand, emphasizing the failings in employers, rather than young people. A setting unfit for the implementation of active labour market policies completes the picture, prompting a substantial Matthew effect to arise from the measure (Pintelon *et al.*, 2013), that is favouring the least-marginalized profiles. In terms of the Italian Youth Guarantee implementation, the programme proved more beneficial to those young people with better chances to access the labour market rather than those requiring more support.

The analysis presented in this chapter raises doubt regarding the possibility that Italy will be able to effectively profit from the improved human capital of new generations. As such, one must question the sustainability of the Italian social and economic model, as the youth of today will soon be the adult generation. To modify this scenario, we need tailored activation policies that focus on the employability of the person, and interventions to adapt the productive system and sustain the development of advanced business services (i.e. incentives to start-ups, academic spin-offs, fostering industrial policies aimed at sustaining creative industries and knowledge-intensive services) and high-tech manufacturing to foster better labour-market opportunities for new entrants. A stronger political intervention aimed at changing the nature of labour demand in the Italian context would assist in the effective development of social investment measures, buttressing human capital and increasing the labour market participation of the younger generations.

Notes

1 The data presented in this section can be accessed through the Eurostat database of indicators at: http://ec.europa.eu/eurostat/data/database.
2 See the Youth Guarantee implementation in Italy: http://ec.europa.eu/social/main.jsp ?catId=1161&intPageId=3340&langId=en
3 See the European Commission – Fact Sheet EU Youth Guarantee: Questions and Answers: http://europa.eu/rapid/press-release_MEMO-15-4102_en.htm
4 Ibid.
5 Data was taken 28 April 2016. After this date, the monitoring system no longer published the trends in jobs placement via Youth Guarantee.

References

ANPAL. (2018). L'attuazione della Garanzia Giovani in Italia. Rapporto trimestrale. 4, 2017. Available at: https://www.anpal.gov.it/documents/20126/41601/Rapporto+ trimestrale+GG+N+4.pdf/55a0ba84-d517-4cf5-a1ab-61855bad68db.

Balduzzi, P. and Rosina, A. (2011). Giovani talenti che lasciano l'Italia: fonti, dati e politiche di un fenomeno complesso. *Rivista delle Politiche Sociali*, 43–59.

Ballarino, G. and Scherer, S. (2013). More investment-less returns? Changing returns to education in Italy across three decades. *Stato e Mercato*, 99, 359–388.

Beblavý, M. and Veselková, M. (2015). Future of skills in europe: Convergence or polarisation? In: Beblavý, M., Maselli, I. and Veselková M. (eds) *Let's get to work! The future of labour in Europe.* http://www.ceps.eu/publications/let's-get-work-future-labour-europe (Accessed 9 April, 2015).

Bernardi, F. and Ballarino, G. (2012). Participation, equality of opportunity and returns to tertiary education in contemporary Europe. *European Societies*, 16(3), 422–442.

Bignardi, P., Campiglio, L., Cesareo, V. and Marta, E. (2014). *Giovani e Lavoro. I quaderni del rapporto giovani.* Milano: Vita & Pensiero editore.

Bison, I., Gagliardi, S. and Girardi, S. (2017). I ritorni occupazionali dei diplomati e dei laureati italiani tra il 1995 e il 2011, Paper presented at SISEC 2017, Rome January 25–28. Paper, available at: http://sociologia-economica.it/wp-content/uploads/2017/02/ Bison-SISEC-2017-panel-8-Roma.pdf.

Bodnár, K. (2018). *Recent developments in part-time employment*. Available at: https://goo.gl/SL5pcH.

Castellano, A., Kastorinis, X., Lancellotti, R., Marracino, R. e Villani, L.A. (2014). *Studio Ergo Lavoro. Come facilitare la transizione scuola-lavoro per ridurre in modo strutturale la disoccupazione giovanile in Italia*. Available at: http://www.mckinsey.it/idee/practice_news/la-ricerca-mckinsey-studio-ergo-lavoro.view.

Chauvel, L. and Schroder, M. (2014). Generational inequalities and welfare regimes. *Social Forces*, 92(4), 1259–1283.

Chevalier, T. (2016). Varieties of youth welfare citizenship: Towards a two-dimension typology. *Journal of European Social Policy*, 26(1), 3–19.

Colli, A. (2010). Dwarf giants, giant dwarfs: Reflections about the Italian 'industrial demography' at the beginning of the new millennium. *Journal of Modern Italian Studies*, 15(1), 43–60.

Cuzzocrea, V. (2014). Projecting the category of the NEETS into the future. In: CoE-EC Youth Partnership (ed) European Youth Partnership Series 'Perspectives on Youth', Thematic issue: '2020 – What do YOU see, Council of Europe.

Cuzzocrea, V. (2015). Occupabili' Più Che Occupati? Ambiguità Di Un Concetto Di Policy Nel Caso Italiano. *Sociologia Del Lavoro*, 185(2), 55–68.

Esping-Andersen, G. (2002). *Why We Need a New Welfare State*. Oxford: Oxford University Press.

European Commission. (2013). Communication from the Commission to the European Parliament, the Council, the European Economic and Social Committee and the Committee of the Regions Towards Social Investment for Growth and Cohesion – including implementing the European Social Fund 2014–2020, 20 February 2013, COM(2013) 083 final. Available at: http://ec.europa.eu/social/BlobServlet?docId=9761&langId=en.

Fellini, I. (2015). Una «via bassa» alla decrescita dell'occupazione: il mercato del lavoro italiano tra crisi e debolezze strutturali. *Stato e Mercato*, 105(3), 469–508.

Firinu, A. (2015). La flessibilità irregolare: un fenomeno grigio della regolazione del lavoro. *Sociologia del Lavoro*, 138(2015), 37–54.

Firinu, A. and Maestripieri, L. (2019). Lavoro Marginale. In: Croce, C., Prevete, R. and Zucca, A. (eds) *Porte girevoli. Contributi di ricerca e buone pratiche su lavoro marginale e le nuove vulnerabilità sociali*. Milano: Giangiacomo Feltrinelli editore.

Gallie, D. (2013). *Economic Crisis, Quality of Work, and Social Integration: The European Experience*. Oxford: Oxford University Press.

Gozzo, S. and Sampugnaro, R. (2016). What happens? Changes in European youth participation. *Partecipazione e Conflitto*, 9(3), 748–776.

Hemerijck, A. (2015). The quiet paradigm revolution of social investment. *Social Politics*, 22(2), 242–256.

Ibáñez, Z. (2011). Part-time employment in Spain: A victim of the 'temporality culture' and a lagging implementation. In: Guillén, A.M. and León, M. (eds) *The Spanish Welfare State in European Context*. London: Ashgate, 165–186.

Kazepov, Y. and Ranci, C. (2017). Is every country fit for social investment? Italy as an adverse case. *Journal of European Social Policy*, 27(1), 90–104.

Lodigiani, R. and Santagati, M. (2016). Quel che resta della socializzazione lavorativa. Una riflessione sulle politiche per l'occupazione giovanile in Italia. *Sociologia Del Lavoro*, 2016(141), 141–157.

Maestripieri, L. and Ranci, C. (2016). Non è un paese per laureati. La sovra-qualificazione occupazionale dei lavoratori italiani. *Stato e Mercato*, 108(3), 425–450.

Marques, P. and Salavisa, I. (2017). Young people and dualization in Europe: A fuzzy set analysis. *Socio-Economic Review*, 15(1),135–160.

Morel, N., Palier, B. and Palmer, J. (eds) (2012). *Towards a Social Investment Welfare State?* Chicago: Chicago University Press.

Nolan, B. (2013). What use is 'social investment'? *Journal of European Social Policy*, 23(5), 459–468.

Ortiz, L. (2010). Not the right job, but a secure one: Over-education and temporary employment in France, Italy and Spain. *Work, Employment & Society*, 24(1), 47–64.

Pintelon, O., Cantillon, B., Van den Bosch, K. and Whelan, C.T. (2013). The social stratification of social risks: The relevance of class for social investment strategies. *Journal of European Social Policy*, 23(1), 52–67.

Reyneri, E. and Pintaldi, F. (2013). *Dieci domande su un mercato del lavoro in crisi.* Bologna: Il Mulino Editore.

Rizza, R. and Maestripieri, L. (2015). *Giovani al lavoro: I numeri della crisi.* Milano: Giangiacomo Feltrinelli editore.

Rosina, A. (2013). Politiche di attivazione delle nuove generazioni e incoraggiamento di scelte positive nel corso di vita. *Rivista delle Politiche Sociali*, 1(2), 50–60.

Sánchez-Sánchez, N. and McGuinness, S. (2015). Decomposing the impacts of overeducation and overskilling on earnings and job satisfaction: An analysis using REFLEX data. *Education Economics*, 23(4), 419–432.

Scherer, S. (2004). Stepping-stones or traps?: The consequences of labour market entry positions on future careers in West Germany, Great Britain and Italy. *Work, Employment & Society*, 18(2), 369–394.

Schwander, H. and Hausermann, S. (2013). Who is in and who is out? A risk-based conceptualization of insiders and outsiders. *Journal of European Social Policy*, 23(3), 248–269.

Seghezzi, F. (2016). 'I dieci motivi per cui Garanzia Giovani non decolla', In: Rosolen, G. and Seghezzi, F. (eds) Garanzia Giovani, due anni dopo. Analisi e proposte. ADAPT Working papers. Paper, Available at: http://moodle.adaptland.it/pluginfile.php/26949/mod_resource/content/3/ebook_vol_55.pdf.

Sergi, V., Cefalo, R. and Kazepov, Y. (2018). Young people's disadvantages on the labour market in Italy: Reframing the NEET category. *Journal of Modern Italian Studies*, 23(1), 41–60.

Chapter 6

The synchrony of temporary young workers

Employment discontinuity, income discontinuity and new social inequalities in Italy

Sonia Bertolini and Valentina Moiso

6.1 Introduction and theoretical approach

In Italy, young people often have to deal with *both* employment and income discontinuity. This co-existence is characteristic of Italy more than any other European country because it encompasses the employment experiences of young workers with a variety of skill levels, including those with higher qualifications, and it lasts over time. In other European countries, young people can rely on public support during unemployment even if they have had precarious jobs (e.g. Germany or Sweden). This condition represents an area of *social risk* that has not been fully conceptualized as such, and which we posit as the object of this chapter. In particular, the chapter aims to analyse some of the coping strategies that young Italians use to deal with income discontinuity, given the framework of opportunities and constraints that informs their actions.

Young people's coping strategies, relative to representations, meanings and feelings were investigated through semi-structured interviews on two different samples of 100 young people in total, drawing from the projects 'Online training for the development of women's managerial skills. Women Online' and 'Except – Social Exclusion of Youth in Europe: Cumulative Disadvantage, Coping Strategies, Effective Policies and Transfer'.[1] A qualitative analysis allows for a more in-depth study of the different nuances of the problem. The study was concerned with both self-employed workers and workers with atypical contracts, as well as those with problems of precariousness and low labour-market attachment, and with different levels of education. What they had in common is that they were all lacking a so-called *typical* contract, in the sense of being permanent, dependent and full-time, and the workers being young (18–30 years). Being *atypical* on the Italian labour market and young at the same time are two conditions that in Italy, as in other European countries, are strongly linked. Comparative research (Mills and Blossfeld, 2003; Blossfeld *et al.*, 2011a) has shown that young Europeans are increasingly subject to forms of temporary employment. They are at higher risk of unemployment and take longer to reach stable and continuous working conditions. This has led to the postponement of important decisions in their private lives and in the transition to adulthood.

Our starting point is that young Italians leave the parental home much later than their counterparts in any other European country, and that the length of postponement and the effects on other life domains depend strictly on the institutional context. *Institutional filters* can mediate young people's economic risks, leading to significant cross-national variations in the degree to which the life courses and career paths of individuals become insecure and unstable (Blossfeld *et al.*, 2011a, 2011b; Bertolini *et al.*, 2014).

Some institutional changes that have occurred in the Italian labour market and the welfare state have penalized young people. We refer to the way in which flexibility was introduced in the labour market and to the lack of *flexsecurity* (i.e. the lack of unemployment benefits for atypical workers). These factors intertwine with restrictions in welfare-state provision. Universal measures to sustain people during periods of unemployment have been missing in Italy for a long time. Moreover, the issue of irregular payments and delays in being paid are widespread problems among workers with atypical contracts.

In the literature, less attention has been given to the role of *private* solutions to the lack or discontinuity of income, or even whether financial instruments have also become crucial to the family budget (Zelizer, 1994; Fourcade and Healy, 2013; Perrin-Heredia, 2011; Lazarus and Luzzi, 2015; Ossandon, 2014). Access to money and credit is recognized as one of the new axes of inequality (Crompton, 2000; Bandelj *et al.*, 2017). The use of credit to cover a range of expenses relating to education or health, daily living expenses or even larger purchases, such as buying a flat, are examples of the complex intertwining among public and private spheres and financial institutions that Martin calls the *financialization of daily life* (Deville and Seigworth, 2015; Martin, 2002; Aalbers, 2008; Montgomerie, 2009). Access to credit, for example, may be necessary not only for renting or buying a house but also for starting a business or financing training to improving one's employability. Focusing on the link between labour market position and access to financial services, the divide between atypical and typical workers becomes particularly evident in terms of limited access to credit and increased costs[2] (Langley, 2009; Lacan *et al.*, 2009; Flaherty and Banks, 2013; Ducourant, 2014). Due to institutional and regulatory differences, the extent of this divide differs across countries. In France and Italy for example, the national system of access to credit is linked to working conditions: precarious workers do not normally have access to credit. On the contrary, in other countries such as the UK, the requirements are less tied to contractual conditions; for example, credit is granted to students and depends more on an assessment of the possibility of repaying the debt based on present and expected income. On the other hand, in this case, the risk of overindebtedness increases, especially for younger generations. The issues in accessing credit intersect with other aspects. If we look at leaving the parental home in some countries, such as Germany, where renting rather than ownership is the general pattern, almost all young people leave their family home in this way. Anticipation of this pattern therefore favours young people's transition, since it is less linked to the problem of access to credit. In the

Italian context, where there is typically a preference for home ownership, this involves the mortgage system and the requirements for accessing credit become another important factor to be considered.

This chapter directly investigates young people's strategies and representations, taking into account their framing in the macro context that structure the opportunities they have. In the next section, we outline the links among labour-market regulation, access to credit and housing market patterns, which are all macro variables to consider in analysing the processes through which young Italians leave the parental home and become economically autonomous. In the subsequent section, we show specific formal and informal strategies deployed by young people when facing the transition to adulthood. The Italian case is an interesting example of this transition, given the context of income instability and irregularity and a welfare state that provides low levels of formal protection.

6.2 The Italian institutional context: income discontinuity and access to a credit system

The Italian model for regulating the labour market was built around the centrality of subordinated employment and permanent contracts. The state regulated the relationship between the two; for example, it guaranteed payment terms and protected the worker, insofar as a citizen was able to fully enjoy rights to the welfare state. Wages were seen as a guarantee of the survival of the workforce and was the responsibility of the employer and the state (Bologna and Banfi, 2011). The entire private banking system and the private sector in general also operate on the same assumptions. For example, the access to credit is more difficult for workers with atypical contracts, the banks do not provide specific instruments taking into account the needs of people working without regularity of payments and the payment system of both salaries and bills are regulated on a *monthly basis*. Moreover, what is happening today is that many workers, especially young people, cannot rely on regular payments and at the same time cannot turn on public support. Irregular payments, weakness of welfare interventions, low dynamism of the labour market, especially for young people, who furthermore see a proliferation of atypical forms of contract, and lack of innovation in the bank system, these are all factors that define the specificity of the Italian case. This is a case in which young people experiment cumulative inequalities in terms of the possibility of having regular income that allow them to reach economic autonomy and a decent lifestyle (Meo and Moiso, 2018).

A deepened view of these dynamics could help to better understand them. The model based on the male breadwinner family arose from the typical contract. It was the adult male who, as head of the family, worked with a permanent contract, and the security of his income protected the rest of the family. Therefore, it was his income that was protected by the state. The wife would take care of the housework and family members, and the children were protected by the family while they were studying but also when looking for their first job.

Salary payment and access to credit were also punctuated by the monthly salary deadlines, and the security of the permanent contract had become the criteria for access to credit. In recent years, credit has allowed many families to become home owners through mortgages on their first house since homeownership in Italy is one of the major systems of protection from financial risk and for the intergenerational transmission of assets. In addition, the state has supported this system through other elements, such as the reduction of transaction costs on the purchase of the first home and preferential value-added tax (VAT).

In the last decade, with the diffusion of precarious contracts, this system has entered into crisis. Deregulation policies have been highly selective, burdening the already disadvantaged labour market outsiders, while leaving the rights of labour-market insiders almost untouched. Given the strong protection guarantees for *insiders*, flexibility was selectively transferred to those people without safe labour-market anchorage, namely those entering the labour market (see Blossfeld *et al.*, 2005, 2011b; Barbieri and Scherer, 2009), a strategy frequently referred to as *flexibility at the margins* (e.g. Buchholz *et al.*, 2009).

In Italy, a rapid introduction of temporary employment contracts, combined with very low and targeted social protection, affected the life of young people differently than in other countries where such changes were slower or accompanied by higher levels of social protection (Bertolini, 2011). Furthermore, in a dual and segmented labour market, young people – with more temporary and atypical contracts – often could not access active and passive labour-market policies. This happened for two main reasons: for a long time, temporary contracts had been excluded from social labour protection, such as unemployment benefits. Moreover, workers with discontinuous working paths, mainly young people, had difficulty achieving minimum requirements to access protection. Berton and colleagues (2009) provocatively called this system *Flexinsecurity*. This is an important factor of dependency upon families for younger generations.

In this way, the reforms of the labour market at the turn of 2000 – the Treu Law of 1997 and Law 30 of 2003 – were directed at removing protection from those whose job and income were holding the rest of the family system together. However, this was done without shifting towards a new model, such as investing in the insertion of young men and women into the labour market. These reforms occurred alongside other processes of change. For example, family models had become increasingly complex; the gender roles of dual earners were no longer well defined, especially for young people where there was also a postponement of the traditional stages in their transition to adult life.

Finally, there was a lack of a facilitated rental policy to support the housing autonomy of young people. As stated by Rabaiotti (2011), a housing policy that encourages youth autonomy should support a low-cost and temporary solution, features that property ownership did not have. In Italy, 70% of people were homeowners, while 17.8% were renting at market prices. However, 17% of owners had a current loan or mortgage (Banca d'Italia, 2018). In other countries, homeowners where only 53.2% of the population, such as Germany (Sweden 68.0%, the Netherlands 59.5% and Denmark 52.7%). These differences in housing were reflected in the ways and timings in which young people left their parental home. Some studies pointed out that the Italian youth population was excluded from the housing ladder, because of the difficulty in obtaining mortgages. Youth became a *rental generation*. There was a debate about the possibility of intergenerational conflict between housing poor young people and the rich elderly (Mckee and Hoolachan, 2015), especially in Northern Europe. This was intimately connected to the question of the future of the welfare-state system. In particular, leaving parental home to rent was not considered an efficient solution in countries where homeowners were predominant. This further delayed the time of departure from the family home because of the difficulty of access to credit for this part of the population. In Southern Europe, the prolonged permanence with the family was seen as a way to avoid depleting the resources of the family: you left home only when you were able to afford to buy a new house or you inherited parents' or grandparents' home. Therefore, for young Italians, contractual discontinuity was associated with the discontinuity of income and difficulty in accessing credit and home ownership, which was a system of protection against financial risk.

In the terms described above, we intend to deal with the repercussions on income and financial management that derives from this structure of integration, or lack of integration among the welfare system, the labour market and access to credit.

6.3 The financialization of young Italians

The role of the banking sector in shaping the opportunities of young Italians has evolved as a recent research interest, possibly because the involvement of families in the financial sector is relatively recent. In other terms, the credit market for families is underdeveloped in comparison to other countries: families have higher savings[3] (Dagnes, 2010; Cannari and D'Alessio, 2006), and even after financial crisis they continue to save, except younger families (Banca d'Italia, 2018). Until recently, they showed higher levels of wealth in the form of property investment. Up until the Second World War, Italian families were less concerned with banking, or rather they benefited much less from banking products and services compared to today, and they were also not very indebted. In 1967,[4] the percentage of people in debt was 18%, of whom only 15.2% had turned to a bank and 5% went to non-banking financial institutions. The main source of loans came from friends and family members; 31.7% of those who needed money used to do this. The percentage rose to 39.9% among low-income families, but remained above 20% in high-income families who preferred to turn to banks in 40% of cases. In addition, 40% of low-income people were in debt, and more than 20% of middle- and high-income borrowers had small debts with suppliers and retailers for purchases that were necessary to carry out their profession. There were also accounts opened by families at food shops or for consumer goods, including the first instalment-rate purchases. What is specific to the Italian context was the delay in starting the process of indebtedness.

Over the years, the Italian context has changed. Since the 1990s, the stability of permanent contracts and the high financial solidity of Italian families in terms of savings on the one hand, and the start of the liberalization of the banking system with the Amato Law in 1992 on the other, have created favourable conditions for the growth of the mortgage market in Italy. Initially, small debts, accessed with the guarantee of family patrimony allowed Italian families to afford things in line with their desired lifestyle. However, the number of Italian families with a mortgage did not significantly change: lower than 5% in the 1960s, and up to 5% in the 1990s. In 2008, indebted households rose to 27.8%, of whom only 12.23% had debts with relatives and friends, even though after the financial crisis this trend seemed to have reversed (Banca d'Italia, 2010). The biggest change was related to the widespread access to mortgages amongst new generations: in the 2000s real estate debt had a greater weight in the financial liabilities of young people up to the age of 34, especially if they were employed and graduates. The biggest changes took place after the deregulation of the 1990s: between 1998 and 2007 the money disbursed by banks to households for the purchase of a house rose by an average of 17% per year (Bonaccorsi di Patti and Felici, 2008). This was partly due to the growing number of households applying for a loan, and partly to the increase in the average loan value.

In a study carried out in the 1980s, Jappelli and Pagano (1988) found that the conditions for obtaining a bank loan in Italy disadvantaged young people. In the last 20 years, things have partially changed and the percentage of young people[5] out of the total of those who obtained a mortgage, went from 6.9% in 1989 to 15.4% in 2008 (Banca d'Italia, 2010). Such data confirm the changes in banking policy towards those categories of customers who were previously relatively less involved in the credit market. Following the deregulation in the 1990s, banks have been more likely to grant loans over longer time horizons or in more flexible ways. Therefore, families have borrowed through easier procedures than in the past. However, access to bank credit is not easy for everyone, and banks have certainly expanded access to credit, but they are not willing to give credit to families with no savings or other assets, especially following the 2007 financial crisis.

In this sense, the situation of the Italian banking sector in general, and of the credit sector, in particular, differs from the American one. In Italy, after the financial crisis, liabilities have amounted to 70% of disposable income compared to 100% in France and 132% in the United States, as mentioned previously. Looking at the spread of mortgages among households, the figure in Italy stood at 12.6%, compared to an estimated 25%–30% in France, Germany and Spain, 35%–40% in Ireland and the Netherlands, and over 50% in the United States (Banca d'Italia, 2010). From an institutional point of view, the Italian case presents factors with a contrasting effect on the growth of the mortgage sector for households (Jappelli et al., 2008). On the one hand, in relation to the European context, there is a high degree of information sharing on the financial history of customers, an element that helps to overcome uncertainty regarding the capacity of customers to pay back money, and therefore facilitates the sale of credit instruments, including mortgages, from the banks. On the other hand, the long-term framework of the Italian judicial system and the only recently filled gap in legislation regarding the bankruptcy of households has increased the cost of loans and, to some extent, limited the offer, because they make the recovery of credit by banks uncertain.

Banks have defined households that are still not in debt as an *expanding market*, and the Italian banking sector looks at the backwardness of the Italian credit market compared to the United States as a reservoir with high-growth potential.[6] The inclusion of young people with atypical contracts, however, given the discontinuity of their income, is yet to come. Moreover, after the financial crisis of 2008, the credit crunch, the uncertainty regarding the economic situation and the new international regulatory frame about risk management in banking system did not support an increase in credit access.

In this direction, the Italian State has started to support the credit market, making financial funds as a guarantee for debt given by banks to individuals, especially young people, without the requested features. These funds are used only if young people are not able to cover their debts.[7] Such measures were implemented at a national level, but also by some municipalities. However, the condition to access the protection of these funds still excludes atypical workers (Moiso, 2012).

6.4 Coping strategies linked to work and salary

It is useful to study the practices of family/individual management of money (spending, saving and investment) of young atypical workers in this difficult private and public institutional context, especially focusing on how housing costs are handled. There are many studies on young atypical workers but not many that look at their financial strategy. Using a life-course approach (Elder, 1985) of transitions, a study (Bertolini, 2012) reconstructed the working family and economic careers of women with permanent contracts and women with fixed-term contracts in Turin and Naples. The research showed that, at the same age and with the same qualifications, the aspect that most influenced financial decisions (house purchase, investments in additional pension schemes, etc.) and family life (leaving parents, marriage, cohabitation, first child, etc.) was the contractual form. Atypical workers were systematically a few years late in achieving their private and financial life milestones with respect to those with permanent employment contracts.

An essential point regards the interdependence between different careers and decisions. The atypical workers emphasized the difficulty or impossibility of planning their working careers and, as a consequence, their private lives from a long-term perspective. One of the effects of remaining in atypical employment was the postponement of important decisions in one's private life, as a wide range of literature has shown (Blossfeld *et al.*, 2005). Having to suspend their plans with regard to their work also led to similar behaviour in other dimensions of their private lives. Our results showed that financial investments, such as buying a house or investing money, were also delayed, mainly due to the irregular income effect. Therefore, they lived with short-term planning:

> I can identify comments regarding atypical workers: economic fragility... being treated like consultants, but paid possibly less than the others, makes any future planning difficult, the feeling of a continuous shaky situation, and in my opinion also psychological insecurity. (Paola, 33, training agency, degree in Science of Education, Turin)

Instability in terms of one's job also meant uncertainty about the continuity of income. Those with atypical contracts also suffered from the irregularity of payments. They were often paid at the end of a contract in a single lump sum, while the world they lived in was based on monthly deadlines.

With a lack of institutional protection, and the impossibility of being able to set up basic financial instruments, such as loans, atypical workers activated individual protection strategies. There were essentially two types: the first was precautionary saving; the second was asking their families for help. The first involved saving money without investing it for of fear of there being periods in which they would have no income:

> As I don't have a permanent contract (also close to expiry), I also prefer not to take on any form of payment obligations that are too demanding, but in the long run I have realised that things tend to drag on... in the end, the solution I have adopted is to make temporary sacrifices, putting a bit of money aside and asking relatives for a loan, if possible, paying it back gradually. (Carmela, 28, classroom tutor, Naples)

Sometimes, this precautionary saving might have been excessive in relation to the actual possibility of experiencing periods *without any money*. However, the income uncertainty that stemmed from both the lack of guaranteed job continuity and possible delays in payment frequently blocked alternative actions of those workers who postponed investment decisions. This also concerned investing in a private pension fund, even though these were workers had a greater need to set one up. With regard to this, the study showed that when they were close to 40 years of age, atypical workers acquired a real awareness of their work situation and put into action other protective strategies against present and future risks: they made financial investments, stipulated additional social security arrangements, set up supplementary pensions or borrowed from banks during periods when they were waiting to be paid, or they were thinking about it. Furthermore, some of them had drawn up some solutions with their banks to cover late payments, as overdraft facilities or other more complex financial instruments.

Asking their parents for help in the event of financial necessity was considered *normal* by the majority of youth involved in the study. For instance:

> I am looking for a house with my boyfriend and we want to buy it, so we are looking at mortgages. At the moment, we are just getting started, also because (perhaps) we have found a house, but what prices! Luckily, we can get a mortgage without having to ask our parents to mortgage their home as they are helping us with a tidy initial sum … but what a hassle! (Eleonora, 31, instructor, Turin)

Some participants, when prompted, mentioned the fact that in this way they were delaying their entrance into the adult world. There was also a risk of an increase in social inequality between those who had a family that could support them in buying a house or in arranging a mortgage and those who did not. In addition, those most likely to invest their savings in long-term assets, real estate or government bonds appeared to be stable workers.

Looking at attitudes towards saving, research findings do not necessarily converge: some research findings identified a greater propensity amongst atypical workers towards saving (Bertolini, 2012). Others showed a lower propensity for atypical workers to save (Musumeci, 2011). In this regard, it is helpful if we differentiate between types of saving. Atypical workers used the so-called *precautionary saving*, but the difficulty was in long-term saving, and it was precisely this type that atypical workers could not have. Precautionary saving was short-term and was, by definition, fluid. Such savings were not investable, since they needed easy access to that money for use in emergencies. Permanent workers who could still count on their fixed monthly salary did not express as much of a need for this type of saving.

Here, once again, the relationship with the banking system emerged as crucial: without long-term savings there can be no investment. In fact, research (Musumeci, 2011) showed a lower propensity to invest amongst precarious workers, precisely because the prospect of discontinuity in employment, linked to income discontinuity, and prevented them from planning in the long run, especially with respect to their finances. However, this meant a lower return on one's money and a loss for banks in terms of possible investors. Precautionary savings stayed in bank accounts.

Another study (Paskov, 2011) showed there was lower propensity amongst atypical workers to invest in supplementary pensions, although they needed this more than most. Again, the pension system as it is, penalized those who had discontinuous payments or different funds. In this study, Paskov found that more than the objective labour market situation, the subjective dimension, that is the perception of job insecurity and the fear of becoming unemployed, played a role in financial decisions. Perceived labour-market insecurity reduced the chances of creating retirement savings in the liberal, conservative and southern welfare regimes. People who perceived labour markets as uncertain did not feel that they had the power to make future financial plans, and they were more concerned with thinking about the present (Moiso, 2017, 2018). It also showed they had lessor access to insurance products (home, life, accident, health, supplementary pension and child health).

6.5 The progressive fall into uncertainty of young Italians

It is interesting to compare the findings regarding job insecurity and economic and housing uncertainty emerged in the previously mentioned EXCEPT project to the study on work and money management strategies of the previous paragraph (Bertolini *et al.*, 2018a, 2019; Baranowska-Rataj *et al.*, 2018; Unt and Gebel, 2018). The differences in meanings, feelings and coping strategies related to the overlapping experiences of job and income insecurity, which resulted in increased uncertainty for young people compared to those described above. The dimension of money management emerged as crucial, but at the same time it was framed in a context confined to the family dimension and the present situation.

Regardless of one's age and level of education, the main coping strategy was removing expenses that the young people interviewed deemed to be less essential, such as holidays, unexpected purchases and expensive leisure activities, differing from the research results mentioned in the previous paragraph. Practices of containing expenses were not put in place to attain or maintain economic autonomy, but to manage the *expenses for oneself* while their daily life expenses were covered by the parents with whom they lived. The lack of economic autonomy was in fact strictly linked to the lack of housing autonomy, and it persisted also for those young people who had a job. In fact, while in the Italian sample of EXCEPT there were groups of people living in a poor household to which they contributed financially to domestic expenses, there was also a good share of young people who had never contributed to the family budget because of their parents' denial, and who had saved their money in order to leave the parental home, buy a car or pay for their free-time expenses.

Strategies of money management put in place by young people underlined that those interviewed were undergoing a shift of risk management from the social system to the individual (see Sennett, 1998; Bosco and Sciarrone, 2006; Negri and Filandri, 2010), driven by the problem of job insecurity. The majority of participants were not in a stable position in the labour market and experienced uncertainty with respect to their work and income in a non-linear way. Atypical contracts with irregular duration, periods of unemployment between contracts, non-paid or underpaid jobs and irregularity in payments were all elements that made budget management more complex. Therefore, feelings and perceptions about the individual risk had increased, and the present had become the frame in which decisions were made (Bertolini *et al.*, 2018b).

Going deeper into the macro, meso and micro coping strategies aimed at maintaining economic autonomy (see Baranowska-Rataj *et al.*, 2015), the EXCEPT findings showed some specificities for Italian young people in comparison to past generations, as well as their counterparts in other European countries. At a macro level, despite the fact that some European policies or recommendations had started to consider the financial solutions to improve the social situation of young people who faced labour market insecurities, none of the young participants had been involved in these types of policies. In particular, measures directed at facilitating access to credit could have been useful for some participants in supporting them in self-employment – starting a new professional activity, opening a shop, or becoming an entrepreneur. These were dreams for some of the young people but, for the moment, they totally avoided debt. For those who knew about the possibility of having access to a microcredit programme, it would have been be a *second-step* strategy; for the time being, the goal was to enter the labour market in a more stable way, and a relationship with the banking system was totally avoided. Participants justified this behaviour in reference to their great fear of falling into debt. Moreover, they were aware that in Italy vulnerable workers were more expensive (higher interest rates) and risky to employers.

At a meso level, economic support given by friends and relatives in EU countries characterized between 40% and 90% of the working poor (Perrin-Heredia, 2013b; Lazarus, 2016). The young participants confirmed this with respect to parental support (Bertolini *et al.*, 2018b). For the majority of the participants, this situation led to a loss of housing autonomy, which was connected to a low level of independence in the management of housing expenses, domestic consumption and long-term savings.

At a micro level, going into high-risk debt, such as a credit card or *not paying* some expenses, choosing to pay only what could create short-term sanctions (Perrin-Heredia, 2013a), were not strategies implemented by the Italian participants. This stands in contrast to other European countries, where such strategies were more widespread. In Italy, parental economic support seemed to protect young people from potentially dangerous behaviour (see Rolando and Beccaria, 2018) and more general economic distress (Colombo *et al.*, 2018). Saving emerged as the most-widespread behaviour. Moreover, the meaning and scope of saving was focused on the present and on individual needs. Young people saved to protect themselves in the event of job loss, including personal expenses such as modest leisure activities or car costs. It was short-term savings that allowed young people to cope with high job insecurity. For the youth who had left the parental home, saving was a short-term strategy finalized to survive, given the uncertainty of the duration of contracts, the periods of unemployment and the absence of an adequate system of income support.

To sum up, if we define financial vulnerability as the individual level of exposure to external events or mistakes in individual financial choices, it depends on the intertwines between context in which people live and the decisions they make (Moiso, 2012). Given the overlap between job and income insecurity, the young interviewees became more vulnerable overall from a financial point of view. However, the level of vulnerability was not equal for all young people at a similar position in the labour market but was influenced by a combination of their individual *financial career* or *debt career*, other individual careers such a professional one, the availability and level of parental support, and housing decisions. Above all, financial vulnerability made young people perceive their situation as being worse, by shaping their individual perception of job insecurity and increasing the related stress. In the absence of a protective system other than the informal support of parents, it could affect their decisions about the future, such as remaining in the family home.

6.6 Conclusion

In this chapter, we introduced the main characteristics of the macro context of the Italian labour market and credit systems, then we presented the main results of different research projects that were conducted on similar samples of young people who faced labour market insecurity. By analysing risks arising from the synchrony on employment and income discontinuity, it was possible to draw some conclusions on short- and long-term inequalities, considering the intertwining of labour market, welfare system and financial sector.

This perspective helped us to investigate in greater detail the impact of precariousness on when and how young people in Italy completed their passage to adulthood. Job insecurity increasingly affected the decisions of young Italians in terms of delaying the decision to leave the parental home, given the increased uncertainty on the labour market mainly as a result of income insecurity. Until then, those with wealthy families with savings had been sheltered in terms of access to work, since they were able to implement a strategy of waiting to leave home only when they attained their first stable job.

This configuration risks being unsustainable in the future. Today, we are already witnessing a generation that has no aspirations for social mobility, and who at most aspire to maintain their positions. In addition, many risks are expected for the future pensions of this generation, given the impossibility of long-term savings. The long-term consequences of this situation are also defined in terms of career development with gender difference in resilience, accumulation and intergenerational transmission of economic resources.

Our discussion reveals the presence of new bottom-up strategies based on money management, not supported by institutions (welfare state or banks). It generates further inequalities among precarious workers, engendering a virtuous or vicious cycle. For now, studies have shown that, thanks to their parental economic support, young Italians have generally not entered into a vicious cycle of over-indebtedness.

At a macro level, measures to help workers to deal with the synchrony of employment and income discontinuity have only been introduced in Italy in recent years, following a much more widespread European trend (OECD and EU guidelines). However, fully fledged policies are still lacking. In 2018, the Italian government started a process of introducing a minimum income scheme. The recipients should benefit from an 18-month transfer, provided their availability to be involved in some active labour-market policies and immediate willingness to work.

In this context, a final question arises: would a national policy of easier access to credit help to improve the social situation of young people, who face labour-market insecurities without support from the welfare state? According to the European Commission (2012: 3), credit of small amounts is an 'effective financing channel for job creation and social inclusion'. However, among the young people interviewed, credit was simultaneously seen as an opportunity and a risk. From an analytical point of view, the main risk is that of increasing the financial vulnerability of young people by allowing them easier access to credit. That is, if it were carried out without strong protection from the risk of default, given the predatory behaviour of banks and the potential lack of financial knowledge on the part of young people. On the contrary, we envisage policies aimed at *enabling* rather than *providing*, that is measures aimed at establishing a synergic collaboration among labour policies, social protection system, banking regulations and policies to support individual entrepreneurship, together with support for non-bank operators, especially non-profit. The latter have the appropriate experience to help the beneficiaries to put their skills into practice thanks to the loans received. This scheme has to be completed by a regulation directed at the protection of over-indebted subjects that provide forms of assistance in managing and restructuring personal debts.

Notes

1 All semi-structured interviews were recorded, fully transcribed and analysed according to a defined analytical framework. The first research was the project 'Online training for the development of women's managerial skills. Women Online' carried out by Cirsde in collaboration with Poliedra and Studio Staff, and financed by the Ministry of Labour and Social Policy. A sample made up of 50 young women aged between 25 and 40, with medium-high educational qualifications, mostly degrees or postgraduate specializations, in humanities, residing in Turin and Naples. These were women who worked in the business services sector. Two-thirds of them had atypical contractual forms, CoCoCo or CoCoPro (term-contract workers or professionals), and one-third were typical indefinite time workers. The different careers were reconstructed through the reorganization of the data in a reading grid on the model used from life-course research. The second research was the H2020 project 'Social Exclusion of Youth in Europe: Cumulative Disadvantage, Coping Strategies, Effective Policies and Transfer – EXCEPT' (2015–2018), involving nine countries: Bulgaria, Estonia, Germany, the United Kingdom, Greece, Italy, Poland, Sweden and Ukraine in a mixed-method research study on 400 young people. The Italian sample comprised 50 interviews conducted between December 2015 and November 2016. Samples covered people aged 18–30, balanced by gender and level of education (25 men and 25 women); 25 were aged 18–24, while the other 25 were 25–30. Regarding their educational level, 26 out of 50 interviewees had a secondary level of education (ISCED 3, and only one ISCED 4), 12 had a low educational level (ISCED 0–2) and 12 had a tertiary education (ISCED 5–6). Other information can be found on www.except-project.eu.

2 These limitations currently imply long-standing consequences, that is in relation to pensions: atypical workers have less opportunities to have access to complementary pension plans (Hofäcker *et al.*, 2016; Moiso, 2018).
3 More data is available in the Bank of Italy documents, *Survey on Household Income and Wealth*.
4 All data is from the Bank of Italy, 'Survey on the Budgets of Italian Families – 1965–2008'.
5 Heads of family are under the age of 35.
6 From the talk by Giuseppe Zadra, then Director General of ABI (Italian Banking Association), at the conference Credito alle famiglie (Credit to Families) 2009, Rome, 23–24 June 2009.
7 For example, the funds for access to home mortgage for young couples or the funds for loans to households with newborn children, both of the Department for Family Policy of the Presidency of the Council of Ministers in 2011.

References

Aalbers, M.B. (2008). The financialization of home and the mortgage market crisis. *Competition & Change*, 12(2), 148–166.

Banca d'Italia. (2010). *I bilanci delle famiglie italiane nell'anno 2008 (Survey on Household Income and Wealth-year 2008)*. Roma: Banca d'Italia.

Banca d'Italia. (2018). *I bilanci delle famiglie italiane nell'anno 2016 (Survey on Household Income and Wealth- year 2016)*. Roma: Banca d'Italia.

Bandelj, N., Wherry, F. and Zelizer, V. (eds) (2017). *Money Talks: Explaining How Money Really Works*. Princeton and Oxford: Princeton University Press.

Baranowska-Rataj, A., Bertolini, S., Ghislieri, C., Meo, A., Moiso, V., Musumeci, R., Ricucci, R. and Torrioni, P. (2015). *Becoming Adult in Hard Times: Current and Future Issues on Job Insecurity and Autonomy*. Torino: Academia University Press.

Baranowska-Rataj, A., Bertolini, S. and Goglio, V. (eds) (2018). Country level analyses of mechanisms and interrelationships between labour market insecurity and autonomy. EXCEPT Working Papers, 11, Tallinn: Tallinn University Press, http://www.except-project.eu/working-papers.

Barbieri, P. and Scherer, S. (2009). Labour market flexibilization and its consequences in Italy. *European Sociological Review*, 25(6), 677–692.

Bertolini, S. (2011). The heterogeneity of the impact of labour market flexibilization on the transition to adult life in Italy: When do young people leave the nest? In: Blossfeld, H.P., Hofäcker, D. and Bertolini, S. (eds) *Youth on Globalised Labour Markets: Rising Uncertainty and Its Effects on Early Employment and Family Lives in Europe*. Opladen & Farmington Hills: Barbara Budrich, 163–187.

Bertolini, S. (2012). *Flessibilmente giovani. Percorsi lavorativi e transizione alla vita adulta nel nuovo mercato del lavoro (Flexibly young. Job careers and transition to adult life in the new labour market)*. Bologna: il Mulino.

Bertolini, S., Hofacker, D. and Torrioni, P. (2014). *L'uscita dalla famiglia di origine in diversi sistemi di Welfare State: l'impatto della flessibilizzazione del mercato del lavoro e della crisi occupazionale in Italia, Francia e Germania (The exit from the family of origin in different welfare state systems: The impact of labour market flexibility and the employment crisis in Italy, France and Germany)*. Sociologia del lavoro, 136, 144–125.

Bertolini, S., Deliyanni-Kouimtzi, K., Bolzoni, M., Ghislieri, C., Goglio, V., Martino, S., Meo, A. et al. (eds) (2018a). Labour market insecurity and social exclusion: Qualitative comparative results in nine countries. EXCEPT Working Paper, 53, Tallinn: Tallinn University Press, http://www.except-project.eu/working-papers.

Bertolini, S., Moiso, V. and Musumeci, R. (2018b). The Italian Report: Young adults in insecure labour market positions – The results from qualitative studies. EXCEPT Working Papers, 18, Tallinn: Tallinn University Press, http://www.except-project.eu/working-papers.

Bertolini, S., Moiso, V. and Unt, M. (2019). Precarious and creative: Youth facing uncertainty in the labour market. In: Colombo, C. and Rebughini, P.A. (eds) *The Politics of the Present*. London: Routledge (forthcoming).

Berton, F., Richiardi, M. and Sacchi, S. (2009). *Flexinsecurity: perché in Italia la flessibilità diventa precarietà' (Flexinsecurity: Why flexibility becomes precariousness in Italy)*. Bologna: il Mulino.

Blossfeld, H.P., Buchholz, S., Hofacker, D. and Bertolini, S. (2012). Selective flexibilization and deregulation of the labor market: The answer of Continental and Southern Europe. *Stato e Mercato*, 96, 364–390.

Blossfeld, H.P., Hofäcker, D. and Bertolini, S. (eds) (2011a). *Youth on Globalised Labour Market: Rising Uncertainty and Its Effects on Early Employment and Family Lives in Europe*. Opladen (Germany) and Farmington Hills (USA): Barbara Budrich Publishers.

Blossfeld, H.P., Hofacker, D., Rizza, R. and Bertolini, S., (2011b). Giovani, i perdenti della globalizzazione? (Young People, Globalization's Losers?). *Sociologia del lavoro*, 124.

Blossfeld, H.P., Klijzing, E., Mills, M. and Kurz, K. (eds) (2005). *Globalization, Uncertainty and Youth in Society*. London: Routledge.

Bologna, S. and Banfi, D. (2011). Vita da freelance. I lavoratori della conoscenza e il loro futuro, Milano: Feltrinelli. [Freelance life. Knowledge workers and their future].

Bonaccorsi di Patti, E. and Felici, R. (2008). Il rischio dei mutui alle famiglie in Italia: evidenza da un milione di contratti (The risk of mortgages to families in Italy: Evidence from one million contracts). Banca d'Italia Occasional papers, 32. Roma: Banca d'Italia.

Bosco, N. and Sciarrone, R. (2006). La certezza dell'incertezza. Ambivalenze e rimedi, Meridiana, 55, 9–33 [The certainty of uncertainty. Ambivalences and reliefs].

Buchholz, S., Höfacker, D., Mills, M., Blossfeld, H.P., Kurz, K. and Hofmeister, H. (2009). Life courses in the globalization process: The development of social inequalities in modern societies. *European Sociological Review*, 25(1), 53–71.

Cannari, L. and D'Alessio, G. (2006). *La ricchezza degli Italiani (The wealth of Italians)*. Bologna: il Mulino.

Colombo, E., Leonini, L. and Rebughini, P. (2018). A generational attitude: Young adults facing the economic crisis in Milan. *Journal of Modern Italian Studies*, 23(1), 61–74.

Crompton, R. (2000). *Renewing Class Analysis*. Oxford: Blackwell.

Dagnes, J. (2010). Il requisito della ricchezza (The wealth requirement). In: Negri, N. and Filandri, M. (eds) *Restare di ceto medio. Il passaggio alla vita adulta nella società che cambia*. Bologna: il Mulino.

Deville, J. and Seigworth, G. (2015). Everyday debt and credit, introduction to special issue. *Cultural Studies*, 29(5–6), 615–629.

Ducourant, H. (2014). Why do the poor pay more for their credit? A French case study. In: Guérin, I., Morvant-Roux, S., Villareal, M. (eds) *Microfinance, Debt and Over-Indebtedness*. London: Routledge.

Elder, G.H. Jr. (ed) (1985). *Life Course Dynamics: Trajectories and Transitions, 1968–1980*. Ithaca, New York: Cornell University Press.

European Commission. (2012). Report from the Commission to the European Parliament and the Council on the application of Directive 2006/48/EC to microcredit, 18 December 2012, COM(2012) 769 final, Available at: https://ec.europa.eu/transparency/regdoc/rep/1/2012/EN/1-2012-769-EN-F1-1.Pdf.

Flaherty, J. and Banks, S. (2013). In whose interest? The dynamic of debt in poor households. *Journal of Poverty and Social Justice*, 21(3), 219–232.

Fourcade, M. and Healy, K. (2013). Classification situations: Life-chances in the neoliberal era. *Accounting, Organizations and Society*, 38(8), 559–572.

Hofäcker, D., Hess, M. and König, S. (eds) (2016). *Delaying Retirement: Progress and Challenges of Active Ageing in Europe, the United States and Japan.* Basingstoke: Palgrave Macmillan.

Jappelli, T. and Pagano, M. (1988). Liquidity-Constrained Households in an Italian Cross-Section. Cepr Discussion Paper 257.

Jappelli, T., Pagano, M. and di Maggio, M. (2008). Households' Indebtedness and Financial Fragility. Centre for Studies in Economics and Finance (CSEF) Working Papers 208.

Lacan, L., Lazarus, J., Perrin-Heredia, A. and Plot, S. (2009). Vivre et faire vivre à crédit: agents économiques ordinaires et institutions financières dans les situations d'endettement. *Sociétés contemporaines*, 76(4), 5–15.

Langley, P. (2009). *The Everyday Life of Global Finance.* Oxford: Oxford University Press.

Lazarus, J. (2016). Le tissage de notre vie quotidienne et de la finance. In: Chambost, I., Lenglet, M. and Tadjeddine, J. (eds) *La Fabrique de la finance.* Paris: Presses Universitaires du Septentrion.

Lazarus, J. and Luzzi, M. (2015). Les pratiques monétaires des ménages au prisme de la Financiarization. *Critique internationale*, 69(4), 9–19.

Martin, R. (2002). *Financialization of Daily Life.* Philadelphia: Temple University Press.

Mckee, K. and Hoolachan, J. (2015). Housing generation rent: What are the Challenges for Housing Policy in Scotland? Working paper of Centre for Housing Research University of St Andrews.

Meo, A. and Moiso, V. (2018). Precari e autonomi: un binomio (im)possibile (Precarious and autonomous: a (im)possible pair). In: S. Bertolini (ed) *Giovani senza futuro? Insicurezza lavorativa e autonomia giovanile nell'Italia di oggi.* Roma: Carocci.

Mills, M. and Blossfeld, H.P. (2003). Globalization, uncertainty and changes in early life courses. *Zeitschrift für Erziehungswissenschaft*, 6(2), 188–218.

Moiso, V. (2012). L'accesso al credito come innovazione di welfare e contrasto alla vulnerabilità (Access to credit as a welfare innovation and contrast to vulnerability). *Rivista delle Politiche Sociali*, 4, 313–332.

Moiso, V. (2017). Country case – Italy. In: Hofäcker, D., Schadow, S. and Kletzing J. (eds) *Long-Term Socio-economic Consequences of Insecure Labour Market Positions.* Tallin: Tallin University Press, 77–88.

Moiso, V. (2018). (Im)previdenti? Rappresentazioni e strategie di giovani precari sulle pensioni ((Im)foresighted? Representations and strategies of precarious young people on pensions). In: Caselli, D. and Dagnes, J. (eds) Autonomie Locali e Servizi Sociali – session on 'Salvati dalla finanza? Finanziarizzazione, welfare e benessere', 2, 271–288.

Montgomerie, J. (2009). The pursuit of (past) happiness? Middle-class indebtedness and American financialisation. *New Political Economy*, 14(1), 1–24.

Musumeci, R. (2011). *Consumi di giovani adulti catanesi, Instabilità del lavoro e razionalità nelle decisioni di acquisto, (Consumption of young people from Catania, labor instability, and rationality in purchasing decisions).* Roma: Aracne.

Negri, N. and Filandri, M. (2010). *Restare di ceto medio. Il passaggio alla vita adulta nella società che cambia.* Bologna: il Mulino.

Ossandón, J. (2014). Sowing consumers in the garden of mass retailing in Chile. *Consumption Markets & Culture*, 17(5), 429–447.

Paskov, M. (2011). Labour market uncertainty and Private Pension planning in Europe. In: Blossfeld, H.P., Hofäcker, D. and Bertolini, S. (eds). *Youth on Globalised Labour Market. Rising Uncertainty and Its Effects on Early Employment and Family Lives in Europe.* Opladen, Germany and Farmington Hills, MI: Barbara Budrich Publishers.

Perrin-Heredia, A. (2011). Faire les comptes: normes comptables, normes sociales. *Genèses*, 84(3), 69–92.

Perrin-Heredia, A. (2013a). Le choix en économie. Le cas des consommateurs pauvres. *Actes de la recherche en sciences sociales*, 199(4), 46–67.

Perrin-Heredia, A. (2013b). La mise en ordre de l'économie domestique. *Gouvernement et action publique*, 2, 303–330.

Rabaiotti, D. (2011). La casa come un servizio, Dossier Centro servizi per il volontariato nella provincia di Milano, 2, settembre 2011.

Rolando, S. and Beccaria, F. (2018). Young people and drinking in Italy: The good side of familism. *Journal of Modern Italian Studies*, 23(1), 93–107.

Sennett, R. (1998). *The Corrosion of Character. The Personal Consequences of Work in the New Capitalism.* New York and London: W.W. Norton & Company.

Unt, M. and Gebel, M. (eds) (2018). Synthesis of the main empirical findings of EXCEPT project. EXCEPT Working Paper, 57, Tallinn: Tallinn University Press, http://www.except-project.eu/working-papers.

Zelizer, V. (1994). *The Social Meaning of Money.* New York: Basic Books.

Chapter 7

Young graduates' access to the labour market

Cumulative or trade-off effects between occupational level, contracts and wages

Marianna Filandri and Tiziana Nazio

7.1 Introduction

Recent cohorts of young people entering the labour market upon graduation face increasing risks of wage and job instability. Italy is characterized by one of the highest degrees of uncertainty in the initial steps of employment careers of all European countries (Barbieri, 2011; Hipp *et al.*, 2015). And even though Italy has a relatively low tertiary graduation rate, the Italian productive system cannot offer sufficient employment opportunities, reflecting low investment in this sector (the lowest in Europe) (OECD, 2015). National growth is based more on consumption than on the provision of skilled services or the production of high technology goods (Nolke, 2015). Unemployment benefit rates for younger workers in Italy are often lower and of a shorter duration than those for older workers, thus adding to young people's poorer employment prospects (Leschke and Finn, 2016). Further, the regulatory practices of the 2000s (the Law 92/2012 also known as 'The Fornero Law' and the more recent Law 183/2014 also known as 'The Jobs Act') have reinforced the dualization[1] of the Italian labour market. Reduced working hours, especially for part-time work, reduced contractual guarantees, and low salaries are the basis for such labour-market dualization (Barbieri *et al.*, 2018).

Low levels of state support for the unemployed also add to young people's bleak prospects. Unlike other European countries, until 2019 when a means-tested income-support measure termed 'Reddito di cittadinanza' has been introduced, Italy still lacked a minimum income support measure regulated at the national level (Saraceno, 2016), while parents are made financially responsible for their children irrespective of their children's age (Art. 433 of the Civil Code). Income support measures are also not available to first job seekers, in a welfare system often described as 'residual familistic', where the State guarantees intervention only when the family's resources are exhausted (Saraceno, 1994, 2016). Young people are thus more dependent on their families for support, or more compelled to take the first job offered to them if this support isn't available.

Within this institutional framework, starting a career in a job that is appropriate to their educational credentials may help young people to avoid getting caught in the 'bad jobs' trap (Barbera *et al.*, 2010; Barone and Schizzerotto, 2011). This is a risk that Italy shares with other European countries,[2] where an initial disadvantage in the labour market may have lasting effects on long-term employment outcomes, on career prospects and on upward job mobility. Upon completing education, young people may – or may not – be employed in a job that is consistent[3] with their educational credentials. In this chapter, we ask how this entrance into the employment sector is linked to wage and the type of contracts for graduates in Italy. Does a higher educational qualification correlate with cumulating a higher occupational level, higher wage and higher employment security? Or are there trade-offs between these dimensions? Some young people may prefer to accept lower paying jobs, because they are in line with their educational qualifications, or short-term contracts, because they may lead to better employment prospects in the longer term.

The aim of this contribution is to explore the relationship between wages, employment security and occupational coherence for young Italians. To achieve this aim we: (a) selected employed young people with a completed tertiary education aged between 25 and 34, within 5 years of graduation; (b) devised a typology based on occupational level and its coherence with wage level and type of contract; and (c) explored the association between the typology and young people's social class of origin.

To achieve these aims, we have employed multivariate analyses of *EU-SILC* (*European Statistics on Income and Living Conditions*) survey data for Italy. More specifically, we used the monthly data on employment statuses from the 2005 to 2012 longitudinal waves of EU-SILC to construct individual occupational trajectories covering a period of 36 months following the award of a tertiary degree. We also used the cross-sectional ad-hoc 2011 module on the intergenerational transmission of disadvantage to explore the role of social background on occupational outcomes. The 2011 ad-hoc module was the most recently available source of information on parental education for young people who have already achieved residential independence. We focus on the profile of workers whose occupations are (or are not) consistent with their wages and employment contracts (i.e. short-term contracts) controlling for both individual and family characteristics (gender, age, marital status, number of earners in the household, presence of small children, geographical area of residence and housing tenure).

The chapter is organized into four parts. After presenting the research question and hypotheses, we outline the typology used to distinguish between good and bad jobs in our analyses. Subsequently, we explore the associations with successful transitions to good jobs in Italy. Finally, we examine the impact of family background on the types of transitions young people have made.

7.2 Research question and hypothesis

This chapter explores how experiencing unemployment (after school exit), having discontinuity in employment and entering employment in a low-quality job are associated with young people's occupational conditions later in life. While job quality, unemployment duration or the influence of families on youth transitions has attracted much scholarly attention, the interrelationship between these dimensions has been much less studied. Here we explore the effects of both unemployment duration and employment continuity on the likelihood of obtaining a 'good quality job' up to 5 years after being awarded a tertiary degree. We are also interested in understanding how the associations with the family of origin influence these strategic transitions for different groups of young people. Thus, we will try to understand how the following conditions are associated with future, more adverse employment outcomes:

1. Length of unemployment spells;
2. Employment continuity;
3. Bad entry job; and
4. Social class of origin.

We discuss the association between social class of origin and youth employment achievement in relation to the transition to adulthood. The existence of differences, we postulate, are stratified by social class, between those who have left the parental home and those who still co-reside with (at least one of) their parents. A longer period of residence in the parental home can act as a support for young people from the lower or middle classes while they are initially coping with poor employment circumstances (Bernardi, 2007). By lowering living costs and the pressure to achieve economic independence, co-residence can allow young people to engage in a prolonged search for better employment opportunities, or to pursue an initially poorly paid position for the potential long-term opportunities, pursuing an 'investment' strategy. For young people, a strategy of occupational coherence becomes more likely if human capital accumulation is traded off for lower wages and short-term contracts (training, occasional contracts or even unpaid internships). For tertiary graduates from the upper classes, a state of occupational coherence with higher salaries and open-ended contracts (or self-employment) is more easily achievable due to the direct transmission of higher material and immaterial resources (such as soft skills, social networks, referral for internships, experience in family businesses, etc.). Alternatively, when young people earn lower salaries or work on short-term contracts, higher household resources make it easier to cope with uncertain prospects (Mac Knight, 2015, for the UK).

7.3 Debates on job quality and timing in youth transitions to the labour market

Here, we will situate our perspective within debates on job quality and the timing of transitions to, within and across the labour market in young people's early employment careers. Our focus is in line with a processual view of transitions from education to employment (Blossfeld *et al.*, 2015; Brzinsky-Fay, 2007, 2014) within the ample literature on school-to-work transitions.

7.3.1 Job quality

A considerable number of empirical studies have found that job quality affects well-being and happiness. Being in a 'low-quality job' is associated with lower levels of self-reported life satisfaction and happiness than being in a 'high-quality job'[4]; this is an association that holds true across different institutional settings (Gallie, 2013a; Kattenbach and O'Reilly, 2011). Although those in low-quality jobs seem to enjoy lower-than-average levels of life satisfaction, these levels are often still higher than those experienced by people who remain unemployed (Grün *et al.*, 2010). Overall levels of (dis)satisfaction can be traced back to different factors: overeducation, underemployment and poor employment conditions (contractual forms and salary levels) (Peiró *et al.*, 2010). Several factors associated with job characteristics affect these responses, such as task autonomy, economic and personal rewards, having a stimulating and supportive environment, training opportunities, contract security, work pressure and job control, among other things (Gallie, 2013b; Gallie *et al.*, 2012).

'Good' jobs can be distinguished from 'bad' ones based on a number of characteristics related to material (monetary and non-monetary) and non-material characteristics (Jencks *et al.*, 1988; Keller *et al.*, 2014). Given the limits of quantitative research designs in addressing more subjective aspects of employment relations, and despite acknowledging that the concept of a good job has a long-debated and multidimensional meaning involving both objective and subjective dimensions, we will focus here on the level of employment, the wage and the duration of the employment relation as indicators of good jobs. Higher quality jobs are frequently associated with higher educational levels, involve more task complexity, autonomy and control and offer better salaries and greater security regarding the duration of the employment relationship (setting the stage for more substantial training investments by companies in firm-specific skills). Workers in these positions usually report higher levels of satisfaction.

While these dimensions have been explored for the wider population, less attention has been paid to how they specifically affect young people's access to employment. The extensive literature on the transition to adulthood (Blossfeld *et al.*, 2015) focuses strongly on the timing, pathways and determinants of the school-to-work transition, with particular reference to first jobs. Here we focus on the issues of job quality and early labour market transitions, which become particularly salient when examining occupational segments for recent labour market entrants and those in the early stages of their careers. Some distinctive characteristics of early employment for young people, especially for those in Southern Europe, are their turbulence and the 'flexible' forms of employment they entail, which are frequently associated with 'bad' jobs (Gebel and Giesecke, 2016; O'Reilly *et al.*, 2015). The long-term consequences of skill mismatch in early transitions have been documented, with young people struggling to make up for early mismatch in their later careers (O'Reilly *et al.*, 2017). Further empirical evidence shows that starting a professional career with a 'bad job', that is a low-skilled, low-paid, short-term job or a combination of these, is associated with worse later employment outcomes and can thus become a real career trap.[5] Some authors suggest that any kind of job, be it short-term, part-time or subsidized, is better than no job at all, because it forestalls unemployment hysteresis and deskilling (Hemerijck and Eichhorst, 2010: 327). However, for young people in the first years of their working lives, to what extent is any job better than no job at all? In the long run, is it better for a young person to hold out for a better-quality job opportunity rather than take the first opportunity they find? How long should they wait to find a good match? And what factors affect their capacity to wait for a better match?

The analyses presented in this chapter focus on young individuals up to 5 years after completing education during the period 2005–2012, thus also covering the beginning of a prolonged and severe economic recession. During this period, especially in Italy and other Southern European countries, young people were confronted with substantial job losses (i.e. temporary contracts ceased to be renewed) and scant new job openings (O'Reilly *et al.*, 2017).

7.3.2 How long should they wait?

Longer periods in unemployment are often the result of two different circumstances one can face in the labour market: they result either from the difficulty in entering the labour market (being unable to find a paid job) or from not taking up a job being offered. A preference for selectivity by taking the uncertainty and risk of a long(er) wait instead of accepting 'any' job inevitably postpones the onset of one's (occupational) career and prolongs the duration in unemployment. However, it could also be seen as a strategic move if it leads to comparatively better outcomes over time. This is particularly salient for young people moving into the labour market for the first time. In this respect, when we refer to employment 'strategies' we do not mean that everyone can freely choose between all possible alternatives. Family background and resources play decisive roles in young people's abilities to devise accessible strategies and in their experiences of outcomes (see also Bernardi and Boado, 2014, on educational choices; DiPrete and Eirich, 2006; Tanskanen *et al.*, 2016).

Upward moves in the labour market depend not only on the willingness and availability to take up emerging opportunities, but also on the ability to wait for, and be able to recognize, the 'right opportunity'. Especially during the early stages of a career, poor-quality jobs undertaken initially could lead to better opportunities later.

For example, internships and short-term training contracts might be used as signalling and screening devices by employers, who could later offer better employment opportunities (Scherer, 2004). However, in the process of waiting, young people will incur a longer spell(s) of unemployment, which may actually worsen their prospects of finding a good entry opportunity (Flek *et al.*, 2019).

Young people's individualized choices need to be contextualized in relation to their family resources (Bernardi, 2007, 2014; Contini and Triventi, 2016; DiPrete and Eirich, 2006). Wealthier families have a range of resources that can allow their children to pursue further education, wait longer, be more selective and be guided more effectively towards successful employment outcomes (Mac Knight, 2015). People from less-advantaged backgrounds might need to move into work earlier depending on the resources available from their families or the welfare state. Another possibility is that they may lack the necessary resources to actively pursue and take up employment opportunities, as reflected by the increasing numbers of young people Not in Education, Employment or Training (NEET).

7.3.3 Data and methods

To answer these questions in relation to the Italian case, we use both cross-sectional (2011) and longitudinal data from the EU-SILC surveys from 2005 to 2012. For the longitudinal part, which focuses on the effect of early experiences on later outcomes, we selected all young people (aged 21–34) who successfully completed a spell in tertiary education resulting in the award of a higher educational qualification by their second interview. We followed them for the subsequent 3 years, thus conducting four valid interviews (we have 668 individuals across 2,672 observations). For the cross-sectional part, which explores the effects of family of origin, we selected all young people (aged 24–34) who obtained a tertiary degree within 5 years of the time of the interview, that is 940 individuals for Italy. We adopted this strategy in order to maximize the available sample size and statistical power for the two sets of analyses.

The first multivariate analysis uses logit models to predict the effects of early unemployment on the likelihood of being in a skilled, well-paid or temporary occupation for employed young people up to 3 years after completion of tertiary education. We first explore the overall duration and frequency of unemployment spells (section 7.4). The second analysis tests for correlates with successful transitions to good jobs (section 7.5), while the final set of analyses examines the association between family background and the types of transitions young people have made within 5 years of graduation (section 7.6).

7.4 Good and bad jobs: a typology of successful outcomes

Using the dimensions of occupational level, salary and employment security, we develop a typology of transitions and compare the four possible outcomes we have identified: 'successful' jobs (with high wages and requiring high skills),

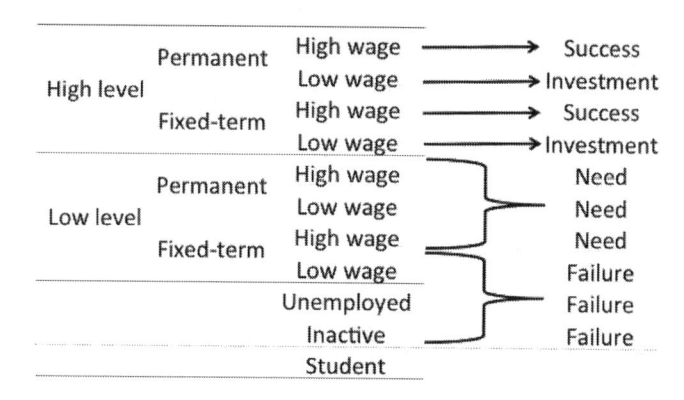

Figure 7.1 Typology of occupational positioning based on skills, contract and wage.

'investment', 'need' and 'failure' jobs (Figure 7.1). Success refers to a situation of occupational coherence and a relatively high wage: a 'successful' state is when young people enter a skilled[6] and relatively well-paid job, with or without a high degree of employment security at this early career stage. Well-paid is defined as pay above the median wage of all employed individuals by all ages, in each country, each year.[7] Investment and need are, by contrast, those situations presenting a trade-off between occupational level and wage or security of the contractual relation. In the case of investment, coherence is achieved at the cost of a lower wage and/or a temporary job; however, it has higher prestige, enables the accumulation of human capital and valuable experience and offers the prospect (or the hope) of future better conditions (contract renewal, opening of opportunities, upward mobility or wage increases). Jobs requiring higher skills or qualifications may initially be poor in quality (entry positions as a screening device) but over time can lead to increasing wage returns. In the case of (economic) need, however, the job obtained is (relatively) well paid or less uncertain due to an open-ended contract, but it is not in a skilled position (in line with the educational qualifications). The opposite of the success condition is failure, in which individuals enter into jobs where low expected qualifications, low wages and short-term contracts coincide. This is the condition that might lead to the 'bad jobs' trap.

7.4.1 Unemployment duration and employment outcomes

Ideally, upon completing university, young people can quickly enter the labour market and maintain continuous employment.[8] But they may instead also end up out of employment for longer periods, either voluntarily, because they choose to wait for better opportunities, or involuntarily, because they are unable to find a job. Italy is a particularly interesting case, because as in other Southern

European countries, labour-market deregulation took place that aimed at increasing the active participation of specific categories of workers, such as women, older workers and young people. The numerous reforms implemented from the mid-1990s have reduced the constraints on hiring, with several new types of temporary contracts emerging, and they have reduced the penalties for companies violating provisions on the transformation of temporary contracts into open-ended arrangements (from the 'Treu package' law n. 186/1997 and Legislative Decree 368/2001 to the more recent 'Fornero Law' n. 92/2012 and the 'Jobs act' law n. 183/2014). These reforms paved the way for an increase in 'atypical' or 'non-standard' jobs, characterized by extremely low social security entitlements and reduced pension contribution rates. Italy has followed what was termed a 'Mediterranean' labour market adjustment strategy (Barbieri, 2009), with the reforms fostering a deregulation process that was 'partial and selective' (Esping-Andersen and Regini, 2000), as it only targeted the 'margins' of the labour market system, that is, non-standard employment. As a result, the Italian labour market is characterized by a higher share of youth unemployment, fixed-term contracts and a higher rate of NEETs than the average European Union country. The more difficult entry pathways for young people into the labour market makes Italy a particularly salient case for our analysis.

In this section, we test the effect of (total) unemployment duration in the early phases of young people's careers on each of the three dimensions comprising the typology separately. We first independently estimate the probability of accessing a high-wage occupation, a skilled occupation, or a fixed-term position, the three dimensions that comprise our typology. In a second stage, we will focus on the occupational outcomes directly (as resulting from Figure 7.1).

We codified the overall duration of unemployment over the 48 observation months (Figure 7.2). 'None' refers to individuals who had either no periods of unemployment, or who spent a maximum of one month in unemployment. 'Short' refers to those with up to 6 months of unemployment and 'medium-long'

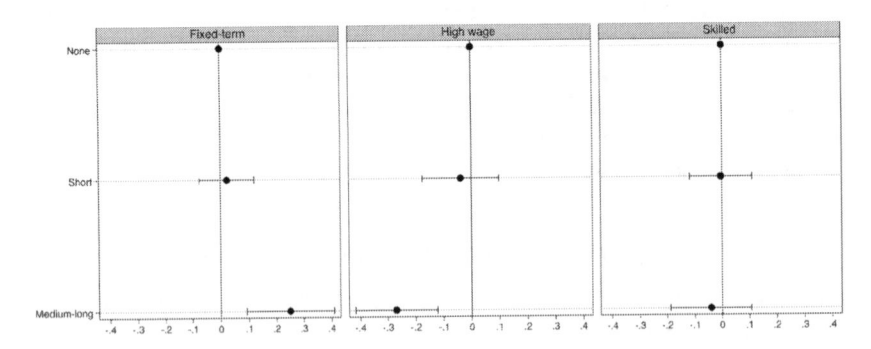

Figure 7.2 Predicted probability of being in a fixed-term, high-wage or skilled job by unemployment duration. (Source: Authors' calculation based on EU-SILC longitudinal data [2005–2012].)

to those who experienced a total period of unemployment spell(s) lasting longer than 6 months. The sample comprises all individuals with four completed interviews who were employed in the last observation.

We ran separate logit models on EU-SILC longitudinal monthly data, predicting the occupational condition reached 3 years after completing a tertiary qualification for those employed. The results for the effect of the average duration in unemployment of the three models are shown jointly in Figure 7.3. All models control for age, gender and number of employment interruption episodes.

We find no significantly observable differences in any of the outcomes analysed for those who had been unemployed for up to 6 months (short unemployment) compared to those who had never been unemployed. Differences in the effect of unemployment duration were more perceptible on wage attainment than on being in a skilled occupation after 3 years (central and right graphs). The probability of having a high-wage position after 3 years (central graph in Figure 7.2) was considerably lower for those who were unemployed for more than 6 months (a medium-long duration) than it was for those who had never been unemployed (none) or who had been unemployed for 6 months or less (short unemployment duration). Conversely, individuals with medium-long unemployment durations seemed to incur a higher risk of fixed-term employment (left graph in Figure 7.2). However, no statistically significant differences could be observed in either case for total unemployment durations of six months or lower. We also observed no difference between groups with different unemployment durations in achieving skilled employment (right graph in Figure 7.2). This might mean that prospective employers may factor in some initial turbulence, especially in periods of economic crisis and in countries like Italy, where employment inclusion of young people in their early career stages is comparatively more difficult than elsewhere (Brzinsky-Fay, 2007). No significant penalty seems to be associated with a short- to medium-term (up to 6 months) unemployment duration.

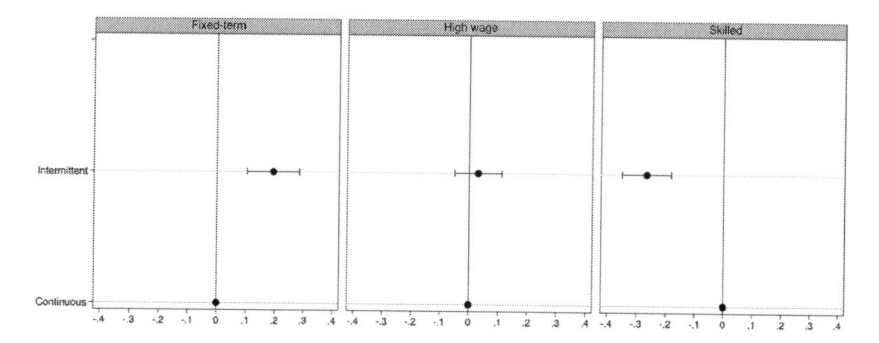

Figure 7.3 Predicted probability of being in a fixed-term, high-wage or skilled job by continuity in employment. (Source: Authors' calculation based on EU-SILC longitudinal data [2005–2012].)

7.4.2 Continuity in employment and employment outcomes

We now further explore any effects of the entry process on employment outcomes 3 years after obtaining a qualification. Specifically, we tested for any effects linked to the timing of unemployment. We have examined the effect of continuity in employment, where 'continuity' is defined as having at most one spell of unemployment. In other words, the 'current' employment situation (at the time of the last interview) was achieved with no employment interruptions or with only one rather than with more frequent interruptions (intermitted employment).

The results (Figure 7.3) show that continuity in employment does not have any clear statistically significant effects on the salary enjoyed 3 years after obtaining a tertiary degree. However, skilled occupations are more likely to be held by those who have been continuously employed (right graph in Figure 7.3) and fixed-term contracts are more likely for those who experienced intermittent employment (left graph in Figure 7.3).

This points to a small positive effect of a quick entry, that is for those with one unemployment spell at most after leaving education: the shorter the search, or the quicker the entry after finishing education, the slightly more likely the individual of being found in a skilled occupation with less-uncertain employment conditions. These results suggest that both employment continuity and taking less time to find a first job are associated with some advantages, but these are not as big as we might have expected in the Italian case.

In sum, we detected some small effects on the different dimensions of the employment outcomes investigated (high wages, skilled employment or fixed-term contracts) from entering quickly or not spending too long in unemployment during this relatively short window of observation (three years after completing a tertiary degree). This could be specific to the early career stage, confirming that, despite a clear but weak advantage of continuous employment and an early start, a short-term period of unemployment does not appear to negatively affect subsequent outcomes as much as we might have expected. However, it is the medium-long-term experience of unemployment (of 6 or more months over the 3 years) and intermittent employment that have a more substantial impact. Whether this experience is of a single short spell or of a collection of several shorter spells, longer periods of unemployment clearly have a negative effect on occupational success chances, especially in terms of employment insecurity (fixed-term employment) and wages (Figure 7.2). A slightly longer initial wait before first entering employment or a turbulent beginning (Figure 7.3) seems to negatively affect both the security of the employment relation and the associated skill level. Having examined the likelihood of transitions into jobs with different dimensions of successful entry measured in terms of their wages, skill profiles and fixed-term employment relations, we now turn to examine the access to occupations after graduation and the factors associated with the kind of job achieved 3 years later.

7.5 Comparing employment outcomes across countries

The analyses presented so far seem to support the idea that a quick transition into any job is always better than joblessness, although the effects are not very big and are mostly statistically significant only for longer unemployment durations. But the empirical evidence presented so far is not enough to show that young people are not trapped in poorly paid and low-skilled jobs. What we have shown so far is that there seem to be career tracks (early entrance and few interruptions) that lead to more favourable outcomes overall. To enrich our understanding, we now further explore young people's initial positioning in the labour market. We explore the effect of occupational conditions at the point of entry on the job held 3 years later (using the typology devised in Figure 7.1). We estimate a series of multinomial logit models with EU-SILC longitudinal data, controlling for age and sex.

For every initial condition (left of figures), the results in Figure 7.4 show the difference in probabilities for every final occupational status as compared to being a student. In other words, positive (on the right of the central vertical line) or negative (on the left of the line) estimates illustrate how more(/less) likely an individual is to be found in the occupational condition in question (Success, Investment, Need, Failure or Student) rather than in education after 3 years, given the initial condition (y-axis of each graph). The figure shows high stability over time for all states. Only the student and failure states seem to have a more transitory character. Being in a failure state is associated with a higher probability of entering a need condition after

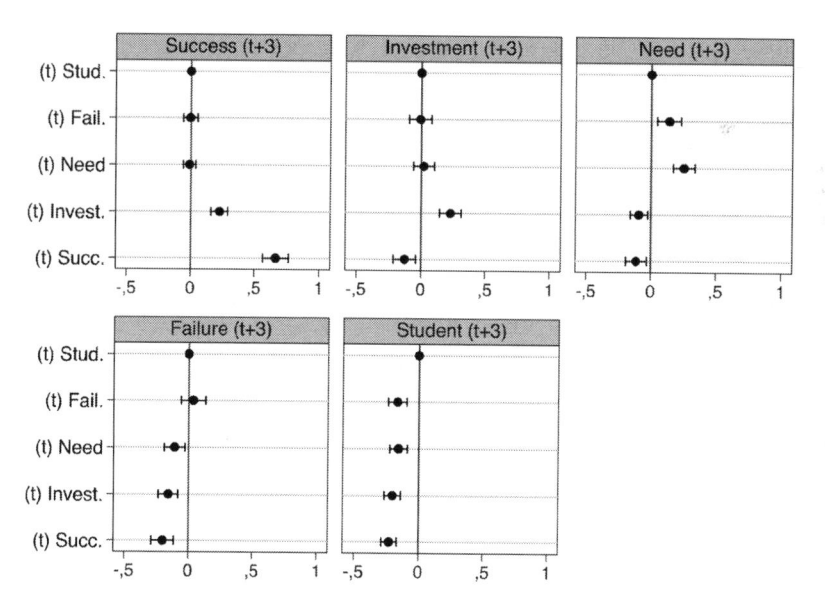

Figure 7.4 Difference in probabilities for each occupational status as compared to being students. (Source: Authors' calculation based on EU-SILC longitudinal data [2005–2012].)

3 years (Need+3 graph in Figure 7.4, the point on the right to the line). Conversely, young Italian graduates in the need, investment or success conditions are less likely to be found in the failure condition after 3 years. A high degree of stability is also found for all other statuses: need, investment and success. However, as can be seen in the graph at the top-left part of the figure, those who were initially in the investment state also have significantly higher chances of being found in a success state later (Success+3 graph in Figure 7.4, investment line).

To summarize, we found a high persistence in statuses over the initial years of young Italians' employment careers, which stresses the relevance of the characteristics of the entry job. We also found that accepting an appropriate job, even if poorly paid at the beginning but with increasing returns over time, qualifies 'investment' choices as a real strategic move in the Italian labour market for tertiary educated individuals; investment choices are additionally linked to a higher likelihood of ending up in the success condition. Similar results were also found for other countries (Berloffa *et al.*, 2016; Filandri *et al.*, 2019).

7.6 What difference do families make to how long you can wait?

The probability of being in one of the four outcome states of the proposed typology (Figure 7.1) varies according to the duration of unemployment experienced, the continuity of employment and the conditions of entry into the labour market. To understand how this varies according to young people's social class of origin, we use the cross-sectional EU-SILC 2011 data, which contain an ad-hoc module on intergenerational transmission of disadvantage. Here, it is possible to obtain information on the educational level achieved by young people's parents, even for those who have already left their family of origin.[9] As stated previously, the subsample for our analysis comprised all young people below 34 years who had obtained a tertiary educational qualification less than 5 years before the survey. We now present the association between social class of origin and the share of people in one of the four states illustrated in the typology we described in earlier paragraphs (Figure 7.1). The social class of origin is defined on the basis of the highest educational level obtained by young people's mothers and fathers (criteria of dominance, Erikson and Goldthorpe, 1992). Social class of origin, as based on education, is classified within three categories: high (tertiary), middle (upper secondary) and low (primary and lower secondary). The data are stratified based on young people's living arrangements, either living independently or with their parents.

Figure 7.5 shows a clear effect of social class of origin on young people's occupational outcomes within 5 years of obtaining a tertiary educational qualification. Among those who left the parental household, we see that belonging to a high social class is associated with a larger presence in the success and investment states, and a lower presence in the need and failure states. Living with one's parents, by contrast, is more weakly associated with the class of origin, although differences across status' are smaller. These results point to the better capacity of

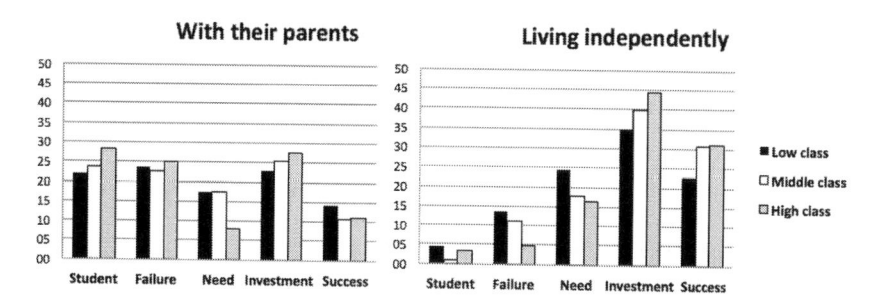

Figure 7.5 Share of occupational outcomes by social class of origin and living arrangements. (Source: Authors' calculation based on EU-SILC cross-sectional data [2011].)

wealthier families to help their children to proceed more frequently and quickly into skilled, well-paid and secure occupations (being it through counselling, guidance, referrals, soft skills or social networks). On the contrary, children from other backgrounds seem to pursue consistent employment through a strategy of longer co-residence with parents and relying on initially low paid occupations.

Our findings point to the persistence of a certain class divide for young people. In the pursuit of 'higher profile' career paths, skilled jobs in this case, it seems easier for youth from higher social classes, while staying longer in the parental home could be a strategy for securing better employment prospects for children from the middle classes. The prospects do not seem as promising for children from the lower classes, who were more likely observed in the need condition and less in the success condition, especially when residentially independent. We can imagine that the increasingly older ages at which young Italians attain residential independence, initially in response to other structural constraints, might also be a rational response from the middle classes to enable their children to obtain/accept skilled jobs, even if they are (at least initially) poorly paid. These findings are broadly consistent with the observations made in Chapter 10 of this book, where the authors note that the social class and educational levels of the family of origin are significant in determining the transitional process to adulthood.

7.7 Conclusions

In this chapter, we have shown that an early start and continuous employment are associated with more favourable outcomes. In particular, we observe a lower rate of fixed term-employment and more skilled occupations for young Italian graduates who are continuously employed, and higher wages and less fixed-term employment for those with short unemployment durations. However, these effects are relatively small and do not support the idea that any job is necessarily always better than joblessness in the face of the risk of a poor skills match. We have also shown that, due to a high degree of status stability over time, the initial job is highly predictive of subsequent outcomes. This predicts that a well-matched start in terms of skill level, even when traded off for a lower salary (or for a longer job search), often seems a better strategy for securing better outcomes in the long run, especially for those with tertiary education (trade-off effects are also found for Germany by Voßemer and Schuck, 2016). Overall, careful and well-informed career planning for young people might well come with a risk of some initial turbulence or a slightly longer period of unemployment caused by rejecting unskilled job offers, but helps to secure better prospects and more successful employment in the longer term.

Exploring the effects of initial occupations on later outcomes, we have also revealed that being in a (initially) poorly paid but skilled occupation (an investment strategy) can constitute an opportunity for young people that can allow them to successfully position themselves in the labour market. Instead, unskilled occupations for skilled young people (need and failure strategies) can become an employment trap that is difficult to reverse in the long run (similar findings for the risk of unemployment in Germany are from Reichelt, 2015). In other words, it seems easier to pursue wage increases with tenure (upskilling in line with human capital accumulation or upward mobility) than it is to improve one's occupational positioning on the basis of skill level.

Our analyses find a clear association between the family social background, the strategies pursued, and the occupational conditions achieved by young individuals within 5 years of completing their education. The results reveal a lower incidence of need conditions among those from the higher social class and a higher incidence of the success and investment conditions. These findings suggest a strong familial influence on young peoples' (un)successful employment outcomes. They point to mechanisms related to greater success for higher class families, which relate to informing (through advice and guidance), supporting (possibly through social networks, aspiration building, more effective guidance through the educational and employment systems) and potentially backing up (through economic support and/or longer co-residence) young peoples' employment strategies (Filandri et al., 2016, 2019). We have shown that the most-effective strategies, those more likely to lead to better outcomes, often entail initial losses, such as higher risks (longer periods or greater likelihoods of unemployment) or greater investments (lower pay). This implies that young people can enjoy a differential access to resources, other than education, that allow them to pursue these strategies depending on their family background. This form of further compensatory advantage adds to the more studied association between family social origin and occupation through education (Bernardi and Ballarino, 2016) and stresses that, though desirable, educational investments per se are not sufficient to secure increased equality of opportunities. Despite the already comparatively very low rate of university graduates in Italy compared to in other European countries (OECD, 2015), we observe a heterogeneity of young graduates' outcomes based on family background. We show that higher levels of education do not seem sufficient to gain access to successful employment outcomes on an equal footing. Whereas children from well-off families can enjoy the double benefit of higher graduation rates and better success in employment, children from lower social backgrounds seem to have to cope with a double penalty in access and completion of tertiary education first, and in mobilizing family resources to pursue 'investment' strategies later.

There is one other important aspect of this economic crisis affecting young people still to be explored: they tend to be hit harder than adults by recessions and stagnation. This is not only because young people's unemployment rates rise more than adults' rates during a recession, but also because young people caught by the crisis are more vulnerable to its effects. They are likely to suffer an economic downturn for longer (being unemployed or underemployed) and to have its effect spill over onto their subsequent career steps (reduced contributions, lower career opportunities, higher unemployment risks). Young people will also have more time to endure the consequences of their current fragility because they are at a formative stage in their lives (O'Higgins, 2010). We limit our analysis to the initial 3 to 5 years due to data availability, but further analyses should explore the longer-term consequences. The quality of employment is also important. We considered wages, skill levels and contractual security with long-term prospects as important aspects for young people's transitions to adulthood (Bernardi and Nazio, 2005). The growing incidence of temporary employment contracts is an issue of concern, particularly in those countries more strongly hit by the crisis in Europe. Although temporary jobs may facilitate the entry of young people into work, they might get caught in such contracts rather than obtaining permanent employment (Berloffa et al., 2016; Gebel and Giesecke, 2016; O'Higgins, 2010).

While the financial crisis has not yet been overcome, given that it has spilled over into rising unemployment and cuts in public services and welfare spending, the capacity of families to respond to these challenges and ensure their members' well-being is strongly segmented by their available resources. This makes the need for resilient employment and social policy more urgent than ever. As for now, having a flexible job in Italy (agency work, fixed-term contracts, part-time work and some forms of self-employment) entails the risk of becoming a member of the lower segment of the labour force. Flexible jobs cater especially to young people but are unable to protect them from the risks of falling into a 'bad job trap', with little protection in case of unemployment, parenthood or illness, nor the ability to provide a secure income in old age. As suggested by the literature (O'Reilly et al., 2015), relaxing hiring and firing legislation without compensating with generous social protection and active labour market policies, while simultaneously increasing retirement age, risks affecting young people's capacity to establish themselves in employment (Barbieri and Cutuli, 2016; Leschke and Finn, 2016), thus further stratifying their life opportunities along their class of origin. This is especially the case for countries like Italy and Spain, which face higher youth unemployment and higher shares of NEETs. We show that these stratifying effects persist for young university graduates facing precarious employment, lower growth and reduced demand for skilled jobs (Emmenegger et al., 2012; Grotti et al., 2019).

To sum up, our findings suggest reinforced patterns of stratification where young people coming from higher social class families were able to make better transitions in terms of job quality than those from lower-class families. The analysis of the relation between social class of origin and the devised typology clearly illustrates, for Italy, the impact of social class on the occupational outcomes of young graduates within 5 years of completing their education. Our results show that, among young graduates who have left the parental home, those from the upper and middle classes have greater chances of being in a success state. In other words, success is more likely for the more advantaged strata of young people, in a process of reproduction of social (dis)advantage (as for Mac Knight, 2015). Figure 7.5 shows that, among those who reside in their parents' households, those in the most promising conditions, like the further education and investment states, are more commonly found among the middle and, especially, the upper social classes. Our results point to later emancipation as the coping familial strategy of the lower and middle classes. Remaining longer in the parental home might be an effective means of obtaining, or accepting, skilled positions in the labour market, especially in an initial career phase, when job offerings are more likely poorly paid or short-term. Finally, ending up in the failure state is a less likely outcome for young people from higher social classes and equally likely to for those from both the middle and lower classes who still live with their parents. Young Italians from the lower and middle classes are instead over-represented in the need condition. This reveals how young people from the lower classes (even if there are a smaller share of them with a completed tertiary education) are structurally more exposed to the 'bad job' trap. Further, our analyses show that, if not born in a higher social class, remaining in the parental household for longer might be the most effective strategy in order to pursue 'high level' career paths (i.e. skilled job positions). Cumulative positive effects are observed for the more advantaged strata of young people, since younger labour market entrants are more frequently exposed to preliminary steps through intermediate 'trade-off' occupations, which require support strategies involving informal family resources (like co-residence or other forms of familial support). However, this prolonged dependence on family resources can further postpone economic independence and the transition to adulthood.

The overall empirical evidence emerging from this study also suggests that, from a policy perspective, we need to target an integrated set of policies on different dimensions. On the one hand, it is desirable to reform the labour market so as to promote skilled labour demand in order to reduce unemployment levels and the rate of NEETs. On the other hand, if Italy wants to converge with non-Mediterranean countries, it would be desirable to devise a set of income support measures to allow young people to enter and progress through the labour market without urgent economic need. The absence or scarcity of income support measures for first job seekers and early labour-market entrants seems indeed to stratify young people's strategies according to their social origins, adding to the well-known effect of social class on educational achievement. If it is true that 'any job' is not necessarily always better than unemployment based on later outcomes, the salience of the early steps in the labour market makes it vital to ensure that all young people are allowed to strategically move through the labour market on an equal footing.

Notes

1 Our analyses here covers the period up to 2011. The process of labour-market dualization in Italy started around the mid-nineties, but has intensified in recent years.
2 Barone et al., 2011; Blossfeld et al., 2008; Bukodi and Goldthorpe, 2012; Hillmert, 2011; Wolbers et al., 2011.
3 We operationalize coherence as the match between one's educational level and the level required by one's occupation. Our measure aims at detecting the absence of suffering from overeducation.
4 Gallie, 2013; Green et al., 2016; Keller et al., 2014; Sànchez-Sànchez and McGuinness, 2013.
5 Barbera et al., 2010; Barone et al., 2011; Barone and Ortiz, 2011; Barone and Schizzerotto, 2011; Blossfeld et al., 2008; Bukodi and Goldthorpe, 2012; Gash, 2008; Hillmert, 2011; Scherer, 2004; Wolbers et al., 2011.
6 Skilled occupations are defined on the basis of ISCO-88 codes: high-skilled non-manual occupations (ISCO 11–34), low-skilled non-manual occupations (ISCO 41–52), skilled manual occupations (ISCO 61–83) and elementary occupations (ISCO 91–93) (Pintelon et al., 2011). We consider both manual and non-manual skilled occupations.
7 Country and yearly based figures computed on the annual wages of all employed people (i.e. including the self-employed).
8 We modelled employment continuity as the absence of unemployment spells within the 4-year period, thus in this case, it does not necessarily imply continuity in the same job, provided there are no gaps in employment attachment.
9 When building an indicator on the social class of origin on the basis of available EU-SILC data, researchers face two limitations. The first concerns the question asked in the ad-hoc module about parents' educational level when the respondent was aged 14, while for those who live with their parents the measure is taken at the time of interview. The second, more serious limitation is that information on parents for those who live independently are only asked for people aged between 25 and 59. This means we are lacking information for those who had already left the parental home at the time of interview but were not yet 25 years old. In our sample, they amount to approximately 17% of young people.

References

Barbera, F., Filandri, M. and Negri, N. (2010). Conclusioni: cittadinanza e politiche di ceto medio. In: Negri, N. and Filandri, M. (eds) *Restare di ceto medio: Il passaggio alla vita adulta nella società che cambia*. Bologna: Il Mulino.
Barbieri, P. (2009). Flexible employment and inequality in Europe. *European Sociological Review*, 25(6), 621–628. doi:10.1093/esr/jcp020.
Barbieri, P. (2011). Italy: No country for young men (and women): The Italian way of coping with increasing demands for labour market flexibility and rising welfare problems. In: Blossfeld, H.-P., Buchholz, S., Hofäcker, D. and Kolb, K. (eds) *Globalized Labour Markets and Social Inequality in Europe*. Basingstoke, UK: Palgrave Macmillan.

Barbieri, P. and Cutuli, G. (2016). Employment protection legislation, labour market dualism, and inequality in Europe. *European Sociological Review*, 32(4), 501–516.

Barbieri, P., Cutuli, G. and Scherer, S. (2018). In-work poverty in Southern Europe: The case of Italy. In: Lohmann, H. and Marx, I. (eds) *Handbook on In-Work Poverty*. Cheltenham: Edward Elgar Publishing.

Barone, C., Lucchini, M. and Schizzerotto, A. (2011). Career mobility in Italy. *European Societies*, 13(3), 377–400.

Barone, C. and Ortiz, L. (2011). Overeducation among European University Graduates: A comparative analysis of its incidence and the importance of higher education differentiation. *Higher Education*, 61(3), 325–337.

Barone, C. and Schizzerotto, A. (2011). Introduction. *European Societies*, 13(3), 331–345.

Berloffa, G., Filandri, M., Matteazzi, E., Nazio, T., Negri, N., O'Reilly, J. and Sandor, A. (2016). Family strategies to cope with poor labour market outcomes. *STYLE Working Papers, WP 8.2 CROME*. Available at: http://www.style-research.eu/publications/working-papers.

Bernardi, F. (2007). Movilidad social y dinàmicas familiares. Una aplicación al estudio de la emancipación familiar en España. *Revista internacional de sociologìa*, 65(48), 4833–4854.

Bernardi, F. (2014). Compensatory advantage as a mechanism of educational inequality. *Sociology of Education*, 87(2), 74–88.

Bernardi, F. and Ballarino, G. (eds) (2016). *Education, Occupation and Social Origin. A Comparative Analysis of the Transmission of Socio-economic Inequalities*. Cheltenham, UK: Edward Elgar Publishing.

Bernardi, F. and Boado, H.-C. (2014). Previous school results and social background: Compensation and imperfect information in educational transitions. *European Sociological Review*, 30(2), 207–217.

Bernardi, F. and Nazio, T. (2005). Globalization and the transition to adulthood in Italy. In: Blossfeld, H.P., Mills, M. and Kurz, K. (eds) *Globalization, Uncertainty and Youth in Society*. London: Routledge.

Blossfeld, H.P., Kurz, K., Buchholz, S. and Bukodi, E. (2008). *Young Workers, Globalization and the Labor Market: Comparing Early Working Life in Eleven Countries*. Cheltenham, UK and Northampton, MA: Edward Elgar.

Blossfeld, H.-P., Skopek, J., Triventi, M. and Buchholz, S. (2015). *Gender, Education and Employment: An International Comparison of School-to-Work Transitions*. Cheltenham: Edward Elgar.

Brzinsky-Fay, C. (2007). Lost in transition? Labour market entry sequences of school leavers in Europe. *European Sociological Review*, 23(4), 409–422.

Brzinsky-Fay, C. (2014). The measurement of school- to-work transitions as processes. *European Societies*, 16(2), 213–232.

Bukodi, E. and Goldthorpe, J. (2012). Decomposing 'social origins': The effects of parents' class, status, and education on the educational attainment of their children. *European Sociological Review*, 29(5), 1024–1039. doi:10.1093/esr/jcs079.

Contini, D. and Triventi, M. (2016). Between formal openness and stratification in secondary education: Implications for social inequalities in Italy. In: Blossfeld, H.P., Buchholz, S., Skopek, J. and Triventi, M. (eds) *Models of Secondary Education and Social Inequality. An International Comparison*. Cheltenham, UK: Edward Elgar Publishing.

DiPrete, T. and Eirich, G.M. (2006). Cumulative advantage as a mechanism for inequality: A review of theoretical and empirical developments. *Annual Review of Sociology*, 32, 271–297.

Emmenegger, P., Häusermann, S., Palier, B. and Seeleib-Kaiser, M. (eds) (2012). *The Age of Dualization: The Changing Face of Inequality in Deindustrializing Societies*. Oxford: Oxford University Press.

Erikson, R. and Goldthorpe, J. (1992). *The Constant Flux: A Study of Class Mobility in Industrial Societies*. Oxford: Clarendon Press.

Esping-Andersen, G. and Regini, M. (2000). Why deregulate labour markets? *British Journal of Sociology*, 53(4), 693–696.

Filandri, M., Gábos, A., Medgyesi, M., Nagy, I. and Nazio, T. (2016). The role of parental material resources in adulthood transitions. STYLE Working Papers, WP8.4. CROME, University of Brighton, Brighton. Available at: http://www.style-research. eu/publications/working-papers.

Filandri, M., Nazio, T. and O'Reilly, J. (2019). Youth transitions and job quality: How long should they wait and what difference does the family make? In: O'Reilly, J., Leschke, J., Ortlieb, R., Seeleib-Kaiser, M. and Villa, P. (eds) *Youth Labor in Transition*. New York: Oxford University Press.

Flek, V., Hála, M. and Mysíková, M. (2019). How do youth labor flows differ from those of older workers? In: O'Reilly, J., Leschke, J., Ortlieb, R., Seeleib-Kaiser, M. and Villa, P. (eds) *Youth Labor in Transition*. New York: Oxford University Press.

Gallie, D. (2013a). *Economic Crisis, Quality of Work, and Social Integration: The European Experience*. Oxford: Oxford University Press.

Gallie, D. (2013b). Skills, job control and the quality of work: The evidence from Britain. *Geary Lecture*, 43(3), 17.

Gallie, D., Felstead, A. and Green, F. (2012). Job preferences and the intrinsic quality of work: The changing attitudes of British employees 1992–2006. *Work, Employment and Society*, 26(5), 806–821.

Gash, V. (2008). Bridge or trap? Temporary workers' transitions to unemployment and to the standard employment contract. *European Sociological Review*, 24(5), 651–668.

Gebel, M. and Giesecke, J. (2016). Does deregulation help? The impact of employment protection reforms on youths' unemployment and temporary employment risks in Europe. *European Sociological Review*, 32(4), 486–500.

Green, F., Felstead, A., Gallie, D. and Inanc, H. (2016). Job-related well-being through the great recession. *Journal of Happiness Studies*, 17(1), 389–411.

Grotti, R., Russell, H. and O'Reilly, J. (2019). Where do young people work. In: O'Reilly, J., Leschke, J., Ortlieb, R., Seeleib-Kaiser, M. and Villa, P. (eds) *Youth Labor in Transition*. New York: Oxford University Press.

Grün, C., Hauser, W. and Rhein, T. (2010). Is any job better than no job? Life satisfaction and re-employment. *Journal of Labour Research*, 31(3), 285–306.

Hemerijck, A. and Eichhorst, W. (2010). Whatever happened to the Bismarckian welfare state? From labor shedding to employment-friendly reforms. In: Palier, B. (ed) *A Long Good-Bye to Bismarck*. Amsterdam: Amsterdam University Press.

Hillmert, S. (2011). Occupational mobility and developments of inequality along the life course. *European Societies*, 13(3), 401–423.

Hipp, L., Bernhardt, J. and Allmendinger, J. (2015). Institutions and the prevalence of nonstandard employment. *Socio-economic Review*, 13(2), 351–377.

Jencks, C., Perman, L. and Rainwater, L. (1988). What is a good job? A new measure of labor-market success. *American Journal of Sociology*, 93(6), 1322–1357.

Kattenbach, R. and O'Reilly, J. (2011). Introduction: New perspectives on the quality of working life. *Management Revue*, 22(2), 107–113.

Keller, A.C., Semmer, N.K., Samuel, R. and Bergman, M.M. (2014). The meaning and measurement of well-being as an indicator of success. In: Keller et al. (eds) *Psychological, Educational, and Sociological Perspectives on Success and Well-Being in Career Development*, Dordrecht: Springer, 171–193.

Leschke, J. and Finn, M. (2016). Tracing the interface between numerical flexibility and income security for European youth during the economic crisis. STYLE Working Paper WP10.1a, CROME, University of Brighton, Brighton. Available at: http://www.style-research.eu/publications/working-papers/.

Mac Knight, A., (2015). Downward mobility, opportunity hoarding and the 'glass floor'. *Research report*. London: Centre for Analysis of Social Exclusion (CASE), London School of Economics.

Nolke, A. (2015). Economic causes of the Eurozone crisis: The analytical contribution of Comparative Capitalism. *Socio-economic Review*, 14(1), 141–161.

O'Higgins, N. (2010). The impact of the economic and financial crisis on youth employment: Measures for labour market recovery in the European Union, Canada and the United States. ILO: Employment Working Paper, 70.

O'Reilly, J., Eichhorst, W., Gábos, A., Hadjivassiliou, K., Lain, D., Leschke, J., McGuinness, S. et al. (2015). Five characteristics of youth unemployment in Europe. *SAGE Open*, 5(1), https://doi.org/10.1177/2158244015574962.

O'Reilly, J., Moyart, C., Nazio, T. and Smith, M. (eds) (2017). *Youth Employment: STYLE Handbook*. Brighton: CROME. Available at: http://style-handbook.eu.

OECD. (2015). *OECD Economic Outlook*, Volume 2015 Issue 1. Paris: OECD Publishing.

Peiró, J.M., Agut, S. and Grau, R. (2010). The relationship between overeducation and job satisfaction among young Spanish workers: The role of salary, contract of employment, and work experience. *Journal of Applied Social Psychology*, 40(3), 666–689.

Pintelon, O., Cantillon, B., Van den Bosch, K. and Whelan, C.T. (2011). The social stratification of social risks: Class and responsibility in the 'New' welfare state. GINI Discussion Paper, 13.

Reichelt, M. (2015). Career progression from temporary employment: How bridge and trap functions differ by task complexity. *European Sociological Review*, 31(5), 558–572.

Sànchez-Sànchez, N. and McGuinness, S. (2013). Decomposing the impacts of overeducation and overskilling on earnings and job satisfaction: An analysis using REFLEX data. *Education Economics*, 23(4), 419–432.

Saraceno, C. (1994). The ambivalent familism of the Italian welfare state. *Social Politics*, 1(1), 60–82.

Saraceno, C. (2016). Varieties of familialism: Comparing four southern European and East Asian welfare regimes. *Journal of European Social Policy*, 26(4), 314–326.

Scherer, S. (2004). Stepping-stones or traps? The consequences of labour market entry positions on future careers in West Germany, Great Britain and Italy. *Work, Employment & Society*, 18, 369–394.

Tanskanen, A.O., Erola, J. and Kallio, J. (2016). Parental resources, sibship size, and educational performance in 20 countries: Evidence for the compensation model. *Cross-Cultural Research*, 50(5), 452–477.

Voßemer, J. and Schuck, B. (2016). Better overeducated than unemployed? The short- and long-term effects of an overeducated labour market re-entry. *European Sociological Review*, 32(2), 251–265.

Wolbers, M.H.J., Luijkx, R. and Ultee, W. (2011). Educational attainment, occupational achievements, career peaks. *European Societies*, 13(3), 425–450.

Chapter 8

When age is academically constructed

The endless status of 'young researchers' in Italy

Rossella Bozzon, Annalisa Murgia and Caterina Peroni

8.1 Introduction

This contribution aims to discuss the ways in which the concept of age is developed within institutional and organizational discourses in academia. Based on the findings of research conducted in a university located in Northern Italy, the chapter analyses the different discursive constructions of age that are mobilized at the national level and how they are translated in two university departments – one of which was science, technology, engineering and mathematics (STEM) and the other, social sciences and humanities (SSH). These disciplines strongly differ in terms of resources and career perspectives, with STEM fields usually receiving more funding and offering better job conditions (i.e. wages). To understand how the concept of age is culturally constructed within Italian academia, an overview of how such a concept is discursively formulated within the last university reform is provided in relation to the recruitment processes in the early stages of career in a global context defined by growing competitivity, work casualization, public spending cuts and research marketization. Drawing on data from a study conducted in 2014–2016, the chapter focuses on how the institutional discourse of age is adopted, modified or challenged within the organizational discourses.

The chapter is structured as follows: First, the last university reform is introduced, illustrating the dominant rhetoric used about age at an institutional level. To better contextualize the conducted case study, and to understand how the concept of age is developed in a specific academic system, an analysis of how the average age of entry in the assistant professor position has progressively increased in Italy in the last decades is offered. Second, to analyse the contradictions between institutional and organizational discourses, and to show that chronological age is an insufficient operationalization of how age is conceptualized within organizations,

This chapter is an entirely collaborative effort by the three authors. If, however, for academic reasons individual responsibility is to be assigned, Rossella Bozzon wrote section 8.2; Annalisa Murgia section 8.4.2, Caterina Peroni section 8.4.1. Sections 8.1, 8.3 and 8.5 have been written jointly.

attention is paid to the different discourses about age developed in one STEM and one SSH university department, particularly referring to recruitment of early-career researchers. On the one hand, on the basis of interviews conducted with full professor members of recruitment committees, the role played by age in the selection processes for a position of assistant professor is analysed. On the other hand, how early-career researchers discursively positioned themselves *vis-à-vis* the department discourses on age is critically discussed. In the conclusion, a reflection is offered on the discursive construction of the 'young researcher' in the current Italian academic context, and on its effects both on the organizational practice of recruitment and on the working conditions experienced by non-tenured researchers.

8.2 'Young on paper': The Italian reform of the university recruitment system

The ageing of academic staff in Italy is a core issue in the debate on the sustainability and quality of the scientific productivity of the academic system (Anvur, 2016). Over the years, the mean age of academics with a permanent position has constantly increased, reaching the age of 52 in 2016, ranging from 59 for full professors, to 52 for associate professors, up to almost 47 for assistant professors (Miur, 2018). The comparison with other European countries shows the particularly problematic situation of the Italian academic context. For example, Italy (together with Greece) ranks last among all European countries in terms of presence of academic staff under 35, whilst academics under 35 represent 43% in Germany, 34% in the Netherlands, 16.2% in the United Kingdom, 12% in France, and in Italy they are only 4.6% (European Commission/EACEA/Eurydice, 2017). The scarce presence of young researchers in the Italian context is a result of discontinuous recruitment policies, mainly due to spending cuts and cost rationalization of academic and research work, and of the ageing of the academic staff recruited in the first part of the eighties. This cohort has recently started to retire, but are not compensated by new entrants into the profession (Bozzon *et al.*, 2015; Pavolini and Viesti, 2016).

In the light of this picture, the last university reform (L. 240/2010) explicitly stated that one of the priorities for reforming the Italian academic system was precisely to rejuvenate the academic staff. This was meant to be done mainly by introducing new recruitment procedures and by flexibilizing the first stages of the career path, with the aim of pushing the Italian 'protective' academic career model closer to a 'tenure track model', typical of more competitive university systems (i.e. the US, the UK and the Netherlands). In such a way the only permanent positions are those at the top of the academic hierarchy, similarly to countries with a Humboldt tradition of academic chairs (e.g. Austria, Germany, Switzerland and Belgium) (Le Feuvre *et al.*, 2019).

By 2005, the previous university reform (L. 230/2005) had pushed out permanent positions in the first grade of the academic career and introduced, for the first time in Italy, fixed-term positions for assistant professors. Continuing in this direction, the 2010 reform has established an 'ideal career path', lasting a maximum of 12 years between the end of the PhD and obtaining a position as associate professor. More precisely, at the beginning of their academic careers, PhD holders are supposed to be employed with three different fixed-term employment contracts: as postdoctoral fellows (for a maximum of 6 years); as fixed-term and non-tenured assistant professors (for 3 years, renewable only once for two more, lasting a maximum of 5 years in total); and finally as assistant professor on a tenure track (lasting 3 years).[1] At the end of the 3 years, and upon obtaining the 'national scientific qualification (known as ASN, i.e. Abilitazione Scientifica Nazionale) in his/her own scientific sector, an assistant professor is due to be hired as associate professor, the first permanent position in the Italian academic system.[2] This means that a researcher who starts a PhD immediately after his/her master's degree is expected to obtain his/her first permanent position (as associate professor) at the age of 38.

Even in the 2 years before the approval of the law, during the Senate hearings,[3] the minister in charge reiterated the urgent need to rejuvenate the university body and to implement a new system that could finally allow young scholars to access academic careers. However, despite an institutional discourse strongly focused on the renewal of academia, the implementation of the reform made the expected generational change difficult to achieve, because of the introduction, at the same time, of a strong turnover reduction (the possibility of hiring only one new member to replace every five retirees), and of robust cuts in public funding to the national higher education system (Triventi, 2009; Peroni *et al.*, 2015). In fact, looking at the recruitment trends in the last decades, the average age of entry into the assistant professor position has continued to increase over time, up to 39.5 in 2015 (it was 33 in 1989 and 36 in 2007, immediately before the reform) (Figure 8.1).

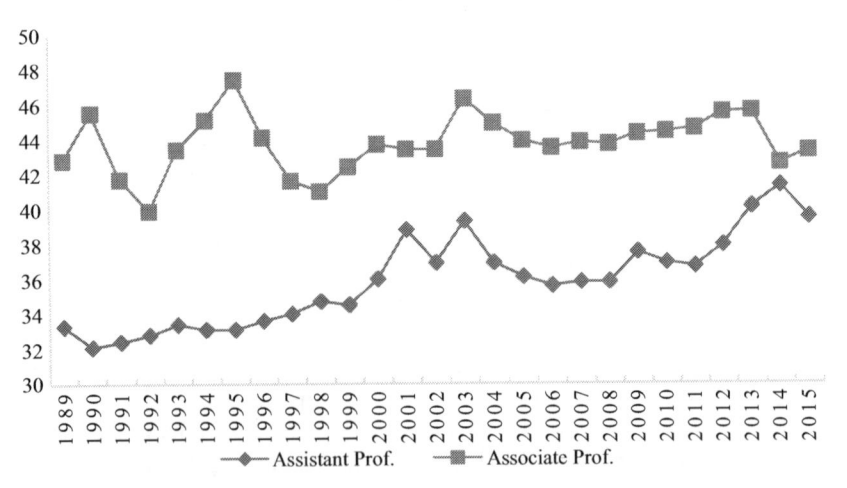

Figure 8.1 Mean entry age to the position of assistant professor and associate professor in the Italian university (1989–2015). (Source: Anvur, Rapporto sullo stato del sistema universitario e della ricerca, Rome. Available at: http://www.anvur.org/index.php?option=com_content&view=article&id=1045&Itemid=708&lang=it, 2016, on Miur data.)

Table 8.1 Academic research staff. Italy 2010 and 2015

	2010	2015	var% (2010–2015)
Permanent positions			
Full professors	15,851	12,877	−18.8%
Associate professors	16,956	20,048	+18.2%
Assistant professor (until 2013)	24,934	17,444	−30.0%
Total permanent staff	*57,741*	*50,369*	−12.8%
Temporary positions			
Assistant professors (from 2010)	1,280	4,608	+260.0%
Postdoctoral fellows	13,168	13,250	+0.6%
Total temporary positions	*14,448*	*17,758*	+22.9%
Total	*72,189*	*68,227*	−5.5%
% Fixed term. Asst. prof./Total	1.8%	6.8%	
% Postdocs/Total	18.2%	19.4%	

Source: Ministry of Education, University and Research (MIUR) data.

Another trend recorded after the introduction of the last university reform was the reduction of academic staff with a permanent position (by −12.8% between 2010 and 2015, see Table 8.1), mainly caused by a massive trend towards retirement across the Italian university system and at the same time by the growth of temporary positions. In 2015, fixed-term contracts accounted for 27.2% of the total academic staff (composed of academics with a permanent position, fixed-term assistant professors and postdoctoral fellows), while their incidence was around 20% in 2010. In particular, temporary positions are widely represented by postdoctoral fellows whose age is constantly increasing (from 33.9 in 2013 up to 34.8 in 2015). This trend seems to be mainly due to the proportion of postdoctoral fellows older than 40, accounting for 13% in 2013, and growing to 16.6% in 2015 (Anvur, 2016).

Despite the attempt to move Italian academic careers towards a 'tenure track model' – in which careers are defined by *up or out* selection procedures and by a short path to obtain a permanent position (Le Feuvre *et al.*, 2019) – the last university reform has mainly fuelled a process of fragmentation and precarization of academic careers. This is a trend shared by almost all of the academic systems in Europe, but in Italy this leads to extreme consequences on the job perspective of early-career researchers. This is mainly due to weak and residual support in managing employment instability, typical of Southern European welfare systems; to the higher risk of being trapped in temporary and low-paid job positions; and to the general lack of competitive job options outside of academia (Bozzon *et al.*, 2017). In contrast to other European countries, such as Germany, Switzerland, Belgium and the Netherlands, where doctoral qualifications are recognized and rewarded on the non-academic labour market, in Italy there is a lack of qualified job options outside of academia for PhD holders, who therefore have limited opportunities to deploy the knowledge and skills previously acquired (Le Feuvre *et al.*, 2019).

The institutional discourse on the modernization of the university, and on the need to open the floodgates to young researchers, therefore, comes up against a situation that remains one of – if not *the* – most problematic across Europe. On the one hand, the reform's supporters interpret the various legislative initiatives as measures needed to make access for young researchers easier, to limit malpractice and distortion – such as irregular recruitment processes, collusive behaviours and unfair use of financial resources – widely documented in the Italian university system (Froio, 1996; Perotti, 2008). On the other hand, its main opponents see the reform as a further step towards the privatization of the public university system and the precarization of the university workforce, which places young researchers in an even more vulnerable position (Zamponi and González, 2017; Coin *et al.*, 2017).

In order to understand how the institutional discourse about age is translated within specific university departments, and how the introduction of fixed-term assistant professors have been actually implemented in recruitment procedures, in the following sections – after a brief description of the research design – organizational discourses about age in one STEM and one SSH department are illustrated and analysed.

8.3 Study design and methodology

Our analysis draws on data from a 3-year European project focused on early-career researchers, carried out between 2014 and 2016, entitled 'GARCIA – Gendering the Academy and Research: combating Career Instability and Asymmetries' (Murgia and Poggio, 2019).[4] With the aim of understanding how age has been discursively constructed within organizations after the university reform was introduced in 2010, we analysed a set of eight qualitative interviews conducted with members of recruitment committees, and 40 interviews conducted with early-career researchers across two departments – one belonging to SSH and one to STEM disciplines – of a university in Northern Italy.

The analysis focuses specifically on how the concept of age is mobilized in academia, with reference to the recruitment process for a fixed-term position as assistant professor. In the SSH department – comprised of 48 professors – from the beginning of 2010 to the beginning of 2014, a total of six assistant professor positions became available. In the same period, only two similar positions became available in the targeted STEM department, comprised of 44 professors. During the GARCIA project, all the professors involved in the recruitment procedures in these two departments were interviewed (the committees were comprised of three professors, of whom only one was internal to the department). Moreover, in order to also understand the perspectives of potential candidates, interviews were conducted with 40 early-career researchers (32 postdoctoral fellows and eight newly employed assistant professors with fixed-term employment contracts) working in the same departments between 2010 and 2014.

We then conducted a discourse analysis, focusing on interview talks and transcripts as social practices and therefore on the resources that are drawn on to enable such practices (Potter, 1996). Different discourses, in fact, might privilege some actors and penalize others within the same organization. A discourse analysis, therefore, allows for a better understanding of power relations within organizations (Clegg *et al.*, 2006). In our case, such a methodological approach has allowed us to explore, in the studied university, how age is constructed in the different discursive practices mobilized in the targeted SSH and STEM departments. Both the discursive position of committee members involved in recruitment procedures (associate and full professors) and that of the potential candidates (early-career researchers) have been analysed and critically discussed.

8.4 The case study: when the 'young researcher' is (only) a discursive construction

We now turn to discuss, in the frame of the last Italian university reform, the ambivalent discursive construction of age within two departments. It is nowadays well established in social sciences, as well as in other academic fields, that age is never merely a number (Calasanti, 2008; Thomas *et al.*, 2014). Bourdieu (1984) argued that *la jeunesse n'est qu'un mot* ('youth is just a word'), underlining how generational categorizations refer more to sociological conceptualizations, rather than fixed categories developed on the basis of chronological age. Taking this perspective into account, it is interesting to analyse the average age of researchers in Italian academia, where we can locate a disfavourable trend towards young people. However, it is also interesting to see how age is discursively constructed and used to legitimize power relations that have concrete effects on the organizational decision-making process, and how that might be seen as constituting a layer of disadvantage for early-career researchers.

8.4.1 Constructing the 'right age' to obtain a tenure track

As argued by Garcia and Hardy (2007), recent reforms in higher education have pushed the organizational culture in universities towards an enterprise culture, new public management and marketization. Therefore, processes such as the commodification of research activities, higher investment in the STEM field, and the preponderance of applied science that fits the demands of the market occur transversally at the global level. However, the results of such trends and their effects are not the same in all countries, because they are mediated by previously existing institutional structures, access to financial resources, the regulation of academic careers and labour markets, and how these factors act as filters for these global pressures (Enders and de Weert, 2009; Bozzon *et al.*, 2019).

In the Italian case, the new recruitment system introduced by the last university reform has been implemented within a highly bureaucratic and co-optative academic system. This means that at the organizational level there is currently a sort of coexistence between two opposing cultures, described by one of the interviewed professors as 'bureaucratic and professional' at the same time:

> These two logics coexist in the professional bureaucracies, because on the one hand it has always been a protective and warranting logic, which assumes that one's career must be evaluated based on seniority and productivity [...]. On the other hand, the professional logic aims to valorize potentialities and not to reward the previous career. So, the first logic is accountable, the second one is clearly not: How can I account for a 'promising young researcher'? (7_SSH_woman)

According to this participant, on the one hand the need for accountability leads to a strong bureaucratization of recruitment procedures, which mainly valorizes seniority and the 'quantitative' evaluation of curricula. On the other hand, there is an investment in potentialities that cannot be quantified when hiring new assistant professors. This is the reason that candidates who have recently completed their PhD, as well as the postdoctoral fellows with a long experience in research and teaching, often apply for the same position as an assistant professor. In the university departments studied, this had resulted in broad age ranges of candidates, which varied between 30 and 50 in the positions that had become available between 2010 and 2014.

The coexistence of such broad-ranging academic profiles makes the required criteria to obtain a position as assistant professor a space of negotiation and/or conflict. In particular, in the departments studied, we identified different organizational discourses about 'senior' and 'promising young' postdoctoral fellows. Among professors who were members of recruitment committees, there are those who mainly valued the seniority of applicants with a longer academic curriculum and long-lasting involvement within the department where the selection had taken place, and those who privileged the potentialities expressed by 'young researchers', who often have more mobile, international profiles. However, these organizational discourses were not present to the same extent in the two departments studied, which greatly differed in the construction of dominant organizational discourses about age.

In the SSH department, there was a tension due to the presence of the two co-existing, competing organizational discourses. Despite these polarized positions, it is interesting to highlight that both discourses were situated in the frame of precarization of academic careers and of ineffective recruitment policies in the public university. In fact, the willingness to invest in 'young talents' goes hand-in-hand with the awareness that many researchers had been working as postdoctoral fellows for several years.

> Somehow a young researcher is penalized, because the problem is that there are not enough positions to recruit non-tenured researchers, so there are no possibilities to access the academic career for a young scholar. (5_SSH_man)

The issue related to the opportunity to hire precarious researchers is not a bad idea in itself. I mean, giving to young researchers the opportunity to work with fixed-term employment contracts to demonstrate their skills, I think it's fine. What doesn't work is the fact that 'young' scholars are not young any longer. (8_SSH_man)

The organizational discourse thus overlaps with the institutional one, both in the declared willingness to hire younger researchers (and to lower the average age of the department) and in considering the fixed-term contract for the assistant professors as an opportunity for them. At the same time, the discourse on the modernization of the department must deal with the high average age of post-doctoral fellows applying for positions as assistant professors. The introduction of the reform, in fact, counts the 12 years between the end of the PhD and the obtaining of a position as associate professor from the date on which the new law came into force, thus not considering postdoctoral fellowships prior to 2010. This explains – together with the limited number of available positions – the growing number of 'senior' postdoctoral researchers (with long academic experience) in Italian academia. Therefore, it is not surprising that in several interviews the recruitment committee members commented on the precarious situation of early-career researchers who were 40 or older.

It is true that we face people aged more than 40 together with people who just got the PhD, but it is obvious that age cannot be considered a criterion for the recruitment. I mean, University has not the function of placing people who have been excluded, right? (5_SSH_man)

This is a contradiction that will always stay unresolved, because if it is true that there is a responsibility of the department in having 'used' a person for a long time, at the same time we cannot stop her/his career just not to encourage further delusions. Where is the responsibility in that? [...] This discourse, meaning to take charge, or the sense of institutional responsibility that we have to assume, is still relevant. I mean, for example, if I were in a selection committee in the field of Anthropology [*where there is a relevant presence of 'senior' postdoctoral fellows*], obviously I could not impose the investment in young researchers as a dominant criterion, because there is an élite of 40- to 50-year-old researchers still waiting for a position assistant professors, so I should use other criteria... (2_SSH_woman)

In the SSH department, there was then also an organizational discourse that somehow, though not explicitly, supported the candidates who had spent many years within the same department. At the centre of this organizational discourse is the concept of age, in terms of years spent waiting for a permanent position, which may or may not correspond to the advanced age of the researchers with a temporary position. Although the participant did not explicitly refer to her own department, rather the situation of the academic community of anthropologists more generally, she was introducing the topic – well-known in the Italian university – of the 'queues' of non-tenured researchers. The logic of the queue is based on the length of the wait and on loyalty to the department (or to a specific professor). Being in academia for many years often means having a more competitive scientific profile compared to younger colleagues, both from a biographical and academic point of view. However, in this manner, weaker scientific profiles can be rewarded, precisely because queuing is more a matter of time than a matter of how time has been used whilst waiting.

In contrast, in the STEM department, the organizational discourses mobilized about age were much more homogeneous, being strictly connected to the public representation of the department, described – even by the university advertising – as 'dynamic, young and international'. Indeed, the interviewed recruitment committee members often referred to international research curricula, underlining the serious delay of the Italian university, mainly due to how academic careers are structured.

> The reason why [*I think that in the Italian university*] we are mediocre? Recruitment is the problem of the Italian university! If you become associate professor at 40 or 50, it is too late, you are too old to be open-minded, to have seen the world... The path must be that either you become associate at 35, 36 or 37 or you are out. If you are 40 years old and you are still there [*in a non-tenured position*], you are going to unlearn the job of professor. You are not attractive in the labour market anymore [...]. Unfortunately, this is an awful system, when you are a postdoc you must build your expertise, you have to travel all over the world, talk, know, build your network... obviously, if you stay only with 'your' professor, when you become associate at 40 or 50, you damage yourself and also your university. (9_STEM_man)

> *Interviewer:* What do you mean that they are 'quite old'?
> *Participant:* It means that in a fair system they [*non-tenured researchers*] would already have a permanent position, a salary and access to all employment benefits. I don't think that a bank would give a loan to a researcher with a fixed-term contract, so consequently if someone who is 35 or 40 years old participates in a competition of this kind [*as non-tenured assistant professor*], it means that we really are at the end of our tether. (10_STEM_man)

In the STEM department, which has a much more international composition than the SSH one, 'being young' was at the centre of the dominant organizational discourse. It is also associated with concepts such as internationalization, networking, dynamism and self-entrepreneurship. Therefore, experienced researchers, who are still in the early stages of their academic career, are associated with mediocrity and considered close-minded and even responsible for the bad reputation of their university in an international context.

Despite the different discursive constructions of age formulated within the two departments, they both have to deal with the structural characteristics of the Italian higher education system, such as the limited positions and career opportunities for young researchers and severe budget cuts. Moreover, it should be stressed that, in Italy, a postdoctoral fellowship is not a proper employment contract, rather a sort of scholarship funded directly from the university or from a grant (e.g. EU research funds) to develop research activities on a specific topic for at least 1 year. People entering this position are not entitled to employment benefits, parental leave or other welfare provisions; the only exception being that of compulsory maternity leave. Only in 2017, after a strong mobilization of the precarious scholars' networks and unions, the Italian government approved a reform that allowed postdoctoral fellows to receive unemployment benefit like the one allocated to freelancers[5] (Bozzon et al., 2019). Therefore, even if different organizational discourses are developed to support either 'young' or 'senior' early-career researchers, in both departments the interviewed professors showed concern for the growing precariousness in academia and research and for the financial disinvestment in the public university.

8.4.2 Challenging the discourse on 'young researchers'

After having analysed how the concept of age had developed within the organizational discourses in the two studied departments – mainly focusing on the discursive positions of associate and full professors who had been part of recruitment committees for assistant professors – we now pay attention to how non-tenured early-career researchers positioned themselves vis-à-vis the dominant organizational discourses on age.

Holding a PhD in a STEM or SSH discipline places PhD holders in very different positions. In STEM, finding a job outside academia that recognizes the acquired skills is easier than in SSH, and the career progression within university departments is relatively quicker, precisely because of the higher mobility and the possibility of looking for interesting and very well-paid jobs in other professional contexts. However, it was possible to identify elements that were applicable to the two contexts, despite the differences. The two excerpts that we introduce belong to the stories of two postdoctoral fellows who are somewhat similar: women, aged 36, both in long-lasting relationships, without children and, at the time of the interview, with limited chances to obtain a permanent position in academia.

From this euphoria of freedom and wellbeing, it becomes after a while a bit... very heavy. I've finished my PhD long ago, most of the people who now hold a postdoc are younger than me, with less years of contract. They are aware of their precariousness, but there is still this sense of freedom; they feel young. If you ask them to teach courses or supervise theses and exams, they are happy; they don't think that they are working for free.[6] Then you feel this *click*, and you understand how the world works. They feel privileged, but then they turn 40, like me, and they don't know what to do. (3_SSH_woman_36)

I've finished my 2 years of postdoctoral fellowship and with the new law I'm fine, because I can have another 4 years, and this means that I accomplish 4 years over the five of the European project on which I should work. But in any case... I'm young! *[sarcastic tone]* and I must put the name of the professor on the projects I write. For the moment I'm fine here; some years ago, there was the idea of running away and going abroad, even though in my experience not everything is also rosy abroad. But maybe we will do it, to run abroad, who knows... Looking back, anyway, I do not complain, because I've always had a decent salary and I will find something, in one place or another. (18_STEM_woman_36)

The two participants shared a similar position within the university, but they formulated quite different discursive constructions on how age can be experienced. In the first case, within the SSH department, the participant described her younger colleagues' behaviours to reflect on her own experience. The desire to enter an academic career pushed her to look for job satisfaction and pleasure in the short-term, without thinking too much about the future. In this case, the interview became an opportunity to take some distance from her own professional aspirations, as she believes that the supposed freedom experienced as a postdoctoral fellow is at the same time a source of insecurity, which easily leads to a precarious condition (if one cannot get a position as assistant professor in a short time).

The second story is instead more oriented to the entrepreneurial logic, which was typical of the STEM department in this study: a researcher in this field should be able to create her own job opportunities. Therefore, on the one hand, the fact that experienced researchers are still employed as postdocs, and often work invisibly, is strongly criticized. On the other hand, the participant's uncertainty about future prospects, and the fact that she would probably have to move abroad – a recurrent topic in the interviews – did not erode her academic aspirations. Her different positioning, in comparison to the one of the colleagues within the SSH department, should be understood also in relation to the already mentioned different labour markets available for SSH and STEM PhD holders. Those from STEM work in more international contexts, have higher salaries and more opportunities to work outside academia. This difference is particularly relevant concerning the higher risk to which SSH non-tenured researchers are subjected, if they want to have an academic career. This allows STEM non-tenured researchers to be more confident about their future, even if they are no longer 'young researchers'.

There's no future for young researchers. Unfortunately, that's the way it is at present. Everyone eventually goes to Google because it's the only option. Or if they really want to have an academic career, they go to the oil-producing countries because they offer good jobs and even well-paid ones. But it is not that people want to go and earn a lot, it's just that they can't find jobs here. They should increase permanent positions at university [...] Now [*after the last university reform*] you can't have a postdoctoral fellowship for more than 6 years, and getting an assistant professorship is extremely hard. So, we are all very insecure, we're all in a bad position concerning the employment contracts, it's not about salary, it's about contracts. (29_STEM_woman_37)

The length of the period in a non-tenured position in Italy is longer than abroad. [...] When researchers get a position – which is also temporary – as assistant professor, quite often their curricula are very solid, and if they weren't in Italy, they'd have higher positions, in some cases comparable to an associate professor in Italy. (5_SSH_woman_37)

As happened with the recruitment committee members, the non-tenured researchers also focused mainly on their seniority and acquired competences, rather than their chronological age. The gap between the academic experience of the participants, and the fact that they are still in the early stage of their academic career, is a discourse frequently mobilized – in this research as well as in various others on the same subject – in order to describe the struggle associated with such a long period in a precarious position and with such a hectic pace of work (see Ackers and Gill, 2005; Davies and Petersen, 2005; Bozzon *et al.*, 2017).

We find this dynamic even more explicit in the stories of those who had left academia. In fact, amongst the interviewed non-tenured researchers who worked in the two departments studied between 2010 and 2014, there were also some people who, at the time of the interviews (conducted between 2014 and 2016), had abandoned the academic career.

There's a rather widespread but not very healthy attitude among non-tenured researchers. I mean, it's very easy to load yourself down with work, publications, and so on, because you feel insecure, you feel under pressure. You think that you have to do more if you don't want to be left out. This is what I've always felt. I've always been a workaholic. But on the other hand, I like my job, it's difficult for me to stand still... but today I'm much less like that... now I can say 'no'. As long as you're young you can do it, but then it becomes very stressful. Because in Italy, paradoxically, the insiders with permanent positions are relatively free, but if you want to get in, you have to publish ten times more! (13_SSH_man_42)

I still publish, not that the company lets me, but it's my relationship with myself, the company and the boss which has helped me create that space. [...] Thinking about when I was at university, I never felt so physically stressed. I often left home at eight and returned at half past eleven [...]. Now maybe I'm calmer... but it's difficult to compare, because I'm more mature, I'm older and not so young. I don't do emails at the weekend, if I'm on holiday I don't check the company's email, which I used to do when I was at university. (27_STEM_man_34)

The first participant obtained a permanent position as associate professor in another European country, in an SSH department. The second left the university to work in the private sector. Therefore, both currently had a more secure position, which allowed them to limit the overflowing of work activities in their private lives, especially at night, and during weekends and holidays. The reasons for having left Italian academia, in both cases, are connected to the opportunity to build a safer professional career, and to the perception that working conditions at university were too demanding and meaningless for a researcher with such a long and consolidated experience, but still employed as a postdoctoral fellow.

A final aspect that we want to highlight concerns the organizational discourses about the 'age of the department' in which the participants worked. Although the average age of the postdoctoral researchers was quite high in both departments,[7] the SSH one was described by most of participants as 'old', whereas the STEM department was described as 'very young'.

> The goal is one thing, the practice another one. Like all the others, this department strives for excellence and multidisciplinarity. That said, I find there's a huge gap between discourses and practices. The department gives limited support to the entrepreneurship and innovativeness of young researchers. There's a small group of people who've made a commitment to the department, including myself, people who've worked for years to value basic research. I find that the department never directly involves early-career researchers, but there's this brokerage layer that sooner or later will sink the department. This is my perception, we're always shielded in some way, and if you're not protected by some professor, you'll never be able to obtain a position [...] These are power games played by older males, maybe of different political orientations, but with similar lifestyles. Here they're all Italian, white and middle class. It's a cohesive group very concerned to protect itself. (1_SSH_woman_34)

The SSH department was described by the participant as governed by 'older males [...] all Italian, white and middle-class'. However, what she was challenging was not only the relative advanced age of the academic staff but the organizational culture of the department, based on co-optation and rigid hierarchies. As the preceding excerpt illustrates, in many of the interviews, the SSH department was represented as an old and tired academic context. Meanwhile, a different representation was constructed regarding the STEM department, which was described as 'young' and much more 'easy-going'.

> There's the usual hierarchy like everywhere else, but I think it's very informal. I worked at *** [another STEM department in Italy] and then I came here, which is a lot more easy-going and more human. I'm not saying that the other departments were inhuman, but they were more formal, they addressed

each other using 'Lei' [*the formal pronoun*], here I can use 'tu' [*the informal pronoun*] with everyone. In my opinion, this department is very distinctive in the Italian scenario. The Italian universities are very hierarchical: there's the full professor and the associate professors who do what he tells them, then there are the assistant professors, then the postdoctoral fellows, then the PhDs. And this pyramid is very strong. This department is very young, very American: the assistant professors do not have a boss; they're heads of their groups. [...] I think that such a flat organizational structure can encourage young researchers to be productive. In other departments there's the full professor who tells you what to do. Here less so, and for young researchers this is amazing. (1_STEM_man_37)

Thus, despite the advanced age of the postdoctoral fellows, the STEM department where we conducted the interviews was represented by most as a stimulating environment for the researchers who worked there: a 'young', informal department, with a flat organizational structure and good pay levels. Still problematic, however, is the pace of work, on the one hand, and the opportunities to obtain a tenure track or a permanent position, on the other. In fact, the average age of the postdoctoral researchers was still also rather high in the STEM department, and many postdoctoral fellows decide to look for other employment, because they perceive themselves to be too 'mature, older and no longer young' to afford the pace of work which, although sustained by academic love, is perceived as too convulsive and sometimes endless.

8.5 Discussion and conclusions

In this contribution, we discussed how the concept of age is mobilized within institutional and organizational discourses in Italian academia. First, despite the dominant rhetoric conveyed by the last university reform on the need to renew Italian academia and lower the average age of its members, we have shown that the investment in young researchers remains merely a statement on paper. Italy continues to be the country with the highest average age of academics in Europe. In fact, the lack of financial investments and the limited availability of permanent positions keep early-career researchers in a structural condition of precariousness (Toscano *et al.*, 2014; Bozzon *et al.*, 2017).

This is the framework in which specific organizational discourses are situated. In our research, we studied two departments – one belonging to STEM and one to SSH disciplines – of a university in Northern Italy. With the aim of investigating the discursive construction of age, recruitment committee members and early-career researchers were interviewed. This allowed for a focus on the entry age into academia, which can be conceptualized as a peculiar space in which individuals who occupy different positions establish conflicted power relations by (re)producing cultural and political discourses (Thomas *et al.*, 2014). In fact, by understanding how the meanings and importance ascribed to age were produced in two specific university departments, we have been able to analyse the discursive and material effects connected to the introduction of new recruitment procedures.

Concerning the point of view of the professors who were members of recruitment committees, at the SSH department we observed a tension between the support of 'senior' and 'young' postdoctoral fellows who applied for positions as assistant professors. The dilemma was in having to choose between candidates in a context of limited positions: postdoctoral fellows, who had relatively recently completed their PhD and showed promise as researchers (as well as having more international experience), and postdoctoral fellows, who had spent several years in the same department (and have mainly local or national experiences). Therefore, in the mobilized organizational discourses, the quandary is how not to penalize young researchers and at the same time avoid relatively senior early-career researchers being pushed out of academia. In contrast, in the STEM department the entrepreneurial logic prevailed, and what emerged was a clear tendency towards the pole of 'young researchers', represented as a priority for achieving high-quality research standards and competing in a globalized academia. In this case, being 'young' did not refer so much to the age of candidates but rather to an organizational model based on dynamism, enthusiasm and constant availability.

These organizational discourses on age affected and were intertwined with the self-representations of the non-tenured early-career researchers who were interviewed. In interpreting how they positioned themselves, crucial factors were the pay gap between STEM and SSH departments as well as the different opportunities to obtain a qualified job outside academia. Similar experiences, in fact, can be re-elaborated in very different ways by subjects, depending also on structural factors, such as the availability of academic positions, the job opportunities in a specific sector and level of income and workers' rights. However, what the participants had in common, in the two departments studied, was the frustration of frequently being labelled as 'young researchers', despite being close to, or exceeding, 40 years of age. This implements a process of downgrading and infantilization related to their lack of autonomy and their persisting dependence on the professor(s) responsible for the renewal of their contract or their future academic career.

Beyond the different opportunities available to researchers in STEM and SSH disciplines, we should reflect on the multiple consequences of the organizational model that are imposed on researchers who are at the beginning of their academic careers. The fact that early-career researchers with a fixed-term contract are passionate about their jobs (Busso and Rivetti, 2014; Coin, 2017) should not justify the expectation of being constantly available, forever young and always industrious and enthusiastic. In fact, regardless of their chronological age, for early-career researchers, being 'young' means being dependent on someone else. Finally, the issue is not whether those who apply for an assistant professorship are too young or not young enough, but rather the fact that a whole generation of PhD holders – composed of both the young and not-so-young – run the risk of being left out of the Italian academic system. The hope is therefore that investment in research does not just remain at the discursive level, but is also implemented in the practices and policies of the national higher education system.

Notes

1 These contracts are defined in Italy as *assegno di ricerca* (postdoctoral fellow); RTD-a (fixed-term and non-tenured assistant professorship) and RTD-b (assistant professorship on a tenure track).
2 University reform L. 240/2010 not only introduced fixed-term positions for assistant professors, but also new rules for academic staff recruitment procedures, organized in two steps. First, at the national level, the national committees (one for each research field) select candidates that deserve the 'scientific qualification' for associate professor. Second, at the local level, each department can decide – within the next 6 years – to open a local competition to either recruit or promote somebody as associate professor in that specific research field. This two-step procedure also applies (separately) to full professorship. These national committees are composed of five members: four extracted from a list of all professors (available to be included in these national committees) who meet in their research field some minimum scientific requirements (identified by biblio-metric indicators) and one external professor (working abroad) designated at the central level (identified in terms of international reputation) (Bozzon *et al.*, 2015).
3 With regard to this, see the work of the 7th Permanent Commission (Public Education, Cultural Heritage) between the end of 2008 and the beginning of 2009 (http://www.senato.it/Leg16/browse/3538?seduta_anno=2008).
4 The GARCIA project was financed within the call *Science in Society* of FP7 Programme of the European Commission (Grant Agreement n. 611737).
5 If a postdoc works for 1 year, s/he will be entitled to an allowance of 6 months maximum of 700–900 euro per month, according to the amount of the scholarship.
6 In the Italian academic context, postdoctoral fellows are often informally required to 'collaborate' with professors in their duties (teaching activities, supervisions, administrative tasks, etc.), without being paid and under threat for the renewal of their contract.
7 On 31 December 2014, there were 13 postdoctoral researchers in the SSH department, seven of whom were aged 30–34, two were 35–39 and four over 40. Working in the STEM department in the same period were 41 postdoctoral researchers, of whom 25 were aged 30–34, 12 were 35–39, and four over 40.

References

Ackers, L. and Gill, B. (2005). Attracting and retaining 'early career' researchers in English higher education institutions. *Innovation*, 18(3), 277–299.

Anvur. (2016). Rapporto sullo stato del sistema universitario e della ricerca, Rome. Available at: http://www.anvur.org/index.php?option=com_content&view=article&id=1045&Itemid=708&lang=it.

Bourdieu, P. (1984). *La jeunesse n'est qu'un mot. Questions de sociologie.* Paris: Éditions de Minuit, 143–154.

Bozzon, R., Donà, A., Villa, P., Murgia, A. and Poggio, B. (2015). Italy. In: Le Feuvre, N. (ed) *Contextualizing Women's Academic Careers: Comparative Perspectives on Gender, Care and Employment Regimes in Seven European Countries.*

GARCIA working papers 1, University of Trento. Available at: http://garciaproject.eu/wp-content/uploads/2014/07/GARCIA_report_wp1D1.pdf.

Bozzon, R., Murgia, A. and Poggio, B. (2019). Gender and precarious careers in academia and research: Macro, meso and micro perspectives. In: Murgia, A. and Poggio, B. (eds) *Gender and Precarious Research Careers: A Comparative Analysis*. London: Routledge, 15–49.

Bozzon, R., Murgia, A. and Villa, P. (2017). Precariousness and gender asymmetries among early career researchers: A focus on stem fields in the Italian academia. *Polis*, 31(1), 127–158.

Busso, S. and Rivetti, P. (2014). What's love got to do with it? Precarious academic labour forces and the role of passion in Italian universities. *Recherches sociologiques et anthropologiques*, 45(2), 15–37.

Calasanti, T. (2008). A feminist confronts ageism. *Journal of Aging Studies*, 22(2), 152–157.

Clegg, S.R., Courpasson, D. and Phillips, N. (2006). *Power and Organizations*. London: Sage.

Coin, F. (2017). When love becomes self-abuse: Gendered perspectives on unpaid labor in academia. In: Taylor, Y. and Lahad, K. (eds) *Feeling Academic in the Neoliberal University: Feminist Flights, Fights and Failures*. London: Palgrave Macmillan.

Coin, F., Giorgi, A. and Murgia, A. (2017). In/disciplinate: soggettività precarie nell'università italiana. *Culture del lavoro*, 4. Available at: http://edizionicafoscari.unive.it/it/edizioni/libri/978-88-6969-137-9/.

Davies, B. and Petersen, E.B. (2005). Intellectual workers (un) doing neoliberal discourse. *International Journal of Critical Psychology*, 13(1), 32–54.

Enders, J. and de Weert, E. (2009). *The Changing Face of Academic Life: Analytical and Comparative Perspectives*. New York: Palgrave Macmillan.

European Commission/EACEA/Eurydice. (2017). Modernisation of Higher Education in Europe: Academic Staff – 2017. Eurydice Report. Luxembourg: Publications Office of the European Union.

Froio, F. (1996). *Le mani sull'università*. Roma: Editori riuniti.

Garcia, P. and Hardy, C. (2007). Positioning, similarity and difference: Narratives of individual and organizational identities in an Australian university. *Scandinavian Journal of Management*, 23(4), 363–383.

Le Feuvre, N., Bataille, P., Kradolfer, S., del Rio Carral, M. and Sautier, M. (2019). The gendered diversification of academic career paths in comparative perspective. In: Murgia, A. and Poggio, B. (eds) *Gender and Precarious Research Careers: A Comparative Analysis*. London: Routledge, 50–80.

Miur. (2018). Il personale docente e non docente nel sistema universitario italiano – a.a 2016/2017. Available at: http://ustat.miur.it/media/1127/focus-personale-universitario_2016-2017.pdf.

Murgia, A. and Poggio, B. (eds) (2019). *Gender and Precarious Research Careers: A Comparative Analysis*. London: Routledge. Available at: https://www.taylorfrancis.com/books/9781351781428.

Pavolini, E. and Viesti, G. (2016). Università: ricercatori in bilico, La Voce. Available at: https://www.lavoce.info/archives/40642/sempre-meno-docenti-alluniversita/.

Peroni, C., Murgia, A., and Poggio, B. (2015). Italy. In: Herschberg, C., Benschop, Y., van den Brink, M. (eds) *Constructing Excellence: The Gap between Formal and*

Actual Selection Criteria for Early Career Academics. GARCIA working papers 2, University of Trento. Available at: http://garciaproject.eu/wp-content/uploads/2014/07/GARCIA_report_wp2D1.pdf.

Perotti, R. (2008). *L'università truccata.* Torino: Einaudi.

Potter, J. (1996). *Representing Reality: Discourse, Rhetoric and Social Construction.* London: Sage.

Thomas, R., Hardy, C., Cutcher, L., and Ainsworth, S. (2014). What's age got to do with it? On the critical analysis of age and organizations. *Organization Studies,* 35(11), 1569–1584.

Toscano, E., Coin, F., Giancola, O. et al. (2014). Ricercarsi – Indagine sui percorsi di vita e lavoro del precariato universitario. Report di ricerca. Available at: https://arca.unive.it/retrieve/handle/10278/3684126/95223/Ricercarsi.pdf.

Triventi, M. (2009). Luci e ombre del dibattito sulla riforma dell'Università in Italia. *Sociologica.* Available at: www.sociologica.mulino.it/news/newsitem/index/Item/News:NEWS_ITEM:146#_edn1.

Zamponi, L. and González, J.F. (2017). Dissenting youth: How student and youth struggles helped shape anti-austerity mobilisations in Southern Europe. *Social Movement Studies,* 16(1), 64–81.

Part III

Moves, transitions and representations

Chapter 9

Young Italians

Individualization, uncertainty and reconquesting the future

Carmen Leccardi

9.1 Introduction

Recent decades have seen profound transformations, both in the ways in which time is experienced and in the ways that young people ascribe meaning in their lives. The significant linkage between these two dimensions is evidenced by the changes that affect biographies, understood as forms of narration (Kerby, 1991), which through language are structured in time and through time. They are, it can be said, inscribed in time. The ways of constructing them are rapidly changing in accordance with the redefinition of links that are identified between the individual and a collective past, present and future. In turn, biographical time and identity are closely bound to one another, and it could not be otherwise. Personal identity, just like biographical time, is in fact the outcome of the dialectical relationship between permanence and change, between continuity and discontinuity (Leitner, 1982).

This interweaving scenario forms a backdrop to the heightened conditions of existential and social uncertainty faced by young Italians in the second decade of the new century. As we shall see, this uncertainty is synthesized in the growing difficulty of establishing a positive relationship with the future. A lack of recognition from the labour market of skills and competences gained is intertwined for these young people with the well-known dynamics of destandardization of entry into adult life that the sociology of youth has for some time analysed and placed at the centre of collective attention (for a summary, see Wyn and White, 1997; Furlong, 2009; Woodman and Bennett, 2015; White *et al.*, 2017). These two forms of uncertainty combine to problematize the vision of the future. The main argument of this chapter is that young people must develop new strategies to cope in the face of this uncertain future. Among these strategies, a crucial role is performed by forms of individualization that characterize the contemporary period. For this reason, they will be subject to specific attention in the discussion that follows.

On this premise, the chapter first discusses the usefulness of the temporal approach in illuminating the specificity of youthful experiences. In particular, it examines how this entails a redefinition of biographical coordinates and identities that are increasingly less attuned to the medium-/long-term future as a central biographical reference. The focus of attention will then be on the dynamics of contemporary individualization, as discussed above. This is an important factor in understanding the existential strategies and biographical constructs of not just young Italians, but young Europeans more generally. The chapter closes with a reflection on one of the strategies with which young Italians today face the uncertainty of social life and the difficulties in relating to the world of work: the decision to look for work outside Italy. Redefinition of temporal coordinates and strong pressure for individualization, it will be argued, are central to an understanding of these experiences.

9.2 About time: social and biographical

Formulated by Durkheim (1912/1968) at the beginning of the last century, the concept of social time refers to the existence of a highly normative temporal dimension that regulates, gives rhythm to and unifies the various activities of social life (Zerubavel, 1981; Adam, 1995). Albeit, invisible to all but the eye of the trained practitioner in the social sciences. Within this analytical framework, it is possible to maintain that social institutions, synchronizing and intertwining their rhythms, jointly contribute to constructing social time. But it should also be underlined that this network of temporal rules, sociohistorical in nature, is characterized by levels of normativity that vary according to the various institutions in question. Time spent in paid work, for example, has a greater degree of normativity greater than in family time; family time in turn is more normative than leisure time, and so on. In short, it can be stated that the interweaving of different institutional times and their normative hierarchies constitute the basis upon which social time is constructed.

Finally, it should be kept in mind that, from modernity onwards, the conception of time that shapes social life has been abstract and empty. In this frame, time is conceived as a linear, irreversible flow separated from every idea of an end and structured exclusively according to a before and an after. This is a time scheme, as emphasized by Agamben (2006), functional to the application of machines to human work. The organization of work in industrial society borrows from the conception of time in the Judeo-Christian tradition. Mundane progress takes the place of spiritual perfection, while the future – removed from the twofold divine and natural influence – is subject to human domination. Formulated by Enlightenment philosophy, the concept of an *open future* was destined, for at least two centuries, to exert a profound and pervasive influence on collective cultural schemes (Koselleck, 2004). Within the conception of the open future, a future subtracted from extra-human influences, freedom and uncertainty become the mirror of each other. Here it must be emphasized that uncertainty is reflective of an idea of the future as a field of infinite possibilities in which 'one can, in principle, master all things by calculation' (Weber, 1919/1946: 139).

We shall see in the discussion that follows how this virtuous connection between uncertainty and freedom gradually changed during the twentieth century, and with an acceleration in recent decades, into a defensive attitude towards the future. Indeed, the contemporary temporal orientation locates it more as an obscurely threatening dimension than an opportunity for action. Although the continuous call for technical and scientific innovation characteristic of the public discourse of our time attempts to exorcise this fear, it nevertheless remains clearly in the background.

Biographical time acquires form and is structured within social time. Its cadences and phases are necessarily structured in terms of institutional times. With regard to young people, this would be from starting school to the beginning of their working life. This means that biographical time cannot evade the temporal rules that structure social institutions; those that determine and define, for example, the different ages of life and construct their meanings. The duration of these phases, their degree of constrictiveness and their social representations vary according to the historical moment (Heinz *et al.*, 2009). Nevertheless, the normative imprint of social time never completely disappears. Not even when, for example, the traditional stages of transition to adulthood seems to be destructured, as is happening today (Furlong, 2009). This destructuring appears to be the most suitable way to attune biographical time to the characteristics of social time in the new century. The contemporary temporal structures in fact appear marked by an evident process of acceleration amid economic-financial, technological and social-change processes (Rosa, 2013). This process makes the past an alien dimension, contracts the present (Lübbe, 2009) and 'burns' the future from the outset. In this scenario, the very identity of institutions, linked to continuity and projection in the long-term future, is eroded.

As a form of narration, biography is required to connect personal events to meanings, and both to existential goals as they are constructed. Personal identity is the outcome of this process, linking meanings and the changing existential experiences. Goals, in turn, are the result of the relationship that each subject establishes with social institutions, and the ability to build forms of satisfactory mediation between personal time and institutional times. The costs associated with this mediation work, starting from the deferral of gratification, can be accepted only insofar as the future offers a space capable of accommodating existential goals and open to possibilities. To put it another way, these costs are acceptable if the construction of forms of biographical planning is not precluded by an all-pervading uncertainty.

To adopt the perspective of social phenomenology, plans can be considered emblematic of both biographical time 'an individual's biography is apprehended as [...] a plan' (Berger *et al.*, 1973: 71) – and of personal identity. This positive relationship between plans, biographical time and identity, however, encounters difficulties when the future is not only foreshortened, as happens in acceleration society, but the general mastery of time becomes more problematic. Put another way, when the accidental and the fortuitous can no longer be controlled by means of medium/long planning, as a form of insurance against the future, due to the exponential growth of the speed of social change and the subsequent increase in social uncertainty, then the capacity of planning in the traditional sense is compromised. Yet even if the project is understood simply in terms of a design, scheme or programme (Boutinet, 1990), and even if one considers medium/short-term planning, contemporary social time requires that this key dimension of biographical construction be rethought. This alters the temporal structure of identities, creating fertile ground for redefinition of their postulates.

In short, because of these new temporal coordinates, we are faced with a transformation of the processes of 'subjectivization of time' that the construction of biographical time implies. The accelerated social time in which young people live redefines the modes of biographical construction, imposing new directions in the construction of identities. At the centre of this process of redefinition of biographies, there undoubtedly lies a changed meaning of the future. The consequence of living in a high-speed society (Rosa and Scheurman, 2009) is that the future folds back into the present, it is absorbed within it and is consumed before it can really be conceived. This imposes the restructuring of project forms and a redefinition of the idea of control over time, a dimension taken for granted since the Enlightenment. As we shall see, the experiences of the young Italians considered here casts new light on the strategies by which control over biographical time has been constructed in recent years in this distinct context (Leccardi, 2017).

9.3 Individualization, temporality and uncertainty

The uncertainty that characterizes our time has a different quality from the uncertainty of early modernity. For the latter, living with doubt and affirming the fallibility, in principle, of every certainty appeared above all to be a conquest (Privitera, 2002). Today, the pervasiveness of uncertainty embraces all social institutions, questioning their quality as 'programmes for action' in the future. Uncertainty is fostered by the acceleration of processes of social change, which involve and question what is taken for granted in an increasing number of areas of experience. In particular, in regard to the topic of this study, the pervasive social uncertainty necessitates forms of subjective processing so as to at least curb the risks associated with growing up in this social scenario.

The paradox here is the need for young people to cope with these uncertainties whilst, above all, projecting themselves into the future through individual choices and decisions. And yet, this is precisely at a time when the future is becoming increasingly evanescent as a result of growing uncertainties. Behind the paradox, therefore, lies the nexus between uncertainty and dynamics of contemporary individualism. On this last dimension, it is now necessary to focus attention, starting from the concept of individualization.

With the term *Individualisierung* – translated into English as 'individualization'– Beck and Beck-Gernsheim (2002) allude to a process of institutionalized individualism. As emphasized in the preface of their book *Individualization* (2002), while the Anglo-American use of the term refers to the neo-liberal idea of the 'free-market individual', the perspective embraced by Beck and Beck-Gernsheim (2002) takes a different analytical position. The individual here is not the 'entrepreneur of him/herself' as in the liberal tradition. Rather, s/he is the result of institutional dynamics characteristic of the contemporary era of globalization. As an effect of the loss of normative force, institutions oblige individuals to reflexively construct their life trajectories, identifying biographical solutions to systemic problems. This is without individuals being able to rely on the welfare system, being forced at the same time to deal with all-pervading precariousness in work and life in general. The constant work on oneself and one's identity that individuals today must undertake appears to be primarily an institutionally constructed dynamic.

This analytical proposal furnishes an ambivalent picture of contemporary individualism. On the one hand, the institutional obligation towards individualization impoverishes the ability to construct qualitatively significant links between the individual and the social. On the other hand, however, the need for an ongoing definition of self, also in response to the demands of central institutions such as work and family, opens the way to a ceaseless reflexive approach with open outcomes. It goes without saying that individual responses to this comparison are strongly influenced by the diversity of economic, social and cognitive resources to which individuals have access. This form of reflexive individualization therefore also draws unprecedented maps of inequality. In parallel, however, the new reflexivity required by this form of social production of individuality can generate dynamics of critical knowledge and civil participation.

Elliott and Lemert (2006) (see also Elliott, 2016), among the best-known analysts of the individualism of our time, propose a different analytical approach that is of particular interest for our purposes here. According to the two authors, the key to understanding the dynamics of contemporary individualism resides in addressing the theme of contemporary temporal dynamics. To be fully understood, it must first be related to the strong pressure to accelerate that characterizes the present, marked by the speed of financial markets, virtual communications and the pace of everyday life. In this context, the theme of the constant reinvention of oneself together with the refusal to defer gratification is configured as a true normative ideal.

In tune with this *zeitgeist*, the individualism described by Elliott and Lemert (2006) requires the ability to know how to transform oneself rapidly in mind and body, to renew oneself and to be mobile and dynamic (see Elliott and Urry, 2010). As a consequence, every social involvement can only be partial and short-term, consonant with the expectation of change. In addition, the fantasy of the potentially inexhaustible plasticity of the world and of the self inevitably also tends to foster the divorce between the individual so conceived and the citizen. The individualism that the two authors define as paramount in the global age appears closely attuned to the increasingly globalized e-economy and its temporal norms built around the ideal of simultaneity. Exercising effective autonomy in such a setting seems likely to fail precisely because of incessant change. How can one construct, for example, a biographical project in a social setting shaped by the search for immediate gratification, within a framework of temporal acceleration that 'burns' the idea of a medium- to long-term future? It goes without saying that the possibility of an emancipatory, non-alienated, individualism in the view of the two authors is called into question. As Elliott and Lemert (2006) stress, one of the most significant aspects of twenty-first century individualism is the search for instant change. Whether it is a matter of work, affective relations, body or identity, the ability to keep up with the speed of change – and, if possible, to anticipate it – is a form of strategic existential control.

To summarize, there are three main interconnected institutional dynamics at the core of the new individualism (see Elliott, 2016). The first is the emphasis on the constant reinvention of the self as an antidote to unstoppable changes that risk undermining identities. Flexibility, the capacity for personal experimentation, self-transformation and self-reorganization become real virtues in this scenario. The impact on the identity of these dynamics is easily predictable: the sense of identity acquires marked features of provisionality. In the age of economic globalization, on the other hand, organizations also comply with this imperative (Thrift, 2006). Individuals are influenced by, and in their own way, influence these trends.

Second, according to Elliott and Lemert (2006), neo-individualism has a positive relationship with the change in the real-time characteristic of our *zeitgeist*, that is to say, instant change. It is not by chance that they use the expression *Instant Generation* to refer to those who grow up and are socialized in this social and cultural climate. Speed appears to be the means with which to negotiate the multiplication of life chances, at least at the virtual level. To follow the idea of the opening of the world to continuous change – and this in a quotidian reality that, for a growing number of individuals, clashes with the harshness of the unequal distribution of resources, and with the growth of widespread feelings of injustice experienced in first person. In turn, consumption is the most immediate resource with which to respond to rapidly changing desires and needs. In keeping with this fascination for speed, even if the personal surroundings appear to be stable, it is nevertheless always considered to be potentially changeable. Consequently, the theme of durability and continuity of change and the traditional theme of biographical narration undergoes profound redefinition. The speed of change that also affects everyday life in turn increases the experiences of contingency.

Third, in this scenario short-termism and episodicity magnify in importance. The previously cited new ethos of the self's constant reinvention has at its basis a cultural orientation according to which the short-term perspective is both desirable and positive. The emotional costs of this process are generally high, eventually producing new forms of alienation (Rosa, 2010). By miniaturizing the social context and emphasizing the internal context, the founding link between individual and social is severed. The fundamental analytical issue here is the evanescence of the contemporary role of the institutions responsible, by definition, for guaranteeing continuity in social life. The result is a crisis of continuity, at the core of the already-mentioned 'institutional individualism'. Moreover, on a biographical level, short-termism prevents the construction of real-life projects. The latter are in fact devised through a close relationship between time and non-presentified existential objectives.

In short, the analysis in terms of the social acceleration of neo-individualism (see also Elliott and Hsu, 2016) pushes it towards loss of the social bond, towards a hypertrophy of the internal environment at the expense of the social one. The active exercise of citizenship thus leaves the horizon of twenty-first-century individualism. The increasingly privatized worlds in which individuals are confined induce them to exclude the other from their visual field; together with the Other, the social world becomes more peripheral. For Elliott and Hsu (2016), neo-individualism therefore becomes synonymous with the privatization of identities: the more that market forces enter social life and dominates its codes, the more explicit becomes the shift to a privatized culture.

This analytical perspective is at odds with the vision of the processes of contemporary individualization proposed by the French sociologist Danilo Martuccelli (2010). According to Martuccelli, although the impoverishment of public discourse and the dominance of the logic of the market are incontestable, privatism is not the main lens through which to read these processes.

To grasp the unprecedented nature of these dynamics, Martuccelli (2010) proposes using the term 'singularity' (*singularisme*). The matrix of singularity is purely social in character. If what matters in individualism is individual independence (and negative freedom), in singularity what is valuable is above all originality, incomparability, being unique and not confusable with anything else. Thus, if privatism is characterized by a loss *tout court* of the sense of the collective, in singularity the relationship with the other is not denied. Rather, it passes through the relationship with oneself and the search for one's uniqueness. The relationship with the social is mediated by the centrality of the relationship with oneself. In this framework, what is collective stems from individualities.

Indignation provoked by the growth of inequalities and offences against the principles of justice can, for example, accompany singularity by opening it to the social bond. This sentiment is the polar-opposite of the 'passion for well-being' characteristic of acquisitive individualism. The 'ethical feeling' through which the indignation is expressed is the result of the deep excavation that the individual performs in and on him/herself. However, this occurs through a process that does not isolate it but rather places it in relation with the world (Hessel, 2010). The relationship with the social therefore does not cease but is built starting from the search for connections between one's own and others' experiences.

Here there arises an aspect of analytical importance highlighted by Martuccelli (2006, 2010). It concerns the role of institutions in social and personal life. Institutions no longer appear to be the drivers of social integration. In the age of indignation and singularity, the relationship with the institutions centres on neither integration nor the simple protection of the rights of individuals. Rather, the institutions are represented as guarantors of personal fulfilment, and considered in a sense 'at the service' of individuals. In this regard, the crisis that today weighs down on individuals becomes an opportunity to explore the difficulty of personal, satisfactory relationships with institutions. The crisis of the European social model can then be addressed in concrete terms in relation to one's life: the demise of a series of provisions guaranteed by welfare entails also the diminishment of personal existential opportunities. The weakening/downsizing of welfare is thus transformed from a question related to public policies to a personal problem.

Indignation is generated and develops in response to these processes of reduction in life chances. Against this and other social injustices – for example, the enormous destruction of wealth caused by speculations on international financial markets – one can take a position of civic engagement. To borrow from the language of the women's movement of the 1970s, the personal and the political merge. Thus, a form of sociological imagination is reintroduced: the possibility of combining biography and history, micro and social dimensions, everyday life and large-scale processes. However, contrary to the contention of Wright Mills (1959), here the starting point and the point of arrival coincide. Personal life and the uniqueness of one's own experiences are indispensable referents in sociohistorical terms. Singularity supersedes privatism.

Following the arguments of Martuccelli (2006, 2010), the singularist perspective tends to modify the prevailing interpretation of contemporary individualism as privatism from several points of view. First, instead of gathering the idea of a separation *tout court* between the individual and social, it looks at the changes that have taken place in the representation of the social. From this perspective, social relations tend to be perceived in terms of human relations, thus transforming conflicts of interest into personal matters. This type of personalization also influences the relationship with the sphere of justice: social injustices are mainly connected to issues of non-recognition and lack of respect (Honneth, 1995).

Second, with regard to the relationship with the institutional system, singularity expresses a demand for institutions able to place themselves at the service of individuals – a view far removed from the one which conceives institutions as a normative and procedural apparatus to whose requirements it is necessary to adapt. Individuals want to 'rely' on the institutions; they want to derive resources for action from the relationship, not constraints. Institutions are asked to recognize the role that individuals play within them, to show awareness of the importance of individual lives for the continuity of their existence (without individuals, there are no institutions). From this perspective, institutions need individuals to be able to survive, not the reverse.

Third, singularity brings with it a strong awareness of personal empowerment and confidence in one's ability to solve problems that generate uncertainty and risks. In relation to collective questions, there is no disinterest, but rather a way of considering them that concerns above all the power of individual action. It is not simply a question of 'individualistic illusion'. Rather, it is a redefinition of the relationship between individual action and collective action in the increasingly interdependent context in which people live. Personal initiative is not conceived as opposing collective initiative but in some way as its expression/ daily extension – unlike political participation *stricto sensu*, considered extra ordinary. Recent analysis of political participation by young people today confirms this interpretation (Pleyers and Capitaine, 2016).

Finally, mention should be made of the complex relationship between singularity and issues of justice. Within singularity, personal situations can be read as questions of social justice, while matters considered *par excellence* in terms of justice cannot be addressed in these terms. For example, injustice can become a synonym for what prevents forms of personal fulfilment. This obviously does not mean that the great social issues that accompany neo-liberalism are not experienced as questions of justice. From the growth of social inequalities to the increase in the precariousness of work, these are processes that have dramatic repercussions on people's lives. But what is emphasized, above all, is the connection between one's own existence and the wider public issues – how personal life is conditioned by macro social issues. This is an approach capable of destabilizing views of individualism in both privatist and utilitarian terms.

9.4 Reconquering the future: young Italians and new strategies for controlling biographical time

Beyond the different interpretations of contemporary processes of individualization, it is indubitable that, for young people living and growing up in Europe in the new century, the individual devising of strategies to cope with an uncertain future is a common practice. For young Italians, this practice is charged with specific meanings, not only because of the continuing negative effects of the economic crisis that hit Europe in the 2010s, but also because of the closure of the labour market to them. Several chapters in this book examine these difficulties in detail, of which brief mention will be made shortly. One consequence of this situation is the prolongation of the semi-dependency of young people on the family of origin – which is a real 'social shock absorber' in Italy. According to Eurostat (2017a), the average age at which young Italians leave their family of origin is 30.1 years compared to a European average of 26.1. Such figures are a clear indicator of these difficulties (Istituto Giuseppe Toniolo, 2018). But it is also important to be aware of the ways in which, even in such a disadvantageous social context, young Italians ensure that they do not lose control over their biographical time.

Perhaps the most significant of these strategies is today the trend for a growing number of well-educated young people to preserve their right to the future by leaving Italy. In looking beyond their national borders, they can make use of acquired skills and competences that they feel are not fully recognized in Italy. Much public discussion revolves around migratory processes particularly from the African continent, which directly involves Italy as the geographically closest European country. However, there is far less discussion – at least outside of Italy – on contemporary Italian mobility.

Data gathered in a recent survey on 'Italians in the world' referring to 2016 (Fondazione Migrantes, 2017) shows that Italian mobility increased significantly in the 10 years between 2006 and 2016, rising by 60%. Moreover, 39% of those who left Italy in 2016 were aged between 18 and 34. With an increase of 23.3% on the previous year, this confirms that such mobility is a constantly growing trend. The main destinations for young Italians are other European countries, with a preference to date for the United Kingdom, Germany, Switzerland, France and Spain. The exceptional difficulties in the labour market for young people in Italy are almost certainly behind these choices. This is evident in youth unemployment data (15–24 years) in March 2018, which although lower than the previous year, revealed a percentage of 31.7% compared to a European average of 15.6% in the same period (ISTAT 2018). And the percentage of young Italians Not in Education, Employment or Training (NEETs) in the same age group is the worst in Europe: one young Italian in four does not study and does not work, reaching 25.7% against a European average of 14.3% (e.g. the Netherlands does not exceed 5.3%) (Eurostat, 2017b).

The mobility choices of young Italians should also be examined in relation to the persistent centrality in Italy of interpersonal relationships as a primary source of economic and social success. Those who benefit from a close connection to the elites through kinship or friendship (in economic-financial, political or institutional, or in general terms) seem to have more chances to emerge. In contrast, those who do not enjoy these forms of support are forced into precarious employment in temporary and mostly underpaid jobs.

The negative aspect of the issue can be summarized in the loss of confidence among young Italians in the institutions that should guarantee their futures. To establish themselves as individuals and citizens, and to see their skills recognized, young people seem to be forced to leave their country, looking elsewhere for adequate opportunities for professional advancement. (For a reflection on the contemporary 'mobility discourse' among young people, see Cuzzocrea, 2019).

However, there is also a positive element to the situation. It concerns the strategies with which some young Italians react to a disadvantaged condition linked to national economic and social dynamics. These young people find the uncertainty in which they are forced to grow up intolerable; they believe that the lack of institutional recognition of their identities as educated and professionally capable young people is an offence to their personal dignity. They react by taking the construction of their biographical time into their own hands – at least as far as possible. Many of the young men and women who invest their professional energies elsewhere in the world are not only amongst the most educated but are also the most aware of their individual and collective rights and responsibilities. Furthermore, they are bearers of cosmopolitan cultures and transnational cultural attitudes (Leccardi, 2016). The latter are nourished by participatory practices able to link subjects, realities and cultures of different countries, traversing physical boundaries. Such practices, it should be emphasized, take shape in global space-time.

In his book *Transnationalism*, Steven Vertovec (2009) rightly points out that this term has gradually accrued a number of different meanings over recent decades. Yet despite this plurality, all the interpretations of the term refer to processes related to the dynamics of contemporary globalization. Namely, the physical and virtual crossing of national borders by increasingly mobile subjects, the changing experiences and cultures that accompany them, and the new subjectivities that take shape and come to the fore as a result of these movements. Mobility flows have undoubtedly played a crucial role in the development of transnationalism. Another key factor in its growth is the use of information and communication technology (ICT) and the disjunction among cultural practices, forms of identification and bonds with a specific physical space. What many individuals and groups now view as 'home' may be far removed in space and time from their physical dwellings. Young people, for example, habitually tend to construct representations and imaginaries that draw on symbols, information flow, cultural practices and networks of relationships that are territorially unbounded (Feixa *et al.*, 2016).

Their hybrid identities bear the mark of this global vision. More generally, it can be said that the intersection of a multiplicity of differences – gender, ethnic, religious and cultural – in a global scenario of increased mobility, and in the context of a daily life that is increasingly globalized, lays the foundations for the development of a 'nomadic subjectivity' (Braidotti, 2011). Fragmented and built around a variety of aspects with no hierarchical order, these subjectivities, particularly in the world of youth, appear to be intertwined with the ability to combine the global and the local.

In short, these young Italians seem able to transform the obstacles that they encounter in their relationship with work into a resource for action (Cuzzocrea and Mandich, 2016). The strongly individualized imprint of their socialization, in conjunction with an uncertain vision of the future, pushes them towards a form of 'reflexive individualization' (Elliott and Lemert, 2006). On this basis, the imperative choice of exercising control over biographical time is expressed mostly through a work of 'subjectivation' (Wiewiorka, 2012; Pleyers, 2016). It is a matter of constituting oneself and one's own choices not only as a principle of resistance to external impositions but also as the ultimate meaning of one's own unique, non-commensurable 'singularity' (Martuccelli, 2010). This happens against the background of a social time characterized by growing speed, which forces people to be flexible in decisions, and to 'seize the moment' when it arises.

9.5 Conclusion

In the difficult social climate of contemporary Italy, a significant proportion of young people, many of whom are highly educated and equipped with professional skills, look outside the country in their efforts to shape their futures and control their biographical time (Assirelli *et al.*, 2018). These young people are highly individualized, well acquainted with uncertainty and eager to experiment with new strategies for constructing their futures despite this uncertainty.

These observations chime with the resilience and adaptability observed amongst some young people in several chapters of this collection. In fact, it is important to consider the direct link between individualization and the 'need for future'. The higher the level of individualization, the stronger this need. The paradox lies in the fact that a high-speed society impoverishes the very idea of a future and hinders the potential to create a direct link between what is possible and what is real. To overcome this paradox, young Italians search for their future in a transnational context, and in a temporal scenario in which the pressure of social speed can be transformed into a choice for action. It is here that 'singularity' comes to the fore. Here, singularity can be dealt with as a positive expression of oneself, as a form of uniqueness and a personalized search for recognition.

In analysing this connection, what must be underlined is the splitting of two central dimensions of young people's biographies: independence and individualization. While independence, especially with regard to economic independence, is only partial and imperfect, individualization is, on the contrary, increasingly strong. Existential plans on a medium to long term, as modernity taught us to consider, seemed to be able to intertwine these two dimensions. This is no longer the case. Italian young people are increasingly individualized and progressively less autonomous. For example, it is rather difficult for most of them to renounce the protection of the family. This specific contradiction is powered by contemporary Italian economic and political uncertainty. Within the European scenario, the populistic Italian government established in 2018 is contributing significantly to creating it. Due to this set of difficult conditions, young Italians' mobility strategies aimed at reconquering the future must be recognized as an expression of strategic intelligence and analysed as a proactive approach in tune with our *zeitgeist*.

References

Adam, B. (1995). *Timewatch: The Social Analysis of Time*. Cambridge: Polity.

Agamben, G. (2006). *Infancy and History: On the Destruction of Experience*. London and New York: Verso Books.

Assirelli, G., Barone, C. and Recchi, E. (2018). "You Better Move On": Determinants and labor market outcomes of graduate migration from Italy. *International Migration Review*. Available at: http://hdl.handle.net/1814/53444.

Beck, U. and Beck-Gernsheim, E. (2002). *Individualization: Institutionalized Individualism and Its Social and Political Consequences*. London: Sage.

Berger, P.L., Berger, B. and Kellner, H. (1973). *The Homeless Mind: Modernization and Consciousness*. New York: Random House.

Boutinet, J.-P. (1990). *Anthropologie du projet*. Paris: Presses Universitaires de France.

Braidotti, R. (2011). *Nomadic Subjects*. New York: Columbia University Press.

Cuzzocrea, V. (2019). Youth, peripherality and the mobility discourse. In: Duggan, S., Finn, K., Gagnon, J., Gray, E. and Kelly, P. (eds) *Social Justice in Times of Crisis and Hope: Young People, Wellbeing and the Politics of Education*. Bern: Peter Lang, 129–141.

Cuzzocrea, V. and Mandich, G. (2016). Narratives of the future: Imagined mobilities as forms of youth agency? *Journal of Youth Studies*, 19(4), 552–567.

Durkheim, E. (1912/1968). *The Elementary Forms of the Religious Life*. London: George Allen and Unwin.

Elliott, A. (2016). *Identity Troubles: An Introduction*. London and New York: Routledge.

Elliott, A. and Lemert, C. (2006). *The New Individualism: The Emotional Costs of Globalization*. London and New York: Routledge.

Elliott, A. and Hsu, E.L. (2016). Accelerated identity: Five theses on the self. In: Elliott, A. (ed) *Identity Troubles: An Introduction*. London and New York: Routledge.

Elliott, A. and Urry, J. (2010). *Mobile Lives*. London and New York: Routledge.

Eurostat. (2017a). Share of young adults aged 18–34 living with their parents by age and sex – EU-SILC survey. Available at: http://ec.europa.eu/eurostat/en/web/products-datasets/-/ILC_LVPS08.

Eurostat. (2017b). Statistics on young people neither in employment nor in education or training. Available at: http://ec.europa.eu/eurostat/statistics-explained/index.php/Statistics_on_young_people_neither_in_employment_nor_in_education_or_training.

Feixa, C., Leccardi, C. and Nilan, P. (eds) (2016). *Youth, Space and Time: Agoras and Chronotopes in the Global City*. Leiden and Boston: Brill.

Fondazione Migrantes. (2017). *Rapporto Italiani nel mondo*. Cinisello Balsamo, MI: Tau Editrice.

Furlong, A. (ed) (2009). *Handbook of Youth and Young Adulthood: New Perspectives and Agendas*. London and New York: Routledge.

Heinz, W.R., Weymann, A. and Huinik, J. (eds) (2009). *The Life Course Reader: Individual and Societies across Time*. Chicago: The University of Chicago Press.

Hessel, S. (2010). *Indignez-vous!* Montpellier: Indigène Éditions.

Honneth, A. (1995). *The Struggle for Recognition: The Moral Grammar of Social Conflicts*. Cambridge: Polity Press.

ISTAT (National Institute of Statistics). (2018). Nota trimestrale sulle tendenze all'occupazione, IV trimestre 2017. Available at: https://www.istat.it/it/files/2018/03/NotaTrimOccupazione-IV_2017.pdf.

Istituto Giuseppe Toniolo. (2018). *La condizione giovanile in Italia: Rapporto Giovani 2018*. Bologna: Il Mulino.

Kerby, A.P. (1991). *Narrative and the Self.* Bloomington, IN: Indiana University Press.

Koselleck, R. (2004). *Futures Past: On the Semantics of Historical Time*. New York: Columbia University Press.

Leccardi, C. (2016). Young transnationalists (and cosmopolitan). Foreword. In: Feixa, C., Leccardi, C. and Nilan, P. (eds) *Youth, Space and Time: Agoras and Chronotopes in the Global City*. Leiden and Boston: Brill.

Leccardi, C. (2017). The recession, young people, and their relationship with the future. In: Schoon, I. and Bynner, J. (eds) *Young People's Development and the Great Recession: Uncertain Transitions and Precarious Futures*. Cambridge: Cambridge University Press.

Leitner, H. (1982). *Lebenslauf und Identität. Die kulturelle Konstruktion von Zeit in der Biographie*. Frankfurt a.M.: Suhrkamp.

Lübbe, H. (2009). The contraction of the present. In: Rosa, H. and Scheurman, W.E. (eds) *High-Speed Society: Social Acceleration, Power, and Modernity*. University Park, PA: The Pennsylvania State University.

Martuccelli, D. (2006). *Forgé par l'épreuve*. Paris: Armand Collin.

Martuccelli, D. (2010). *La société singulariste*. Paris: Armand Collin.

Pleyers, G. (2016). De la subjectivation à l'action. Le cas des jeunes alter-activistes. In: Pleyers, G. and Capitaine, B. (eds) *Mouvements sociaux. Quand le sujet deviant acteur*. Paris: Maison des Sciences de l'Homme.

Pleyers, G. and Capitaine, B. (2016). *Mouvements sociaux. Quand le sujet deviant acteur*. Paris: Maison des Sciences de l'Homme.

Privitera, W. (2002). Incertezza e individualizzazione. In: Rampazi, M. (ed) *L'incertezza quotidiana. Politica, lavoro, relazioni nella società del rischio*. Milano: Guerini.

Rosa, H. (2010). *Alienation and Acceleration: Towards a Critical Theory of Late-Modern Temporality*. Copenhagen: Nordic Summer University Press.

Rosa, H. (2013). *Social Acceleration: A New Theory of Modernity*. New York: Columbia University Press.

Rosa, H. and Scheurman, W.E. (eds) (2009). *High-Speed Society: Social Acceleration, Power, and Modernity*. University Park, PA: The Pennsylvania State University.

Thrift, N. (2006). Re-inventing invention: New tendencies in capitalist commodification. *Economy and Society*, 2, 279–306.

Vertovec, S. (2009). *Transnationalism*. London and New York: Routledge.

Weber, M. (1919/1946). Science as a vocation, In: Gerth, H.H. and Wright Mills, C. (eds) *From Max Weber: Essays in Sociology*. Oxford: Oxford University Press.

White, R, Wyn, J. and Robards, B. (2017). *Youth & Society*. Oxford: Oxford University Press.

Wiewiorka, M. (2012). Du concept de sujet à celui de subjectivation/dé-subjectivation. Working Paper 16. Paris: Fondation Maison des Sciences de l'Homme.

Woodman, D. and Bennett, A. (eds) (2015). *Youth Cultures, Transitions, and Generations: Bridging the Gap in Youth Research*. London: Palgrave Macmillan.

Wright Mills, C. (1959). *The Sociological Imagination*. Oxford: Oxford University Press.

Wyn, J. and White, R.D. (1997). *Rethinking Youth*. Crows Nest: Allen & Unwin.

Zerubavel, E. (1981). *Hidden Rhythms: Schedules and Calendars in Social Life*. Chicago: University of Chicago Press.

Chapter 10

Pathways towards adulthood in times of crisis

Reflexivity, resources and agency among young Neapolitans

Antonella Spanò and Markieta Domecka

10.1 Introduction

This chapter illustrates the pathways towards adulthood for young people living in a metropolitan area of Southern Italy. It is a context of very high unemployment, especially in case of young people, with irregular work and insufficient institutional support. This is also a context that has been particularly affected by the recent economic crisis. We understand adulthood as a life stage when economic independence and a definition of the occupational role have been established. In the conditions where processes of individualization and destandardization have dismantled pathways to adulthood and the crisis has reduced work opportunities, young people are deeply affected by precariousness and uncertainty. Not all of them, however, are equally disoriented or unarmed while facing the fluidity and the constraints of contemporary society. Reflexivity, in fact, seen as the capacity to focus on one's own capacities, possibilities and life course (O'Connor, 2014), turns out to be a crucial resource. Today more than ever this constitutes a key tool to find one's own way to adulthood.

Not all social settings and interactional contexts are equally stimulating for reflexive development. However, differences in the ability to navigate uncertainty and life-management skills are not necessarily class based (Furlong *et al.*, 2011). This means that the paths young people follow differ along lines that do not precisely reflect the class structure. As Farrugia (2013: 686) puts it, 'reflexivity is an important aspect of young people's identities which varies both between and within broad class groupings'. However, focusing on reflexivity does not imply denying the role played by structural factors in shaping young people's destinies. Here we follow the argument put forward by Farrugia (2013), which is that the analysis of different forms of reflexivity is an important way of understanding the new inequalities that have emerged. Also as Threadgold (2011) asserts, reflexivity becomes the medium by which the class is produced and reproduced now. Here, we do not conflate reflexivity with agency, as we recognize that even with high levels of reflexivity, 'successfully fulfilling the trajectory of the self still requires access to socioeconomic resources and opportunities' (Threadgold and Nilan, 2009: 54). In circumstances of structural constraints and a lack of resources, reflection cannot immediately be translated into action. In other words, the positions individuals occupy within power hierarchies do not necessarily affect how reflexive they become, but they do affect their level of agency.

Reflexivity, objectified resources and agency define new axes of inequalities experienced by young people in building an adult life. Importantly, young people are not homogeneously reflexive, and those who are reflexive do not necessarily gain much advantage from this in their lives (Farrugia, 2013), as there are always structural opportunities and constraints at play. Addressing the issue of inequality, an issue that has been and must remain the core of youth studies, thus means analysing the conditions in which reflexivity is generated and agency put into practice. This is exactly the aim of this chapter, empirically based on 50 autobiographical narrative interviews conducted with young people in the Naples area.

In the following sections, the conditions of young people living in the context of Southern Italy are first sketched out, then class and gender issues are outlined. Finally, by focusing on four case studies, the interplay of reflexivity, resources and agency is discussed in order to show how reflexivity and agency become the new axis of inequality reproduction.

10.2 Becoming an adult in Southern Italy

Many comparative studies have shown how the paths followed by young people moving towards adulthood vary across countries according to the structure of the labour market, educational system and welfare regime (Walther, 2006), as well as family culture (Cuzzocrea, 2011). Van de Velde (2011), in her study on different European countries, highlights how the trajectories followed, but also the meaning young people give to their experiences and their definitions of adulthood are socially constructed. In the Mediterranean model, 'youth is characterized by the logic of waiting at home for the necessary conditions for constructing a new home: stable job, marriage, and buying an apartment in the context of a real estate market not inclined towards renting' (Van de Velde, 2011: 225). Elements that have been identified as mutually reinforcing and contributing to the deceleration of young people's independence include: the selective nature of unemployment, which in Italy disproportionately affects young people and women; the theory-oriented educational system, which provides neither a strong sense of orientation nor a clear link between school and the labour market (Banca d'Italia, 2012; OECD, 2014); the dualistic, particularistic and familistic character of the Southern European welfare model (Ferrera, 1996), which offers hardly any support for the young unemployed or precariously employed, and cultural norms, which enhance family ties and intergenerational solidarity.

The characteristics of the national institutional context also affect the ability to respond to globalization processes (Blossfeld *et al.*, 2012). In Italy there has been a precarization rather than a flexibilization of work. Moreover, the welfare system has proved to be completely incapable of overcoming its distortions, protecting against new risks, and strengthening support towards the social groups most affected by the post-Fordist transition: women and young people (Ferrera *et al.*, 2012). In the light of the crisis, the Italian welfare state was unable to correct the penalization of these populations, particularly in the field of employment policies (Gualmini and Rizza, 2013).

The territorial dualism in Italy makes the South particularly disadvantaged, as discussed in Chapter 11 of this collection. Not only is it historically character-ized by a lack of employment opportunities and high structural unemployment but also a greater shortage of welfare provision (Ascoli, 2011). Employment ser-vices are especially lacking in the South, precisely where they are most needed (ISFOL, 2016). Due to all these factors, the situation of Southern Italy in this time of crisis has become severe, especially for young people. As noted in previous chapters of this collection, youth unemployment (aged 18–29) in 2015 reached 43% in the South and was even higher for the 15–24-year-old group, which sat at 54%. The situation for young women is even more dramatic: in 2015 the unem-ployment rate for young adult women (aged 25–34) in the South was 33%, and 58% for 15–24-year-olds (ISTAT, 2015). In sum, the youth situation in the South is a structural problem that has been further aggravated by the crisis.

The structural weakness of the Southern context has a clear impact on the life conditions of young people. Their narratives present a scenario of great economic and existential fragility. Unskilled, fragmented jobs, 'fake part-time' (when one works full-time but is paid only a half wage), irregular work and experiences of unemployment are the norm rather than the exception, and very closely resemble the 'Precariat' described by Standing (2011). Although our qualitative sample is not statistically representative, the picture that emerges accurately depicts the occupational situation of youth in Southern Italy. Among the 50 young people interviewed for this research, there were only two cases of regular employment. The other cases of employment included non-standard contracts, part-time con-tracts, temporary contracts, apprenticeships (15) or no contract at all (9). Among those engaged in self-employment (11), we found craftsmen, professionals and small-business owners. Finally, some participants (5) worked in family business and others (8) were unemployed.

In many cases, conditions of exploitation emerged. These were accepted according to a logic of adaptation to the scarce opportunities in the local market. The exploitation also affected the more qualified young people, who accepted poor working conditions due to the fear that any manifested rigidity would lead to job loss. Remuneration was extremely low for all; consequently, most of the interview-ees still lived with their parents. All the secondary school leavers, who were the youngest of our participants, lived with their family of origin. Also among the university graduates, half still lived with their family, and often even when they lived on their own, they were supported financially by their parents (cf. Cairns *et al.*, 2014). The crucial role played by the family, which has always been impor-tant in Italy and particularly in the South, seemed to be further strengthened by the precarious nature of employment and by the crisis. At the same time, the collected narratives suggest a change in young people's understandings of autonomization, which now does not necessarily mean leaving the family of origin, and shows an interdependence between parents and their children (Wyn *et al.*, 2012), testified by the reversal of roles in case of contingencies, such as a father's job loss.

10.3 Class, gender and their intersections

The crisis seems to have led to a certain uniformization of young people's living conditions, as we saw a generalized situation of uncertainty, precariousness and mistrust. Still, class and gender differences[1] were far from being weakened, as was shown by analysing both the objective living situations of the young people and the ways they experienced them subjectively. Among less-educated young people, all from working-class families, precarious or irregular jobs, conditions of exploitation, and a lack of perspective for the future are more widespread. Moreover, the pathways followed by these young people – which included fragmented schooling, recurrent unemployment and changes in job – appeared much closer to the non-linear model of transition (Furlong *et al.*, 2006; Heinz, 2009) than those of more privileged youth. Difficulty in 'finding a place' both at school and on the labour market is not new for working class young people, especially for those less educated. What has changed in the post-Fordist system is that the old mechanisms of integration into the labour market (the public administration, which for decades in Southern Italy worked as a 'sponge' against unemployment and self-employment after a long apprenticeship) ceased to be effective (Spanò, 2001).

The situation of university graduates was more variegated. Among these, we found the only two cases of standard work (both were graduates in 'strong' disciplines: statistical and managerial economics) and some cases of relatively well-established professional or business activities, but also temporary jobs, overeducation and some cases of unemployment. This can be explained by the greater heterogeneity of the social backgrounds of graduates: they do not always come from families equipped with capital (economic, cultural and social) capable of supporting their children in entering the labour market. In fact, with the transformation of higher education from an elite to a mass system, tertiary students became a more diverse group and graduation has lost its predictive value (Furlong and Cartmel, 2009). In other words, it is not the degree but the social background that makes the difference.

Also gender plays a role, but it reveals its significance through intersectionality with social positioning (Woodman and Wyn, 2015). Young female graduates coming from lower backgrounds were the only ones working with fake part-time contracts or in family businesses without a real salary. In some cases, they also withdrew from the labour market because of discouragement. On the contrary, among the female graduates of higher classes, there seemed to be no gender disadvantages experienced.

Even the meaning of work appeared to differ across classes. For young people from higher classes, work was the central aspect of their project of constructing a satisfying life. This project included a work–life balance. Both higher-class men and women claimed their right to manage their time, and it was considered an essential resource. Unlike lower-class youth, they placed a high value on having control over time, which confirms that having free time for relationships (social capital), and various kinds of experiences (cultural capital) now represents a new way of reproducing social inequality (Woodman, 2012). Also, the expectation of finding in work a source of personal fulfilment and self-expression was shared by young men and women of higher classes. Although aware of the need to earn in order to achieve economic independence, these young people were not willing to forgo expressive aspects of work. In fact, there were cases where participants voluntarily left their job when it was considered unsatisfactory due to inconsistency with the qualifications acquired, scarce autonomy, repetitiveness or an unpleasant working environment. Moreover, even if interested in continuity of work, these young people were not looking for the kind of full-time, full-life jobs by many considered, uncreative and unrewarding.

Finally, higher-class young people commonly experienced temporary internal or external migration for study or work and/or cohabitation with a partner, and subsequent return to the family home. In fact, even housing transitions seemed to have a class connotation: while lower-class young people (both school leavers and graduates) were still living in the parental home (except in two cases) and planned to leave only after marriage, among the higher-class graduates we found a more complex situation (singles, cohabitation with a partner, living with friends, cohabitation with spouse, pendulum movements between one's own and family home). This proliferation of living arrangements was similarly observed in Chapter 12 of this book, in which the authors note that many young people (especially those from more affluent families) take an experimental attitude towards leaving home. Choosing, trying, giving oneself a second or a third chance, not giving up on one's own aspirations seem to be a privilege of more affluent youth. Only for these young people the idea of a choice biography (du Bois, 1995) seemed to be appropriate. In contrast, for the less privileged, the complexity of the life course 'may actually signify a lack of choice and a vulnerability to the adverse effects of flexible labour markets' (Furlong *et al.*, 2006: 227).

It is, once again, family background rather than the level of qualification that makes the difference. In fact, while more qualified young people coming from affluent families did not want to abandon their aspirations in the name of settling for whatever job is available, those coming from working-class backgrounds appeared much more inclined to give up their expectations in name of stability and of economic autonomy. This turns out to be the most pressing need for young people who cannot rely on family support. The following cases clearly show the process through which the aspirations of less-privileged youth decline: the case of a young man who graduated in biology with honours, who worked in an analytical laboratory under exploitative conditions, and at the time of the interview was applying for a two-year apprenticeship in a call centre in order to improve his income and obtain greater stability; or that of a young woman who had graduated from a law school, when interviewed made a living by writing theses and working in the black economy as a tutor in a long-distance teaching university, who was looking for a job as a shop assistant in order to have a stable income.

For university graduates from the lower class, the need to become economically independent is a priority, meaning that their desire for self-realization and finding a job congruent with their qualifications took secondary importance. For school graduates from working-class backgrounds, these aspirations represent a true luxury. For both women and men in this latter group, work was a central aspect of life mainly related to instrumental meaning. Coming from troubled educational pathways that have provided neither professional skills nor the basis for the construction of a professional identity, and living in families burdened by economic difficulties, they see employment as a means by which to achieve a 'normal' life, rather than to realize expectations like self-expression, satisfaction or personal fulfilment. Even those who after achieving a diploma nurtured some ambitions ended up renouncing them, pushed by both the will not to be a burden on their families and the increased perception of employment difficulties following the crisis.

Even perceptions of the crisis were influenced by social background. Early socialization in job insecurity and the ways of coping with it due to structural unemployment and widespread poverty that characterized the Southern context also before the crisis seems to have led to a kind of 'normalization' of the crisis. As such, it was not generally experienced as a traumatic event. However, in views regarding the effects of the crisis, class-based differences emerge. In fact, if lower-class young people saw only the negative effects of the economic crisis, those from higher classes often attributed a cathartic effect to the crisis: reaching the bottom in order to revive and rediscover the 'real' values in life. The former, pressed by immediate needs, had a view limited to the present. Whereas, the latter have a more temporally extended vision, which lead them to see in the crisis a long-term process of renovation, which concerns both people (rediscovering the true values of life) and society (overcoming capitalist consumerism, reducing inequalities, strengthening ecological values, etc.).

It is also worth noting that if among higher-class young people gender differences in expectations and meaning of work seem to have been attenuated, amongst those from lower classes, differences in subjectivity between young men and women were more visible. For lower-class young men, in fact, work was the focus of their life, as well as their main concern, and what they sought in a job was primarily stability (there are many who had attempted to join the army or the police hoping to find a stable job). Lower-class females, on the other hand, were interested in developing a model of womanhood certainly different from that of their mothers, as they saw work as an integral part of their biographies, but without questioning the primacy of their domestic roles. In other words, unlike what was found among young people of the higher classes, here the traditional division that attributes men the role of breadwinner and women that of caregiver is still present.

10.4 Reflexivity, resources and agency

Deep structural changes in education and in the labour market result in a situation where young people are faced with the need for reflexivity (Furlong *et al.*, 2006; Farrugia, 2013; O'Connor, 2015) and constant negotiation of the possibilities and impossibilities of the social world. The difficulty of moving in an uncertain context is reflected already in the school paths shaped by a lack of guidance, random decisions and trial-and-error strategies (Wyn and Dwyer, 1999), changes of direction and dropping out. It is not only a question of the lack of linearity in the objective sense (namely, trajectories marked by breaks, divergences or backtracking, Furlong *et al.*, 2006; Heinz, 2009), but it is also the lack of a subjective sense of direction. First work experiences whilst at school and university are often marked by a similar type of contingency: these are diverse small jobs, related neither to each other nor any defined occupational path. However, in this difficult structural context, restricting the time dimension to the present and thus hindering planning, not all young people are disoriented and unable to act strategically. We have examples of young women and men of all social backgrounds who managed to define their educational and occupational projects and invested in them all the resources they had at their disposal. These were lower-class, young adults who had developed their occupational identities through early socialization of working in micro family businesses, through vocational education and learning-by-doing. These were also young people of higher-class backgrounds who had invested in traditional professions (such as law and engineering) and new sectors such as e-commerce, organic agriculture and cooperative work. The difference between the disoriented ones and those capable of defining their life projects cannot be explained only by the amount and type of objective capitals at hand, but also by their subjective resources. The subjective sense of direction, self-understanding, identity construction, orientation and planning are developed through reflexivity, a continuous dialogue people engage in with themselves and with significant others.

We see reflexivity as the type of resource of a higher order central for one's biographical and occupational development. It is the capacity to recognize one's talents and limitations, which is crucial for defining one's life projects. Reflexivity is the ability to mobilize all resources at hand and applying them in innovative ways in order to pursue one's objectives. In an uncertain world, reflexivity is a necessary resource for its navigation (Heinz, 2009), as it allows one to spot opportunities and obstacles, making use of the former and avoiding the latter. Contemporary conditions mean that young people are increasingly confronted with situations that compel them to rethink themselves and their place in the world.

Not all social settings and interactional contexts, however, are equally stimulating for reflexive development. By analysing the life stories of young Neapolitans, we saw that some of them were encouraged to think about their life from early childhood onwards, to reflect and discuss before making decisions and to rethink all they did in relation to the changing context. Others receive less encouragement to reflect. Importantly, this distinction does not follow class or gender inequalities, as we see that reflexivity can be developed both in the lower- and higher-class contexts, irrespective of gender. Indeed, apart from socialization, there were also life experiences and encounters with significant others that had real effects on young people's self-reflection: when finding themselves in new situations or facing unexpected events, they needed to think about what it all meant and what should be done about it. In fact, the role of reflexivity is particularly important when the routine ways of acting are interrupted. Thus, the notion of reflexivity allows us to analyse the differences within seemingly similar social categories, as we found that young people from comparable class backgrounds frequently developed different kinds and degrees of reflexivity.

Reflexivity, however, was not automatically translated into agency, and this is where the impact of social class and gender became evident. Agency required objectified resources in the form of social, economic and cultural capital. We understand agency as the ability of purposive action aimed at adapting one's life to the external environment or at changing the environment in accordance with one's life projects. We do not conflate it with reflexivity, as we recognize that it is possible to reflect (work on one's life experiences in relation to one's context) without having the objective possibility of taking action due to structural constraints and lack of resources needed to confront them. Our argument here is that the location of individuals within hierarchies of power does not necessarily affect how reflexive they may become, but it does affect the amount of resources (thus the level of agency) available to them.

Reflexivity, resources and agency therefore defined new axes of inequalities experienced by young people in the sense of uneven opportunities available to them for constructing an adult life. Young people are not homogeneously reflexive, and reflexivity cannot be directly translated in agency. Still, the effects of a low level of reflexivity varied across backgrounds: while in the higher classes, distortions in reflexivity development can be amortized by family resources and constant family investment, in lower classes they have more severe consequences.

10.5 The case studies

Drawing on the analysis of young people's life histories, we will now discuss four case studies that illustrate the ways in which reflexivity operates in lower- and higher-class contexts and how it gets transformed (and how it does not) into agency. The empirical material, in the form of 50 autobiographical narrative interviews, was collected in a research project[2] carried out in the Naples area from summer 2013 to spring 2014. The sampling strategy was directed by the aim of analysing the paths of young people of different social backgrounds. The study deliberately included 'ordinary' young people, often neglected in youth research (Woodman, 2013), which tends to be more interested in success or failure cases. Even if educational attainment is no longer predictive of young people's destinies, it was chosen as a proxy of social positioning; in fact, all interviewees were repositioned in this regard after the analysis of their narratives. The sample consisted of 26 young women and 24 young men, 32 with a high level of education (university degree or higher) and 18 with a lower level of education (secondary school diploma or lower), all living in Naples and the surrounding areas. Ages varied according to their educational attainment: secondary school leavers and dropouts were between 21 and 24 years of age and university graduates were between 28 and 34. The choice of differentiating age groups according to the education level is due to the aim of comparing young people who left the education system in the same period (2008–2010), that is when the effects of crisis were already tangible. The use of the biographical method was aimed at giving priority to young people's voices in order to grasp the richness of their experiences and to bring out not only their paths but also their understandings and subjectivities.

The goal was to add to the wider literature on how reflexivity makes a difference when other types of resources cannot be mobilized (as in the case of the lower-class participants) and how this, on its own, cannot cancel class inequalities. We focus first on two young men of working-class backgrounds, of whom one had managed to define his life project and follow it with great determination, bringing him a certain level of autonomy and stability; and the other, who was lost in the fragmented and precarious labour market, the impact of which he was unable to counterbalance neither with his material nor his reflexive resources.

Michele was 23 and came from a Neapolitan neighbourhood strongly marked by the presence of organized crime. His father worked as a cook and his mother as a housewife. His whole narrative was constructed around the support, guidance and a good example of his family. His is an example of a project of upward mobility, as Michele's family had invested heavily in his education. The choice of secondary school was the result of the shared family plan: Michele was sent to a hotel and catering school because he was meant to follow in the footsteps of his father. During school he realized, however, that he was not made for working as a chef. Work for him was not supposed to be only a means of income but also a source of fulfilment. After graduating, he took a moratorium period, 'a gap year', in order to give himself the time to reflect on what he wanted to do with his life. His decision was supported by his family, which brings us to the point that reflexivity in some contexts may be developed more easily than in others. Since childhood, Michele loved drawing and when he started reflecting on how he could convert his passion into a job opportunity, tattooing came to his mind. Thanks to his family's social network, he found a tattoo artist available to offer a free year of apprenticeship, which again required the economic support of his family. Michele prepared the drawings and practiced tattoos first on pork skin and then on his friends. Being highly motivated, he quickly learned and soon started earning 'quite well'. After two years, again thanks to the help of his family (he received a loan from his relatives), Michele opened his own tattoo studio. He rented a small place in an elegant quarter of the city centre, refurbishing it, and starting from that point onwards had gone on to operate a successful business.

Carmelo was 27 and, similarly to Michele, came from a working-class family living in a poor neighbourhood. In his narrative, however, the family played a different role, illustrated by the fact that Carmelo avoided speaking about it. Another difference between the two young men was their school experiences. Carmelo's parents did not offer him any guidance or encouragement to continue his studies. At the age of 14, completely disoriented, Carmelo began studying at a hotel and catering school (the same as in case of Michele), but in his case, he took this route simply because he had followed his friends.

At his new school, he soon realized that he had made the wrong choice. Unsupported and unable to change direction, he found a new reference group – a circle of peers who would 'get into mischief'. Carmelo entered into the mindset of 'doing nothing', and after repeating a year twice, he dropped out of school with the feeling of being a 'complete failure'. He started working precariously as a waiter and a bartender. After 3 years, he decided to do a private recovery school in order to get his diploma as he believed that, 'a piece of paper makes you get ahead'. The new school had a completely different profile compared to the previous one and Carmelo graduated as a computer technician, although he admitted that he understood nothing of mathematics or computer science. He got a new job in a private post agency freshly opened by his friend: '…a job that doesn't give you any future, doesn't make you grow, doesn't bring you anywhere'. He worked in the black economy, underpaid. We contacted him a year later after the interview and saw that his situation remained unchanged. He had a dream of a permanent office job, 'with a desk and a computer', or his own business ('a restaurant, a bar or whatever'), but he still had not set in place any stepping-stones towards realizing it.

The cases of Michele and Carmelo show how behind the apparently similar conditions there can be very differently lives, and how reflexivity, stimulated through the guidance provided by significant others, can lead to self-orientation and projectuality. Michele's capacity to reflect on his own abilities and possibilities, together with his perseverance, confidence and mutually supportive social relations allowed him to navigate the particularly difficult structural context in which he lived. Carmelo, on the other hand, had paid a high price for his disorientation. Without support or guidance at home or at school, he had not found sufficient reflexive resources within himself in order to deal with the difficulties and navigate them successfully. His lack of objectified resources, his sense of failure and his fractured reflexivity could not be forged into agency, which made him resentful. He remained trapped in a cycle of underpaid and precarious jobs, unable to construct an alternative life project.

For people who come from the lower classes, where circumstances are characterized by limited objectified resources, reflexivity is the capacity that can make the difference between successful and unsuccessful navigation. For people of higher-class origins, to whom more capital is available, the role of reflexivity changes. It is no longer a matter of success or failure, as navigation is possible on the basis of objectified resources only. We will now present two cases, a young man and a young woman, equipped with comparable capital, and both apparently successful on their paths to adulthood, even though one of them was much less reflexive than the other.

Fabio was a 32-year-old man from an upper-middle-class background. Like many from the well-off families, he attended 'the best schools', and then studied economics at undergraduate and postgraduate level. Fabio encountered many difficulties during his studies and managed to graduate only due to his family's investment in private tuition. After Fabio's graduation, his family continued supporting him in his training, covering the cost of his master's programme, including the cost of living away from the family home. With his educational credentials, he accepted one of the two job offers received, only to quit soon after as his salary seemed to him very low compared to his aspirations.

In fact, Fabio had neither the need nor the desire to work because, as he admits, '[he]'ll never have economic problems'. Relying on family resources and following his sister's initiative, together they started a business, converting a family property into a bed & breakfast. In theory, he worked on the business, but in reality it was managed by his sister whilst he spent his time playing basketball and poker. Fabio had not made any definite plans for his future. Overprotected by his family, pushing him towards a path deemed appropriate for an upper-middle-class young man, he lacked the conditions for the development of reflexivity and responsibility. His is an example of an 'apparent transition'; objectively, Fabio may seem to have moved towards an adult life, but subjectively he remained his 'family's son', entirely dependent on inherited resources.

Seemingly similar, but in fact very different, was the case of 30-year-old Gisella, born to a middle-class family. The downward mobility of her parents, compared to her 'very important grandfather', was Gisella's motivation for taking on the mission of family social advancement. Her family's dynamics and her own experiences (a motorbike accident and her parents' separation) helped Gisella to grow up quickly and become, prematurely, a responsible adult. After a secondary school (of classical profile) she enrolled in law and her dream, shared with her parents, was to become a judge. After graduation, she began a preparatory course for the judicial examinations, but before the results were published she received a job offer from a law firm. She accepted it, viewing it as a tangible opportunity to become autonomous. A year into her job, when she discovered she had passed the first step of judicial examinations, she faced a difficult choice between this concrete career opportunity (work as a lawyer) and pursuing her dream, which might never come to fruition (the career as a judge). She decided to keep her job and to continue working within administrative law, although she knew that in doing so she had betrayed her overall project and her parents' expectations.

When interviewed, Gisella fully identified with her highly absorbing work. It was not by chance that the opening phrase of her main narrative was the following: 'Let's start from the fact that I am a lawyer, I am a lawyer by choice but also a bit by the contingencies of life because I had to give up my dream of becoming a judge'. The reflexivity of Gisella, in the sense of her self-analysis, orientation and projectuality, was very much stimulated by her painful experiences, in particular, the year of inactivity following her accident and by the family cultural capital offering her a clear motivation to succeed in life. She was capable not only of setting her own objectives, but also of weighing them up in the light of concrete opportunities offered by the context she lived in.

10.6 Conclusions

Reflexivity, understood here as biographical resource and a form of cultural capital (Threadgold, 2011), can be compared to a language: everyone uses it but some have the skills and resources to use it better than others (Threadgold and Nilan, 2009). On its own, without the accompaniment of structural resources, reflexivity cannot overcome class inequalities. The role of reflexivity changes according to class-dependent resources young people have at their disposal. For young people from higher classes, it may be enough to follow the family path simply by making use of family capital; whereas for youth from lower classes, the strategic use of limited resources requires significant reflexive effort. Reflexive life management (Furlong *et al.*, 2011) is thus a necessary condition for the mobilization of all possible resources and their conversion according to a biographical project developed in close relation to the opportunities and constraints defined by the structural context. This is especially true in the case of lower-class young people without educational credentials. If they are not supported in the development of their reflexive skills, their attempts to deal with structural insecurity is a day-to-day struggle, which may never translate into agency enabling long-term planning.

We agree with the argument of Threadgold (2011), according to whom people can be infinitely reflexive, but if they cannot put their choices into action, reflexivity becomes an intrinsic part of the experience of inequality (Threadgold, 2011). We found examples of highly reflexive university graduates who had been unable to find adequate jobs due to the lack of structural opportunities. In a situation where there are no real choices or where the possibilies of achieving one's choices are unequal (Threadgold and Nilan, 2009), reflexivity is no longer a life-changing resource. Rather, it is a source of suffering, as young people can be aware of the existing constraints but have little ability to alter their realities (O'Connor, 2015). Biographical research shows the importance of lived experiences of young people in diverse contexts for the understanding of different ways reflexivity takes and the impact it has on individual lives. The analysis of autobiographical narratives allows us to develop a more nuanced understanding of class, going beyond educational attainment and occupation as primary proxies. It remains true that class is defined by the amount and type of objectified resources at hand, but young people's journeys and their reflexive negotiation and interpretation of their experiences may be a poor reflection of their objective positioning within social structures (Furlong *et al.*, 2011). Through the reconstruction of biographical processes and subject positionings, it is possible to explain how agency is constructed as a result of the interplay between individual reflexivity, objectified resources and structural opportunities and constraints (Ruokonen-Engler and Siouti, 2016). The structural fragmentation and the lack of institutional support for young people, on the one hand, contribute to feelings of loneliness and disorientation while facing their biographical turning points. On the other hand, they reinforce the role played by family and its resources. Without a process of defamilialization and institutional development, reflexivity, resources and agency will continue defining the axes of inequalities experienced by young people in the sense of uneven opportunities available to them for successful navigation and construction of an adult life. The reflexive development of life-management skills by young people should very much be supported, but it is only one side of the coin. The other are the structural opportunities that are equally important in the process of adult life construction.

Notes

1 Although not discussed in this chapter, our research has shown that also the employment status, the nationality and the territorial context affect young people's career paths and aspirations (Spanò, 2017).
2 The project Pratiche sostenibili di vita quotidiana nel contesto della crisi: lavoro, consumi, partecipazione [Sustainable everyday practices in the context of crisis in Italy: toward the integration of work, consumption and participation] was funded by the Ministry of Education, University and Research. The sample also included 28 interviews with young people of foreign origin that are not analysed here. For the findings concerning the foreign origins of young people, see Spanò (2015).

References

Ascoli, U. (ed) (2011). Il welfare in Italia [The Welfare in Italy]. Bologna: Il Mulino.
Banca d'Italia. (2012). Il capitale umano per la crescita economica [Human capital for the economic growth]. Questioni di Economia e Finanza, 122 (April).
Blossfeld, H.P., Buchholz, S., Hofäcker, D. and Bertolini, S. (2012). Selective flexibilization and deregulation of the labor market: The answer of Continental and Southern Europe. Stato e Mercato, 3, 363–390.
Cairns, D., Growiec, K. and de Almeida Alves, N. (2014). Another 'Missing Middle'? The marginalised majority of tertiary-educated youth in Portugal during the economic crisis. Journal of Youth Studies, 17(8), 1046–1060.
Cuzzocrea, V. (2011). Squeezing or blurring: Young adulthood in the career strategies of professionals based in Italy and England. Journal of Youth Studies, 14(6), 657–674.
du Bois, R.M. (1995). Future orientations of Dutch Youth: The emergence of a choice biography. In: Cavalli, A. and Galland, O. (eds) Youth in Europe. London: Pinter, 201–222.
Farrugia, D. (2013). Young people and structural inequality: Beyond the middle ground. Journal of Youth Studies, 16(5), 679–693.
Ferrera, M. (1996). Il modello sud-europeo di welfare state [The South-European model of welfare state]. Rivista italiana di scienza politica, 1, 67–101.

Ferrera, M., Fargion, V. and Jessoula, M. (2012). *Alle radici del welfare all'italiana. Origini e futuro di un modello sociale squilibrato.* Venezia: Marsilio.

Furlong, A. and Cartmel, F. (2009). *Higher Education and Social Justice.* Buckingham: Open University Press.

Furlong, A., Cartmel, F. and Biggart, A. (2006). Choice biographies and transitional linearity: Re-conceptualising modern youth transitions. *Revista de Sociologia,* 79, 225–239.

Furlong, A., Woodman, D. and Wyn, J. (2011). Changing times, changing perspectives: Reconciling transition and cultural perspectives on youth and young adulthood. *Journal of Sociology,* 47, 355–370.

Gualmini, E. and Rizza, R. (2013). *Le politiche del lavoro.* Bologna: Il Mulino.

Heinz, W.R. (2009). Youth transitions in an age of uncertainty. In: Furlong, A. (eds) *Handbook of Youth and Young Adulthood: New Perspectives and Agendas.* London: Routledge.

ISFOL. (2016). I canali di intermediazione e i servizi per il lavoro [The intermediation channels in employment services]. Research Paper, 31.

ISTAT. (2015). Indagine IFL Indagine trimestrale sulle forze di lavoro, media annuale [Quarterly Labour Force Survey, annual average].

O'Connor, Ch.D. (2014). Agency and reflexivity in Boomtown transitions: Young people deciding on a school and work direction. *Journal of Education and Work,* 27(4), 372–391.

O'Connor, Ch.D. (2015). Classed, raced, and gendered biographies: Young people's understandings of social structures in a Boomtown. *Journal of Youth Studies,* 18(7), 867–883.

OECD. (2014). Education at a glance: OECD indicators. OECD Publishing, Available at: http://dx.doi.org/10.1787/eag-2014-en.

Ruokonen-Engler, M.K. and Siouti, I. (2016). Biographical entanglements, self-reflexivity, and transnational knowledge production. *Qualitative Inquiry,* 22(9), 745–752.

Spanò, A. (ed) (2001). *Tra esclusione e inserimento. Giovani a bassa scolarità e politiche del lavoro a Napoli.* Milano: FrancoAngeli.

Spanò, A. (2015). Il lavoro, il futuro e la crisi nelle narrazioni dei giovani di origine straniera. *Mondi Migranti,* 2, 111–145.

Spanò, A. (ed) (2017). *I giovani del Sud di fronte alla crisi. Strategie di sopravvivenza e capacità di innovazione.* Milano: FrancoAngeli.

Standing, G. (2011). *The Precariat: The New Dangerous Class.* London and New York: Bloomsbury Academic.

Threadgold, S. (2011). Should I pitch my tent in the middle ground? On 'Middling Tendency', beck and inequality in youth sociology. *Journal of Youth Studies,* 14(4), 381–393.

Threadgold, S. and Nilan, P. (2009). Reflexivity of contemporary youth, risk and cultural capital. *Current Sociology,* 57(1), 47–68.

Van de Velde, C. (2011). Diventare adulti in Europa. L'importanza delle società nazionali sui percorsi di emancipazione giovanile. *La rivista delle politiche sociali,* 3, 209–232.

Walther, A. (2006). Regimes of youth transition: Choice, flexibility and security in young people's experiences across different European contexts. *Young,* 14(1), 119–139.

Woodman, D. (2012). Life out of synch: How new patterns of further education and the rise of precarious employment are reshaping young people's relationships. *Sociology,* 46(6), 1074–1090.

Woodman, D. (2013). Researching 'ordinary' young people in a changing world: The sociology of generations and the 'missing middle' in youth research. *Sociological Research Online*, 18(1), 7, Available at: http://www.socresonline.org.uk/18/1/7.html.

Woodman, D. and Wyn, J. (2015). Class, gender and generation matter: Using the concept of social generation to study inequality and social change. *Journal of Youth Studies*, 18(10), 1–9.

Wyn, J. and Dwyer, P. (1999). New directions in research on youth in transition. *Journal of Youth Studies*, 2(1), 5–21.

Wyn, J., Lantz, S. and Harris, A. (2012). Beyond the 'transitions' metaphor: Family relations and young people in late modernity. *Journal of Sociology*, 48(1), 3–22.

Chapter 11

From South to North

Internal student migration in Italy

Dalit Contini, Federica Cugnata and Andrea Scagni

11.1 Introduction

Human capital of the new generations is considered to be the most important resource of advanced economies to create innovation and ultimately economic growth. Despite the significant increase of university graduates in the most-recent generations, Italy is still lagging behind the majority of other European Union (EU) countries in the share of young people with a higher education degree (currently at 27% against 39% in the EU-28 area) (Eurostat, 2018). This is clearly at odds with the EU educational strategy, which is based on the concept of *social investment* (Hemerijck, 2015), aiming at strengthening the younger generation's ability to thrive in a competitive knowledge economy. Indeed, a rise in the number of university graduates might not translate immediately into more employment or higher wages, in particular if the demand for high-skilled labour is low and if higher education qualifications do not meet the needs of a continuously evolving productive world. A crucial issue at stake in this respect is the high existing level of skills mismatch among Italian young workers, giving rise to overeducation on the one side and shortage of skilled specialists on the other (ISFOL, 2012).

Within this complex scenario, a rising number of young Italians are now moving abroad to attain university degrees. International student mobility, generally increasing worldwide, is viewed as an opportunity for students and workers to expand their knowledge of other languages and societies, and to enhance human capital formation, networks and relational abilities. From this perspective, one of the strategic goals of the EU is the promotion of student intra-European mobility. However, Italy has difficulties in attracting students and high-skilled young workers from abroad: outward mobility from Italy is not compensated by similar inward mobility flows (Migliavacca *et al.*, 2015). Issues concerning international mobility are discussed in Chapter 9 of this book, where it is argued young Italians seek opportunities to move abroad as a direct consequence of the limited prospects for professional advancement within Italy. As suggested by a large literature, the net deficit in the migration balance regarding highly qualified workforce may have strong negative effects on the productivity and economic growth of the country (e.g. Faggian *et al.*, 2007; Boffo and Gagliardi, 2017).

Parallel to the rise of international student mobility, internal student mobility has also increased in Italy in the past decades. Attractive areas are mainly in the north and centre, but we also observe some southern provinces with large universities having positive net mobility flows.[1] However, these provinces only attract students from southern regions, and in particular from areas where no higher education institutions exist (Giambona *et al.*, 2017). In the light of the deep North–South divide, mobility can be viewed as a resource and a possible strategy to overcome the disadvantage of being from a relatively economically deprived area of the country (Cuzzocrea, 2018). Possibly due to the economic crisis, the number of students entering university has steadily declined at the national level from 2008 to 2013, particularly in southern regions, and then slightly increased in the most recent years. At the same time, the share of southern high-school leavers enrolling into a university institution outside the macro-area of origin[2] has increased from 16% to 22%. Instead, the share of students from northern and central Italy enrolled in southern universities has been quite stable around 0.2%–0.4% and 2.3%–2.9%, respectively (De Santis *et al.*, 2019). Thus, from the perspective of Southern Italy, internal student migration is a *unidirectional* phenomenon – from south to north.

The structural determinants of internal student mobility in Italy have been addressed by a few studies examining aggregated migration flows of students across Italian provinces. Employing gravity models, Dotti *et al.* (2013) show that universities can be a source of selective migration processes and provide evidence that student mobility depends on the local labour-market conditions in the areas of destination and on the quality of universities. Similar results are found in Bratti and Verzillo (2019), who highlight the role of university research quality on enrolment patterns across the country, and in Giambona *et al.* (2017). In fact, economic theory predicts that student mobility decisions are affected by the local development of the area where universities are located, because these areas guarantee better job opportunities (Bover and Arellano, 2002).

Indeed, unidirectional student mobility represents a critical issue, in particular if movers are more endowed in terms of economic and cultural resources than stayers. The imbalance might trigger a vicious cycle between quality of the student population and educational targets, at the detriment of the quality of the university institutions in the areas of out-migration. In addition, internal student mobility involves a transfer of economic resources from south to north. Contrary to what occurred for the internal migration waves of the fifties and sixties when migrants contributed to the economic well-being of the areas of origin with their remittances, today the flow of resources goes in the opposite direction, as students living outside the home depend on the economic support of their families (Mocetti and Porello, 2010).

Against this background, a crucial issue is what happens to Italian students after they graduate. Where do they employ the acquired human capital? We may speak of a *brain drain* – as opposed to brain circulation, implying a sustained but even exchange of skilled individuals – if a substantial share of southern graduates does not return to the area of origin, at further detriment of southern local economies. The literature identifies local labour-market conditions as a major driver of both student mobility and post-graduate mobility choices. The quality of political and administrative institutions (Nifo and Vecchione, 2013) and university quality (Ciriaci, 2014) also matter; hence, local development strategies complemented by measures aimed at making the work environment more attractive on the one side, and policies aimed at improving the quality of southern higher education supply on the other may help to keep young skilled students and graduates in loco or to favour brain circulation.

Our contribution aims at providing a comprehensive picture of the students' and graduates' internal mobility flows, focusing on the patterns that contribute to the brain drain of the southern regions. Using the data of the national Survey on Upper Secondary Graduates and the Survey on University Graduates,[3] we analyse the internal mobility of southern students to northern regions and the migratory behaviour of university graduates. Our aim is to address the phenomenon from two different perspectives: that of individuals (who is more likely to move?) and of the territories (what is the human capital loss?). Differently from the current literature, we do not analyse mobility with an all-flows encompassing national level model. Rather, we focus on the migrations involving southern students and graduates. First, in an attempt to 'follow' individuals over time, we focus on relevant choices in individuals' educational careers and migration behaviour (see Figure 11.1). More specifically, based on the information available in the surveys, we analyse the individual determinants of university enrolment, the probability of attending university in the south given university enrolment, the dropout probability of movers and stayers within 4 years from enrolment and the probability of living in the south 4 years after degree attainment. Second, to examine mobility from the point of view of territories, we classify university graduates according to their migration behaviour when entering higher education and after college completion. We then provide descriptive evidence on the composition of these groups, in order to evaluate the human capital loss associated to student and graduate mobility investing the southern macro area.

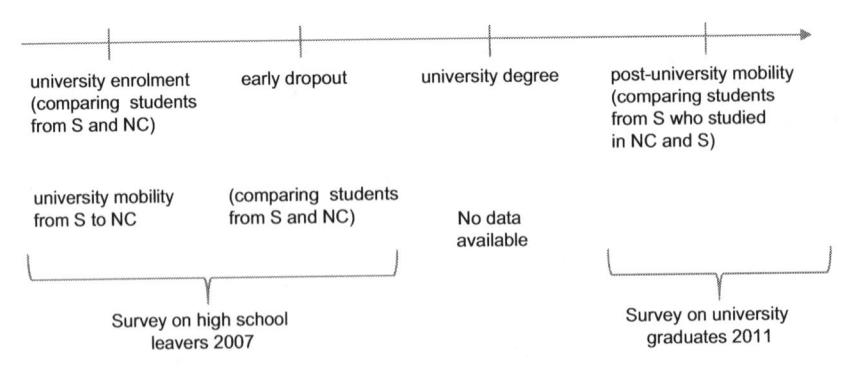

Figure 11.1 Stages of the educational career under study and data.

11.2 Context and data

Italy has long been characterized by out-migration waves. In the nineteenth and early twentieth century, large flows of people from almost all Italian regions migrated to continental Europe, the USA and Latin America in search of better opportunities (Faini and Venturini, 1994). A major change occurred in the 1950s and 1960s, when the industrial boom centred around the automotive industry suddenly increased the demand for low-qualified workers and the northwest started attracting huge migration flows in particular from the southern regions. This mass displacement phenomenon still exerts an influence today, as many southern families have relatives and connections to former migrants now permanently settled in the north.

Concerning education, the Italian school system features 8 years of comprehensive basic school, followed by 5 years of highly tracked upper secondary school (lyceums, technical and vocational schools), with marked differences in curricula and educational targets. Despite that access to tertiary education is open (regardless of grade/ability restrictions) to all students with a 5-year high-school diploma, transition rates are extremely different across tracks: from over 90% of the students from lyceums to around 30% of those from vocational schools.[4]

The university system was reformed in 2001 in accordance with the Bologna Process and now includes 3-year undergraduate courses and 2-year master courses. Universities are mainly public institutions, although there is a very limited number of high-prestige private institutions. Degrees are 'legally equivalent' by law, no matter which university issued them; hence, although differences in university quality exist (as documented by a number of university rankings delivered by a variety of institutions), the degree of differentiation is lower than in most other countries. Altogether, the share of 19-year-olds enrolled in university has varied in the last decade between 46% and 52%, with the lowest figure in 2013 and a small increase afterwards. This share is relatively low as compared to other European countries, such as Germany, the UK and Spain, ranging around 60%–70% in the same years (De Santis *et al.*, 2019).

In this chapter, we employ two national cross-sectional surveys conducted by the Italian National Statistical Institute (ISTAT): the Survey on Upper Secondary Graduates 2007 (ISTAT, 2007) and the Survey on University Graduates 2011 (ISTAT, 2011). Both surveys collect information on educational choices and labour market experiences within a time span of 3 to 4 years from degree attainment. The first survey interviews students who obtained the high-school degree in 2004; the second survey interviews students who graduated from university in 2007. Since the official number of years for the first degree (*laurea triennale*) is 3 years, these data ideally refer to the same cohort of students.[5] In Figure 11.1, we depict the information on the individuals' educational and post-educational careers that are available in these two surveys. The survey on high-school graduates allows studying university enrolment, including mobility patterns, as well as university dropout within 4 years from enrolment. Unfortunately, the data does not identify university completion in itself, with the exception of the limited share of students who attain the degree within 4 years from enrolment. The survey on university graduates allows studying post-university mobility patterns.

Information on the previous educational career, final examination grades, parental education and occupation, as well as a range of personal attributes, is available in both surveys. The university graduates' surveys also contain information on the region of residence before university, university institution and region of residence 4 years after degree attainment.

11.3 The perspective of individuals: determinants of student and graduate mobility

In this section, we investigate which individual characteristics play a role in shaping the size and direction of student and graduate mobility flows. Due to data availability, we focus on young individuals who enrol in university within 3 years from the end of high school. Our definition of mobility encompasses only movement across the two macro areas: north-centre and south. The explanatory variables included in the models (see Appendix for details) include demographic characteristics gender and age, social background indicators concerning parental education and parental social class, and the two main features of the high-school career: the type of high school and the grade at the final high-school examination. To analyse university enrolment and student mobility, we also add dummy variables for the field of study, an indicator of the availability of university degree programs in the province of origin (under the assumption that students living in areas with fewer options might have higher incentives to move), as well as dummy variables for the region of origin, capturing residual territorial effects operating on top of the wideness of the supply of degree programs. To analyse the probability of living in the south after university completion, we further add degree type (*laurea triennale, magistrale, ciclo unico*)[6] and the college graduation mark. Moreover, for post-graduate mobility of student movers, we add the macro-area of university.

We estimate logit regression models and report average marginal effects (Mood, 2010), that is the average probability variations when a covariate increases by one unit, or in the case of dummy variables, when comparing different attributes (e.g. the average probability difference of an outcome for a female and a male). In the following, we briefly summarize the main results, focusing in particular on the role of sociodemographic factors and previous school career.

11.3.1 Probability of university enrolment

According to the survey on Upper Secondary Graduates 2007, the share of high-school leavers enrolling at university is 64% at the national level and is only slightly lower (−1%) among southern high-school leavers.[7] As shown in Table 11.1, females have a higher probability of enrolling than males, confirming

Table 11.1 Probability of university enrolment

Variables	Students from South			Students from North and Centre		
	I	II	III	I	II	III
Female	0.14***	0.042***	0.039***	0.054***	−0.007	−0.008
Age at secondary school graduation – reference is 18–19						
≤18	0.038**	0.003	0.014	0.011	−0.004	−0.006
20–21	−0.216***	−0.071***	−0.074***	−0.214***	−0.064***	−0.066***
≥22	−0.356***	−0.218***	−0.219***	−0.339***	−0.178***	−0.180***
Parental education – reference is tertiary school degree						
Lower secondary	−0.329***	−0.143***	−0.144***	−0.327***	−0.139***	−0.140***
Higher secondary	−0.188***	−0.087***	−0.085***	−0.159***	−0.068***	−0.068***
Parental class – reference is salariat						
Working	−0.177***	−0.086***	−0.083***	−0.219***	−0.114***	−0.113***
Intermediate	−0.101***	−0.044***	−0.044***	−0.096***	−0.055***	−0.054***
Secondary school degree – reference is lyceum						
Teaching school		−0.204***	−0.202***		−0.131***	−0.132***
Arts school		−0.429***	−0.430***		−0.389***	−0.388***
Technical school		−0.306***	−0.308***		−0.308***	−0.308***
Vocational school		−0.495***	−0.494***		−0.491***	−0.490***
Secondary school mark – reference group is 90–100						
60–69		−0.284***	−0.282***		−0.271***	−0.272***
70–79		−0.166***	−0.165***		−0.157***	−0.158***
80–89		−0.117***	−0.118***		−0.089***	−0.089***
n_fields			−0.009			0.004
Region of origin						
Observations	9,259	9,259	9,259	16,621	16,621	16,621

Source: Survey on Upper Secondary Graduates 2007 – MIUR.

Average marginal effects from logit models.
***p < 0.01, **p < 0.05.

the tendency observed in the majority of the OECD countries. However, the gender gap is much larger in southern regions: the difference between females and males is 14 percentage points (p.p.) in the south versus 5 p.p. in the north-centre. Moreover, while in the latter the differential is fully explained by the school type and school grades, in the south a residual difference of 4 p.p. persists after adding these controls. Social background differentials are large and similar between macro areas. Parental education has a larger effect, but social class also matters. Altogether, the enrolment probability of children whose parents have a university degree and belong to the salariat class is 50–55 p.p. higher than that of children whose parents have a lower secondary degree and belong to the working class. This differential reduces but remains dramatically large (23–24 p.p.) when controlling for the individual previous schooling experience. The enrolment probability is positively related to the high-school final examination mark and is highest for students who attended lyceums (in both macro areas approximately +30 p.p. if compared to technical schools, +49 p.p. if compared to vocational schools).

11.3.2 Probability of student mobility

Since our concern is the out-migration from the south, we focus our analysis of student mobility of the high-school leavers from southern regions. The results on the probability of choosing a northern or central university (given enrolment) are shown in Table 11.2. Females have a lower migration probability than males (−3 p.p.), and no substantial change is observed when controlling for school-type and grades. Gender differences in student mobility decisions seem to confirm the more traditional vision of the female role in society, typical of southern regions of Italy (D'Agostino *et al.*, 2019). Further, social background effects are substantial: children belonging to higher status families are more likely to be movers (+14 p.p. when comparing those with university educated parents in the salariat class to those with lower secondary degree in the working class). This gap is only partially explained by school type and grades. Finally, students from lyceums have a much higher migration probability (+7–8 p.p. as compared to technical and vocational schools). High school performance also plays a role, as having received a high grade in the final upper secondary exam (80–100, on a 60–100 scale) increases by approximately 3 p.p. the probability to be a mover. Large differences are also observed between regions and fields of study.

11.3.3 Dropout probability

According to the survey on Upper Secondary Graduates 2007, the average national dropout rate within 4 years from enrolment is 14%, slightly higher if we focus on students from the south (almost 15%).[8] Focusing on the latter, we see that southern students making mobility choices to the northern regions are much less likely to withdraw before degree attainment than those remaining in the south (−8–9 p.p.). Yet, since as we have seen movers are on average more endowed than stayers, it is relevant to assess whether the result is due to composition effects, that is if the difference in the aggregate dropout probability is explained by the different social background and previous school experience of movers and stayers, or if instead it can be ascribed to a different 'behaviour'. As shown in the third column of Table 11.3, the difference observed at the aggregate level is not explained by the more advantaged profile of students migrating

Table 11.2 Probability of enrolling into a northern or central university. High-school leavers from southern regions

Variables	I	II	III	IV	V	VI
Female	−0.0291***	−0.0165*	−0.0353***	−0.0363***	−0.0303***	−0.0297***
Age at secondary school graduation – reference is 18–19						
≤18	−0.0225*	−0.0482***	−0.0516***	−0.0290**	−0.0307***	−0.0296***
20–21	−0.0508***	−0.0466***	−0.0275**	−0.0165	−0.0134	−0.0132
≥22	−0.0146	0.0314	0.0778**	0.130***	0.139***	0.136***
Parental education – reference is tertiary school degree						
Lower secondary		−0.0741***	−0.0511***	−0.0446***	−0.0449***	−0.0451***
Higher secondary		−0.0403***	−0.0248**	−0.0249**	−0.0252**	−0.0256**
Parental class – reference is salariat						
Working		−0.0694***	−0.0563***	−0.0559***	−0.0559***	−0.0542***
Intermediate		−0.0248**	−0.0164	−0.0192*	−0.0188*	−0.0180
Secondary school degree – reference is lyceum						
Teaching school			−0.0379***	−0.0349***	−0.0315***	−0.0311***
Arts school			−0.000596	−0.0106	−0.000127	−0.000142
Technical school			−0.0770***	−0.0832***	−0.0825***	−0.0829***
Vocational school			−0.0580***	−0.0698***	−0.0662***	−0.0667***
Secondary school mark – reference group is 90–100						
60–69			−0.0319***	−0.0294***	−0.0252**	−0.0250**
70–79			−0.0358***	−0.0367***	−0.0326***	−0.0324***
80–89			0.00047	−0.00260	−0.00131	−0.00143
Region of origin – reference is SICILIA						
ABRUZZO				0.204***	0.203***	0.202***
MOLISE				0.305***	0.302***	0.301***
CAMPANIA				0.0187	0.0166	0.0165
PUGLIA				0.143***	0.143***	0.115***
BASILICATA				0.395***	0.391***	0.391***
CALABRIA				0.199***	0.196***	0.194***
SARDEGNA				0.0670***	0.0661***	0.0468**
Field of study – reference is other						
Engineering					0.0364**	0.0365**
Economics and Statistics					0.0415***	0.0401***
Political and Social Sciences					0.0281*	0.0275*
Law					0.0306**	0.0280**
n_fields						−0.0222***
Observations	5,359	5,359	5,359	5,359	5,359	5,359

Source: Survey on Upper Secondary Graduates 2007 – MIUR.

Average marginal effects from logit models.
***p < 0.01, **p < 0.05, *p < 0.1.

Table 11.3 Dropout probability

Variables	Students from southern regions			Students attending university in the north		
	I	II	III	I	II	III
Female	−0.073***	−0.084***	−0.040***	−0.074***	−0.081***	−0.049***
Area of university − reference is region of origin						
North	−0.083***	−0.075***	−0.068***			
Centre	−0.091***	−0.085***	−0.079***			
Other southern regions	−0.014	−0.021	−0.021			
Area of origin − reference is North region of origin						
South				−0.063***	−0.060***	−0.049***
Centre				−0.065***	−0.061***	−0.035
Other northern regions				−0.030***	−0.026***	−0.015
Parental class − reference is salariat						
Working		0.090***	0.057***		0.043***	0.007
Intermediate		0.059***	0.039***		0.016	−0.002
Secondary school degree − reference is lyceum						
Teaching school			0.078***			0.091***
Arts school			0.210***			0.178***
Technical school			0.130***			0.134***
Vocational school			0.245***			0.261***
Secondary school mark − reference group is 90–100						
60–69			0.200***			0.178***
70–79			0.101***			0.092***
80–89			0.053***			0.087***
Region of origin						
Observations	5,356	5,356	5,356	7,796	7,796	7,796

Source: Survey on Upper Secondary Graduates 2007 − MIUR.

Average marginal effects from logit models.
***p < 0.01, **p < 0.05, *p < 0.1.

to the north-centre; in fact, controlling for social origin and previous schooling profile the gap decreases only slightly. Indeed, movers might have more incentives to do well, given the effort sustained by their families due to the higher costs of living outside the parental home. The result could also be due to unobserved compositional effects; if high aspirations are a reason for migration, movers are more positively selected than stayers and this could also contribute to explain their better performance.

In a second stage, we analyse how movers from the south compare in terms of dropout behaviour with the other students enrolled in northern and central universities. Students from the south do better than the others (−5/6 p.p. as compared to students whose area of origin is the north, even when controlling for previous school experience, and social background). This result provides further evidence to the hypothesis that student mobility – in particular long-distance mobility – is attached to motivations and personal characteristics associated to a better performance. Differences might also be related to other reasons, induced by the families' pressure to do well, due to their higher economic investment, or to the beneficial effect of living in a new environment, more centred around university life and potentially more suitable to full commitment to studies.

11.3.4 Probability of living in the south after university completion

Focusing on students from the south, we estimate models for the probability of living in the south 4 years after the degree attainment, distinguishing between those who attended university in the north-centre [for whom we analyse the *back migration* probability (Table 11.4, left panel)] from those who attended university in the south [for whom we analyse the probability of *remaining* in the south vs. moving northbound (Table 11.4, right panel)]. A caveat on the meaning of the outcome 'living in the south after university completion' is in order. Despite being a minority (approximately 12%), some students in the university graduates' survey are still in education (e.g. those who attained a first-level degree might be still enrolled in masters' programs); for these individuals, the post-graduate migration behaviour might not be related to the decision on where to settle, but could still be part of the educational migration project.

Moving to results, we start from gender differences. Females are more likely than males to live in the south after college graduation if they have attended a university in the south (+4 p.p.) and less likely (−9 p.p.) if they have attended a university in the north or centre. These differentials are only partially explained by grades, school type, institution of destination and field of study. Hence, females have lower chances to migrate for study reasons, but if they do, they are more likely *not* to return to their region of origin after degree completion. This result is in line with the evidence on the graduates' migration behaviour in the UK (Faggian *et al.*, 2007). One possible explanation for the higher propensity not to return to the area of origin after the first migration is that women use migration as a means of compensating for their disadvantage in the labour market (ibid.).

Parental education and occupation operate in different ways. Children of more highly educated parents have a lower probability of living in the south, whatever the university attended. Parental occupation, instead, has no effect on the probability of back migration and has an opposite effect on the likelihood of migrating to the northern regions after university, as working-class children are more likely to make post-graduate mobility choices than those from more

Table 11.4 Choices after university completion

Variables	Probability of remaining in the south (southern universities' graduates)			Probability of back migration to the south (students from the south graduating in north-centre universities)		
	I	II	III	I	II	III
Female	0.042***	0.051***	0.037***	−0.094***	−0.063***	−0.052***
Age at degree– reference is 25–29						
21–22	−0.061**	−0.061**	−0.068**	0.068	0.064	−0.020
23–24	0.002	0.005	0.011	−0.007	0.023	−0.011
≥30	0.108***	0.104***	0.097***	0.297***	0.246***	0.170***
Parental education – reference is tertiary school degree						
Lower secondary	0.043***	0.040***	0.038***	0.064**	0.037	0.022
Higher secondary	0.017*	0.015	0.015	0.048**	0.025	0.021
Parental class – reference is salariat						
Working	−0.034**	−0.035**	−0.024*	0.018	0.005	−0.009
Intermediate	−0.021**	−0.029**	−0.016	0.030	0.025	0.010
Secondary school degree – reference is liceo						
Teaching school		−0.034**	−0.038***		−0.035	−0.062*
Arts school		0.050*	0.035		0.13	0.14*
Technical school		0.013	0.0062		0.054***	0.014
Vocational school		0.027	0.020		0.121***	0.073*
Secondary school mark – reference group is 90–100						
60–69		0.030***	−0.004		0.190***	0.105***
70–79		0.001	−0.025**		0.137***	0.085***
80–89		0.018**	0.003		0.122***	0.086***
Field of study – reference is humanities						
Economics and Statistics			0.003			−0.017
Political and Social Sciences			0.024*			0.097***
Sciences			0.003			0.003
Law			0.092***			0.135***
Engineering			−0.093***			−0.0725**
Architecture			0.046***			0.020
Medicine			0.035***			−0.056*
Physical Education			0.038			0.061

(Continued)

Table 11.4 (Continued)

Variables	Probability of remaining in the south (southern universities' graduates)			Probability of back migration to the south (students from the south graduating in north-centre universities)		
	I	II	III	I	II	III
Degree type – reference is laurea triennale						
Laurea ciclo unico			0.002			−0.151***
Laurea magistrale			0.001			−0.113***
Degree mark – reference group is 110 cumlaude						
66–90			0.069***			0.042
91–100			0.045***			0.095***
101–105			0.011			0.083***
106–110			0.031***			0.039*
ch_region			−0.034**			
University in centre (vs. north)						0.089***
Region of origin						
Observations	11,980	11,980	11,980	3,726	3,726	3,726

Source: Survey on University Graduates 2011.

***p < 0.01, **p < 0.05, *p < 0.1.

advantaged classes. Given the prominent role of informal networks in the south, working class children might have fewer job opportunities in the region of origin.

The final university graduation mark has an unclear effect, possibly because performance evaluations are highly dependent on the field of study, department and university institution. Instead, high-school grades and school type have a strong influence on the probability of back migration: better students are less likely to return to the south. This can be explained by their higher chances to find good jobs in the area of the university, or to continue education in masters or postgraduate degrees. Interestingly, students who experienced shorter moves (those who attended university in a southern region different from their own) have a higher likelihood of moving northbound after graduation than those who remained in the region of origin.

11.4 The perspective of the territory: composition of mobility groups

We have shown above that the young individuals moving from south to north to attend university are on average better performing and come more often from lyceums, the most-prestigious high-school types. In this section, we provide descriptive evidence that helps grasping the extent to which this massive student mobility represents a problem in terms of loss of human capital and brain drain. To this aim, similarly to Faggian and McCann (2009), we classify university graduates according to their migration behaviour when entering university and after graduating from university. We define 'mobility' with respect to movements across the macro areas north, centre and south,[9] and identify four different individual profiles: *Stayers* are those who never leave the macro-area of origin. *Early movers* are those who migrate to attend university and do not return to their area of origin after graduation. *Late movers* are those who remain in the same macro area when attending university but migrate outwards after obtaining the university degree.[10] *Back movers* are those who attend university in a different macro area, but return to the macro-area of origin after graduation.

At first, we compare mobility patterns across the country (Figure 11.2). Stayers are much more common among northern students (92%) and among students from central Italy (84%) than among students from the south (62.7%). The latter have much higher chances of being in each of the 'movers' groups. Early and late movers – who eventually will employ their human capital elsewhere – represent 26.7% of the college graduates from southern regions (14.1% are early movers and 12.6% are late movers). The majority of those making student mobility choices towards the north-centre do *not* return after studies (back movers are 10.6% of the total, amounting to 33% of those attending university in the north and 49% in the centre). Instead, among those studying in the south, 83% remain in the south after university, most of which in their region of origin.

Mobility is much more frequent among the 'best students'. In Table 11.5, we show the mobility distribution by distinguishing between lyceum students and other schools, and by the final high-school examination mark. Concentrating on the students with the highest level of academic ability (those graduating with a

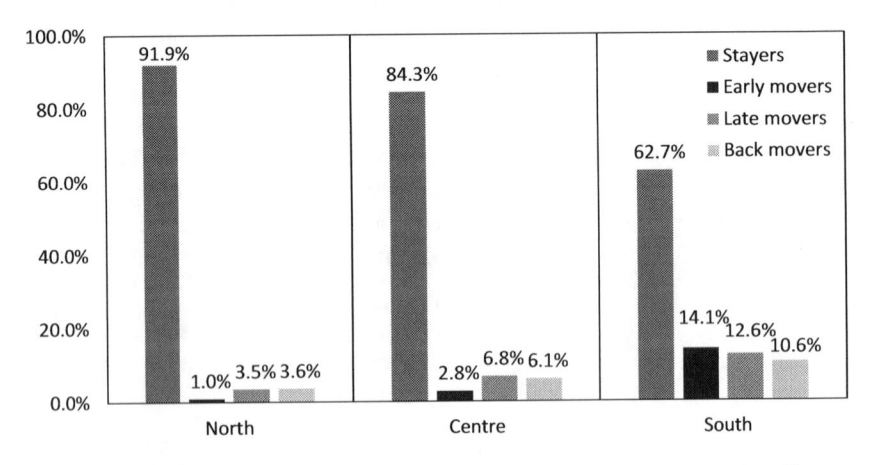

Figure 11.2 Typology of student–graduate migration behaviour by geography. (Source: Own elaboration from the Survey on University Graduates 2011.)

Table 11.5 Probability of belonging to each mobility group by high-school type and final-exam mark

High-school type	High-school exam mark	Stayers	Early movers	Late movers	Back movers	Early/ (Early+Back)
Lyceum	≥90	53.0%	24.4%	13.9%	8.6%	74%
	<90	64.8%	12.0%	12.6%	10.6%	53%
Others	≥90	65.6%	13.1%	12.6%	8.8%	60%
	<90	66.6%	8.8%	11.5%	13.1%	40%

Source: Own elaboration from the Survey on University Graduates 2011.

mark ≥90 from a lyceum), 1 out of 4 are early movers and 74% of those who attend university in the north-centre *do not go back south* (last column). Moreover, an additional 14% leaves the south after the degree attainment. Altogether, almost 38% of this highly selected subgroup leaves the south (potentially for good) at some point.

We now turn to examining the *composition* of the mobility groups (Table 11.6). When focusing exclusively on the high-school profile, we see that nearly 70% of the early movers graduated from lyceums, and almost 40% are represented by the best-performing lyceum students. Late movers have an intermediate profile, while stayers and back movers display the lowest level of academic skills. The share of females within each group is 62% among *stayers*, 57% among *early movers*, 56% among *late movers* and 41% among *back movers*. Because of the tendency of females to move less in the first place (ceteris paribus) but not to return to their home region if they move, *stayers* are composed largely by females and *back movers* by males.

Table 11.6 Mobility group composition by high-school type and final-exam mark

High-school type	High-school exam mark	Stayers	Early movers	Late movers	Back movers
Lyceum	≥90	19.4%	39.7%	25.4%	18.7%
	<90	36.3%	29.7%	35.2%	35.3%
Others	≥90	15.2%	13.5%	14.5%	12.1%
	<90	29.1%	17.1%	24.9%	33.9%
		100%	100%	100%	100%

Source: Own elaboration from the Survey on University Graduates 2011.

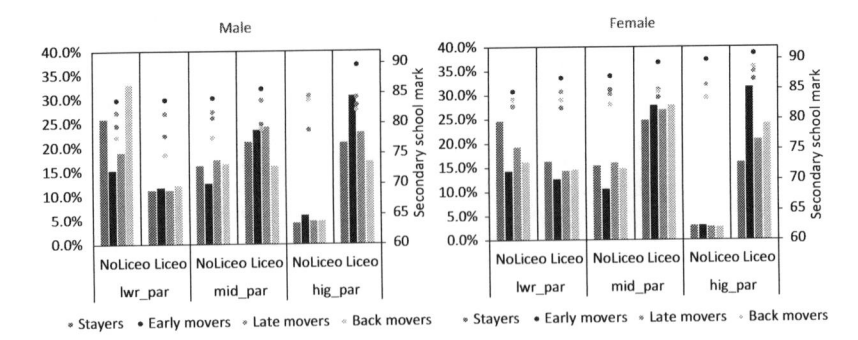

Figure 11.3 Mobility group composition by social background and high-school type. (Source: Own elaboration from the Survey on University Graduates 2011. Left scale (vertical bars): Share within mobility groups. Right scale (dots): Average high-school grade. Social background here defined as: lwr_par = low education & working or intermediate class; hig_par = high education & intermediate or salariat class; mid_par = others.)

In Figure 11.3, we describe the mobility group composition adding social background to the picture. Students of low parental background not graduating from lyceum are the most frequent category among male *stayers* and male *back movers*. Female *stayers* are more polarized: many are of low social origin and not from lyceums, but a large share is also represented by students from lyceums of middle-high social origin. This group is also over-represented among female *back movers*. The most advantaged category among both males and females is that of *early movers*, both in terms of school type and proficiency (the average mark is substantially higher), and of social background.

11.5 Conclusions

In this chapter, we have provided an overview of the students and graduates' internal mobility flows, from enrolment to post-graduate mobility. Focusing on the behaviour of young individuals who obtained the high-school diploma in the South of Italy, we first analyse individual determinants of student and graduate mobility and find that mobility patterns differ by social background and previous schooling: students of more endowed families and coming from lyceums have a much higher probability to attend higher education out of the southern regions. Moreover, movers are more likely to complete university than stayers, even after controlling for previous schooling and social background. After graduation, children of more highly educated parents have a higher probability to remain in the northern regions (if student movers) or flow to the north (if student stayers). Altogether this evidence shows that movers are positively selected in terms of social background, schooling and presumably of motivation and aspirations. Analysing the data from the perspective of the territories, we find that early movers – those who attend university in the northern regions and do not return to the area of origin after graduation – represent 14% of the stock of high-school diplomats and are largely composed by students from lyceums and high marks. If we add to these figures those of students leaving the south after the degree attainment, the share reaches 27%.

Our conclusion is that the human capital depletion of the southern regions is severe. This imbalance is likely to determine a long-term widening of the gap in wealth and economic development that has historically separated the southern regions from the rest of the country, increasing the obstacles to compete successfully on the international context in a medium-long-term perspective. There is urgent need to invert this tendency and transform *brain drain* into *brain circulation*. With few exceptions, southern universities are mostly at the bottom of all national university quality rankings: to attract students from the entire country and abroad, educational policies aimed at enhancing the prestige of southern university institutions should be enforced. Indeed, in the light of the long-standing dualism of the Italian economy, if the Southern Italian productive system lacks the capacity to absorb high-skilled workers, targeted demand-side interventions are also of paramount importance.

Appendix

A.1 Definition of variables included in the models

A.1.1 Common variables

Sources: Survey on Upper Secondary Graduates 2007 and Survey on University Graduates 2011

- Female: gender of the respondent (1 for women, 0 for men)
- Parental education: highest level of education of the parents of the respondent (tertiary, higher secondary and lower secondary education);
- Parental class: highest level of occupation of the parents of the respondents (salariat, intermediate, working class), see Table 11.1;
- Secondary school degree: lyceum, teaching school, arts school, technical school and vocational school;
- Secondary school mark: grade obtained at the end of the secondary school: from 60 to 100; and
- Region of origin: the region where the respondent attended secondary school.

A.1.2 Models (i)–(iii)

Source: Survey on Upper Secondary Graduates 2007

- Age at secondary school graduation: ≤ 18, 18–19, 20–21, ≥ 22;
- Field of study: engineering, economics and statistics, political and social sciences, law, other fields;

- Area of university; and
- n_fields: the number of fields of study offered in the province where the respondent attended secondary school and in the neighbouring provinces. Varies from 0 to 9 (source: Ministry of Education).

A.1.3 Model (iv)

Source: Survey on University Graduates 2011

- Field of study: area of studies chosen at the university by the respondent: humanities, economics and statistics, political and social sciences, sciences, law, engineering, architecture, medical school, physical education;
- Degree type: the type of degree obtained by the respondents in 2007. *Laurea triennale, Laurea magistrale, Laurea Ciclo Unico*;
- University degree mark: from 66 to 110 cum laude;
- Age at degree: 21–22, 23–24, 25–29 and ≥30;
- ch_region: a dummy that identifies graduates who attended university in a region different from that of high school; and
- uni_CENTRO: a dummy that identifies graduates who attended university in the centre.

The parental social class is defined through the EGP classification of job types. University professors, professionals, secondary-school teachers, managers and executives form the *salariat* (upper) class. Infant and primary-school teachers, high- or medium-qualification office workers, company owners, partners in family-owned or mutual companies, small farmers are included in the *intermediate* class. Finally, all dependent and self-employed manual workers without any specific qualification belong to the *working class*. Unfortunately, data provided by ISTAT do not distinguish between large and small company owners who, according to the Erikson, Goldthorpe, Portocarero (EGP) classification, should be included in the *salariat* class and the *intermediate* class, respectively. Since owners of small companies are much numerous than those of large companies, we classify all company owners as belonging to the intermediate class.

Notes

1 Italy is divided into 20 administrative divisions called 'regioni', further divided into provinces. In total, there are 80 provinces in the country.
2 Throughout the paper, macro areas are defined as follows. North: Piemonte, Valle d'Aosta, Lombardia, Trentino-Alto Adige, Veneto, Friuli-Venezia Giulia, Liguria, Emilia-Romagna. Centre: Toscana, Umbria, Marche, Lazio. South: Abruzzo, Molise, Campania, Puglia, Basilicata, Calabria, Sicilia, Sardegna.
3 Full names of these surveys are: 'Indagine sui Percorsi di Studio e Lavoro dei Diplomati' (Survey on the Educational and Occupational Paths of Upper Secondary

School Graduates) and 'Indagine sull'Inserimento Professionale dei Laureati (Survey on University Graduates' Occupational Condition).

4 These figures are derived from the Survey of Upper Secondary Graduates (2007). More recent data from the same survey shows a substantial decline in the track-specific transition rates (in particular for the students from the technical and vocational track), entailing a widening of the gap across tracks.

5 This holds only for students from the laurea triennale graduating within 3 years. Students from the laurea triennale taking longer time to graduate, those enrolled in 5/6-year programmes (ciclo unico) or in master's level programs (laurea magistrale), belong to an older cohort of high-school leavers.

6 Laurea triennale is a 3-year first-level degree, after which students can continue with a 2-year master's level program (laurea magistrale). The laurea a ciclo unico are 5- or 6-year programs, usually in the field of medical science, pharmacology and law.

7 The figures based on administrative data reported by ANVUR (the National Agency for the Evaluation of the Italian University System) are substantially lower. This might be due also to the fact that the administrative individual data on schooling careers is not currently linked to the university database, so to date only indirect calculations are possible. Nonetheless, the overall trends are similar: according to ANVUR (2016), the transition rates at the national level were rather stable around 56% between 2004 and 2010, and then decreased to 53% in 2015 (ANVUR, 2016). According to survey data, the share decreased from 2004 and 2011 from 64% to 63%.

8 According to administrative data (ANVUR, 2016) the overall share of students of the matriculation cohort 2010–2011 who dropped out the system within 4 years from enrolment was over 28% (notice also that there is evidence of decreasing dropout rates over time, so the corresponding figure for earlier cohorts is probably higher). The reason for this discrepancy is likely to be due to survey underreporting of events. The literature that has studied dropout with the Survey on Upper-Secondary Graduates assumes that this phenomenon occurs evenly across sociodemographic groups.

9 Note that no data is available on the post-university migration behaviour of university dropouts. Individuals attending university institutions outside Italy are not observed while those moving abroad after graduation are included among early movers or late movers.

10 Late movers might also include students migrating to attend master's degrees (laurea magistrale).

References

ANVUR. (2016). Rapporto biennale sullo stato del sistema universitario e della ricerca 2016, Agenzia Nazionale di Valutazione del Sistema Universitario e della Ricerca, Roma.

Boffo, S. and Gagliardi, F. (2017). I costi della nuova mobilità internazionale dei giovani laureate italiani: un tentativo di stima. In: Bonifazi, C. (ed.) *Migrazioni e integrazioni nell'Italia di oggi*. Rome: IRPPS, 87–100.

Bover, O. and Arellano, M. (2002). Learning about migration decisions from the migrants: Using complementary datasets to model intra-regional migrations in Spain. *Journal of Population Economics*, 15(15), 357–380.

Bratti M. and Verzillo, S. (2019). The 'Gravity' of quality. Research quality and universities' attractiveness in Italy. *Regional Studies*, 53(10), 1385–1396.

Ciriaci, D. (2014). Does university quality influence the interregional mobility of students and graduates? The case of Italy. *Regional Studies*, 48, 1592–1608.

Cuzzocrea, V. (2018). Rooted mobilities' in young people's narratives of the future: A peripheral case. *Current Sociology*, 66, 1106–1123.

D'Agostino, A., Ghellini, G. and Longobardi, S. (2019). Out-migration of university enrolment: The mobility behaviour of Italian students. *International Journal of Manpower*, https://doi.org/10.1108/IJM-07-2017-0169.

De Santis, G., Pirani, E. and Porcu, M. (2019). Rapporto sulla Popolazione. L'istruzione in Italia. Associazione Italiana Studi di Popolazione (AISP). Il Mulino.

Dotti, N.F., Fratesi, U., Lenzi, C. and Percoco, M. (2013). Local labour markets and the interregional mobility of Italian University students. *Spatial Economic Analysis*, 8, 443–468.

Eurostat. (2018). Education and training in the EU – facts and figures. Eurostat statistics explained. Available at: http://appsso.eurostat.ec.europa.eu/nui/submitViewTableAction.do.

Faggian, A. and McCann, P. (2009). Universities, agglomerations and graduate human capital mobility. *Tijdschrift voor Economische en Sociale Geografie*, 100, 210–223.

Faggian, A., McCann, P. and Sheppard, S. (2007). Human capital, higher education and graduate migration: An analysis of Scottish and Welsh students. *Urban Studies*, 44, 2511–2528.

Faini, R. and Venturini, A. (1994). Italian emigration in the pre-war period. In: Williamson, J. and Hatton, T. (eds) *Migration and the International Labor Market, 1850–1939*. London: Routledge.

Giambona, F., Porcu, M. and Sulis, I. (2017). Students mobility: Assessing the determinants of attractiveness across competing territorial areas. *Social Indicators Research*, 133, 1105–1132.

Hemerijck, A. (2015). The quiet paradigm revolution of social investment. *Social Politics*, 22(2), 242–256.

ISFOL. (2012). Rapporto ISFOL 2012. Le competenze per l'occupazione e la crescita.

ISTAT. (2007). Indagine sui percorsi di studio e lavoro dei diplomati 2004 (Survey on the Educational and Occupational Paths of Upper Secondary School Graduates 2004), Roma, Available at: https://www.istat.it/en/archivio/35940.

ISTAT. (2011). Indagine sull'inserimento professionale dei laureati 2007 (Survey on University Graduates' Occupational Condition 2007), Rome, Available at: https://www.istat.it/en/archivio/94568.

Migliavacca, M., Rosina, A. and Sironi, E. (2015). Condizione lavorativa e mobilità internazionale delle nuove generazioni italiane. *Mondi Migranti*, 2, 53–78.

Mocetti, S. and Porello, C. (2010). La mobilità del lavoro in Italia: nuove evidenze sulle dinamiche migratorie. Questioni di Economia e Finanza: Occasional Papers. Banca d'Italia

Mood, C. (2010). Logistic regression: Why we cannot do what we think we can do, and what we can do about it. *European Sociological Review*, 26(1), 67–82.

Nifo, A. and Vecchione, G. (2013). Do institutions play a role in skilled migrations? *Regional Studies*, 48, 1628–1649.

Chapter 12

Becoming an adult in the new millennium

How the transition to adulthood has changed

Monica Santoro

12.1 Introduction

The process of transition to adulthood is comprised of different phases, such as entry into the labour market, leaving the parental home, forming a first union and entrance into parenthood (Modell *et al.*, 1976; Shanahan, 2000). It is acknowledged that, since the end of the seventies, the transition to adulthood has become more complex and less linear (Billari and Liefbroer, 2010; Kohli, 2007; Settersten Jr. and Ray, 2010). More specifically, the prolongation of educational paths, the difficult conditions of the labour market and the emergence of new family forms have changed profoundly, inducing a shift in the traditional transition model. These changes have occurred in different ways and on differing timescales in various European countries. For example, from the eighties onwards, the tendency to prolong permanence in the family of origin has become more pronounced in the whole Western world, especially among young people aged 25 to 34 (Furstenberg Jr., 2010; Holdsworth and Morgan, 2005), although this phenomenon has had a higher intensity in Southern Europe (especially Italy, Greece and Spain) (Cherlin *et al.*, 1997).

This chapter reports on the findings of two studies carried out in 2003 and 2013 respectively, which both focus on the transition of young Italians into adulthood. The comparison of the two projects provide an insight into several changes in the transitional pathways, especially on how the transition from school to employment and moving out from the parental home are dealt with. Before presenting the results, I will provide some data that will be useful in characterizing the conditions of young people in Italy in contrast to their counterparts in Europe. The data is indicative of transformations that have occurred in the family, education and employment status in the course of the decade from 2003 to 2013.

12.2 Transition to adulthood in Europe

There are two distinctive traits in the transitional model of young people in Italy: the fact that financial independence does not lead to leaving the parental home and the widespread absence of living arrangements that differ from cohabitation with parents prior to marriage. Since the start of the new millennium, cohabitation before marriage or experiencing periods of independent living after achieving financial independence have become increasingly common choices in cities within Central and Northern Italy (Santoro, 2012). However, Italy remains one of the European countries with the highest percentage of young people (aged 18–34) who live with their parents (in 2014 68.8% of male and 57.6% of female adults) (ISTAT, 2015).

Cavalli and Galland (1995) consider the Italian model of transition as an example of the so-called Mediterranean model, counterposed by the Nordic model. Prolonged permanence in the family and the synchronicity of the phases of leaving the parental home and marriage define the transitional model in Southern European countries (Italy, Greece, Spain and Portugal). In contrast, the Nordic model is characterized by a pronounced experimental phase in which young people adopt various living and family arrangements (including cohabitation with friends during the university period, cohabitation with a partner before marriage or solo living).

Because of the recession and the increased rates of youth unemployment in all Western countries, a prolonged permanence in the family of origin has been observed. It is interesting to note that Furstenberg (2008) coined the phrase 'Italianization of transition to adulthood' to indicate how pervasive this trend is in Italy, as observed in previous chapters of this book. As a result of this deferral of home-leaving that frequently occurs in Italy, young people typically enter into a union and parenthood at a later age than in the past. Numerous comparative studies between different European countries have highlighted the widespread nature of this destandardization of the phases of the transition into adulthood (Billari and Wilson, 2001; Elzinga and Liefbroer, 2007).

Recently, social scientists have increasingly focused on the emerging models of transitions to adulthood than the differences between countries. Although they do not deny the differences persisting between Southern, Northern and Central European countries, they have also identified some common trends in the transitional pathways. Billari and Liefbroer (2010) estimate that the new transition model is late, protracted and complex. Late, because many events occur with a delay, and they are protracted because the timespan between leaving the parental home and the birth of the first child has been prolonged, and finally complex, because during the transition many events happen, and some of them repeatedly.

In contexts that are particularly difficult from a labour-market perspective, the experimental dimension characterizes many transitional phases. In such cases, the traditional transition model based on the consequential achievement of different phases and on the separation between youth and adulthood is of little help to understand the orientation strategies of young people. Boundaries between the different transition phases are porous and not all of them appear to lead to taking on adult roles. Young Italians go through experimental phases where they are confronted with adult roles and new experiences. New ways of building their work and family paths emerge, where precariousness and uncertainty are not necessarily a suspension of adulthood (Cuzzocrea and Magaraggia, 2013). This trend has been observed in previous chapters of this book.

12.3 Data on young Europeans

In 2013, the youth unemployment rate in the European Union (EU) peaked at 23% for people in the 15–24 age range. In the years that followed, the steady decrease of this percentage appeared to have marked the end of the recession for most European countries. However, for some countries and most of those in Southern Europe, recovery from the recession has yet to occur. In 2015, the youth unemployment rate in Italy amounted to 40% (30% in the 15–29 age range). This is one of the highest rates in the EU and is only better than that of Greece and Spain. In addition, Italy ranked highest in Europe for the number of those Not in Education, Employment or Training (NEET). In 2015, the percentage of young NEET aged between 15 and 24 was 21.4% (this figure rose to 31% in the 20–24 age range) (Eurostat, 2016b), whereas in Greece and Spain these figures were 17.2% and 15.6%, respectively (Eurofound, 2016).

With regard to education, Italy is far from reaching the targets set in the Europe 2020 Strategy – the EU Strategy for Jobs and Growth – which focuses on increasing tertiary educational attainment to at least 40% and reducing the share of early school leavers to less than 10% by 2020. In Italy, although the share of early school leavers who obtained only a lower secondary level of education has steadily declined over the years, this figure is currently over-target at 15% (23.1% in 2004) (European Commission, 2012; Eurostat, 2016a). Additionally, although the percentage of university graduates continues to increase, it is still far from the European targets: in 2015, only 25.3% of young Italians aged between 30 and 34 had obtained a university degree, compared to a European average of 38.7% (Eurostat, 2016a).

As an effect of the recession, the phenomenon of prolonged permanence in the family of origin has grown substantially, especially among young adults: in 2015, 38.3% of young males and 23% of young females aged between 30 and 34 still lived in the parental home (ISTAT, 2015). Arguably, the decision to remain under the parental roof no longer appears to represent free choice but rather a solution to circumstantial issues. An ISTAT survey examining the reasons for deferred home-leaving reveal a decrease in the percentage of young people stating their satisfaction with living at home, whereas there was an increase in the number of those who declared they remained due to contingencies (especially unemployment, and not being able to afford housing costs) (ISTAT, 2009).

Prolonged permanence in the family of origin has the effect of postponing family choices (ISTAT, 2014a). For example, Italy has the lowest percentage of young people aged between 18 and 34 years who live as a married or cohabiting couple (Mauceri and Valentini, 2010; Eurostat, 2010). The postponement in entering the first union is therefore considered as one of the reasons underlying the very low Italian fertility rate (1.35 children per woman in 2015), together with the low incidence of prenuptial cohabitation (ISTAT, 2016c; Santoro, 2012).

12.4 The case studies

The two pieces of research on which I will draw my analysis herein are both based on qualitative data. The first research, 'Families and transitions in Europe (FATE)', was carried out in 2003 with the funds of the European Commission within the Fifth Framework Programme (European Commission, 2007). It involved in-depth interviews with 40 young people who had finished their educational path in the previous year – or were finishing – and were therefore on the verge of entering the labour market or had just entered employment. At an early stage of the research, a questionnaire had been given to approximately 100 young people attending the final year of secondary school or university. One year later, 24 of these participants (12 females and 12 males) were contacted again for an in-depth interview. The remainder of the sample was comprised of participants who had graduated from university the previous year. The recruitment of the young graduates was obtained using the snowball sampling method. All the participants lived in Milan, the second largest Italian city by territory and population. The age range of the interviewees was between 19 and 34 years (Leccardi *et al.*, 2004). The main aim of the research was to look into the processes through which young people make their most important life decisions in view of their assumption of adult roles. In this respect, there was a specific focus on the school to work transition.

The second piece of research was carried out between 2013 and 2014 and was funded by the Ministry for Universities, in the context of Research Projects of National Interest (PRIN), involving a study of 65 young people aged between 18 and 32. Unlike the sample of participants of the previous study, these participants were contacted 3 years after the completion of their education. The university graduates were recruited using lists supplied by University of Milan and the snowball sampling method; whereas the qualified secondary school leavers and young school dropouts who were attending training courses were obtained through the Afol centres in Milan (Metropolitan Agency for training) and Vocational Training Centres.

In certain respects, the two pieces of research are not immediately comparable. First, a difference is apparent in the differing number of participants, comprising 64 in the second study, compared to 40 in the first. Additionally, a lack of uniformity of educational pathways derived from the differing sampling and recruitment methods. Moreover, in the earlier study, the participants were contacted a year after completing secondary school, meaning that they had all obtained a secondary-school diploma. Whereas in the later study, some participants had no secondary-school qualifications. Having dropped out of school, they were attending training courses with the aim of achieving vocational qualifications. However, this lack of uniformity can also be partially linked to the reform of the educational system that occurred during the intervening decade, which will be described in the following section. In spite of these differences, the analysis of the results has allowed light to be shed on some changes in the transition processes, both at a structural level (transformation of the labour market and the educational system) and at an individual level (biographical choices), which will be developed in the conclusion section.

12.5 The educational system

Within the 10-year time frame from 2003 to 2013, the conditions of young Italians have undergone significant transformations. In the year 2000, the Italian educational system launched the reorganization of university courses. They are no longer based on a single cycle, which variably lasted from 4 to 6 years, but rather consisting of two distinct cycles. The first of which represents an undergraduate qualification and lasts for 3 years, with the option of following on with a postgraduate degree, lasting 2 years. This allowed university students who obtained a (3-year) bachelor's degree to enter the labour market within a shorter timescale than with the previous single-cycle university system. This is the specific reason that in the 2013 research the degree-holding participants were younger than those in the previous study.

In 2003, further reforms to the educational system were implemented. A greater autonomy in terms of the organization of qualifications was conferred to the Regions.[1] In the Lombardy Region, where the participants were based, a professional qualification is awarded after attending a vocational institute for a 5-year course. This type of qualification can only be obtained by the age of 18 or higher and allows access to both the labour market and to university – this latter feature making the system more open in theory than other countries in Europe. Other than this professional qualification, young Italians can opt for other educational institutes, called lyceums and technical institutes. The lyceum is a preparatory school for university, whereas the technical institutes focus more on providing a high standard of vocational training, although they also grant formal access to university. Students who fail to obtain any of these 5-year qualifications and drop out of school earlier are instead steered towards alternative training programmes, combining theoretical lessons with training internships in companies. In this case, upon completion of a 3- or 4-year training course, a vocational qualification is obtained.

12.6 Education and work paths of young interviewees

The first distinctive feature differentiating the two samples concerns the employment status of the participants. In 2003, the most commonly reported status of interviewees was 'student' (12 participants). The decision to enrol in university, especially for those participants who had obtained a professional diploma, took the form of a short-term experimental response while waiting to find employment. This trial-and-error attitude was partially an effect of the then recent university reform, where an increasing number of curricula had been introduced, that were able to better satisfy the demand for specific interests. For the participants, obtaining a degree also represented a key factor for upward social mobility. For the participants' parents' generation, obtaining a university degree was less common, and this explains why families perceived the attainment of a degree by their children as an improvement in their social status. In 2004, only 23% of students had obtained a first university degree, compared with an OECD average of 32% (OECD, 2004). In 2017, the share of young adults aged 25–34 with a tertiary degree was 27%, lower than other OECD countries (OECD, 2018). In this sense, less importance was assigned to the type of subject chosen; what counted most in their accounts was that they managed to obtain a university degree, which was perceived as representing a guarantee to be able to find a job and improve their social status. Moreover, compared to those who attained a secondary-school diploma, a university education also offered greater opportunities for finding a job.

> Until the very last minute, I still didn't know whether to start working and therefore start earning. Then, the fact of standing out from the crowd and gaining more knowledge than others, encouraged me to continue education, also because if you don't have a degree, I don't think you're able to find a job very easily... I like being, well, I think everybody would like to belong to the higher strata of society. (Giovanna, 20 years old, studying Foreign Languages, interviewed in 2003)

Several young people admitted that it was their parents who actively encouraged them to attend university, convinced that a degree, other than offering greater job opportunities, was also a key element of social prestige. In a country where attending university is still a choice for the privileged few and where previous generations had difficulties in accessing university education, a son or a daughter holding a degree represents a conquest. It is an instrument to improve social status.

> Actually, there was some encouragement to start university from my parents; especially dad, he really wanted me to continue my education. (Cinzia, 20 years old, doing Arts and Cultural Management Studies, interviewed in 2003)

A decade later, a university degree is no longer perceived as an instrument providing upward social mobility, nor as a guarantee of accessing the labour market. For young people from a privileged social-economical background, obtaining a degree is a set course that has been planned since the choice of secondary education. At the other end of the spectrum, for young people from less-privileged social strata, the best decision is deemed to be the acquisition of work experience rather than education. More specifically, witnessing friends or family members working in low-paid jobs or in jobs which were at odds with the educational level acquired, had further strengthened the belief in the futility of a university education.

> Nowadays in Italy a degree is useless, no one could care less. My cousin has a degree and what does he do? Nothing, absolutely nothing. Others work as waiters, so what? (Federico, aged 18, apprentice mechanic, interviewed in 2013)

> They always told me that without a secondary school diploma, you're going nowhere. I see people, my friends with a diploma, my cousin with a degree, not going anywhere. They work like I did, as a waiter. And so, I see them and say, what am I supposed to do, do I have to study until I'm 30... you know, there are people who study engineering and then end up working as waiters. (Rocco, aged 21, apprentice plumber, interviewed in 2013)

From this viewpoint, Italy differs from other countries because throughout the decade 2007–2017 the employment prospects for young graduates have worsened. Indeed, the employment rate of young graduates in Italy is much lower than that of the graduates aged about 60 (OECD, 2018). National data confirms the increasing (and worrying) disenchantment of young Italians towards university education, particularly in the central-northern regions, those very areas of the country where employment rates are highest. It has been calculated that between 2003–2004 and 2014–2015 new enrolments in university have decreased by 60,000 students, reaching a record low of less than 260,000 students in total (−20.4%) (Fondazione Res, 2016; ISTAT, 2016a).

Even those who had obtained a university degree expressed deep concerns about a hostile labour market that is also poorly receptive to specific areas of specialization. In Italy, those holding a degree in the arts or humanities are usually the ones who are more highly penalized by the labour market (ISTAT, 2016b). However, the narratives emerging from the interviews were crystal clear about the obstacles that also faced by those holding a degree in several scientific fields. For example, Fausta had a degree in Veterinary Medicine, but had been unable to find employment as a veterinarian. Therefore, she planned to transform her hobby for photography into a business:

> In my sector there's too much competition, too many graduates in Veterinary Science. I'm giving myself one more year to succeed; after that I'm going to try to do something else. Anything else at that point, anything else. I also have a hobby for photography; I must admit that I occasionally work as a wedding photographer. (Fausta, aged 30, interviewed in 2013)

This is similar to the experience of another female respondent, who had a degree in Biological Sciences:

> I was working in the university lab without any type of contract or salary. At the same time, I had begun working in this shop just after my degree, it's a brand in the luxury fashion sector, and they offered me a job with a permanent contract and I accepted without giving a second thought. (Bianca, aged 26, interviewed in 2013)

In Italy, the phenomenon of accepting jobs where the skills required to perform the job are lower than the academic qualifications attained (Murgia and Poggio, 2014), is fairly widespread among younger generations (in 2013, 34.2% of young people in the 15–34 age bracket) (ISTAT, 2014b). In Lombardy in particular, this is especially relevant among people aged 25 to 34 (21.6%) (Cerea *et al.*, 2015). Overqualification is also the subject of Chapter 5 of this collection, by Lara Maestripieri, so I will concentrate here more specifically on the effect of this trend on the more general transition to adulthood.

In 2003, the participants perceived university education as representing the route to achieve an occupation, providing good financial and social rewards. In the same manner, even for those who had attained secondary-school qualifications and wanted to enter the labour market, attaining a vocational diploma was seen as a valid instrument to be able to perform qualified manual work. They managed to move on from their initial low-paid temporary jobs by acquiring work experience and thus improved their employment prospects. Indeed, apprenticeship represented a valid route to obtain regular employment.

> I'm now working as an apprentice accountant in an accountancy firm, which is what I studied to be... The only thing is that they employed me as an apprentice, so they pay me less money... I think that above all, I'll get a regular job, because they assured me they would give me a permanent contract. (Valeria, aged 19, interviewed in 2003)

One decade later, young people with vocational qualifications are the most disadvantaged in the labour market and appear to have lost the opportunity to improve their job prospects, even after acquiring work experience. Their narratives described a range of strategies, such as switching jobs continuously, undertaking employment through short-term contracts lasting just a few months, accepting unpaid working hours and getting involved in difficult relationships with employers and colleagues.

Some exceptions are those young people who were able to create alternative career pathways by fiercely exploiting their skills and setting up their own businesses. For example, Virginia, aged 20, after attaining a lower-secondary-school qualification, attended a regional fashion and tailoring course and then started to design her own patterns. At the time of the interview, she had just opened her own business, together with a partner, in a property she inherited from her grandmother. Or as in the case of Fabio, aged 18, who after attending a car mechanics training course organized by the Region, had undertaken an apprenticeship in a luxury car workshop. He was attending online courses of a renowned car manufacturer, with the hope of being accepted for an internship in the United Kingdom. Two other young degree holders had created their own business ventures. Enrico was 28 years old and a graduate in Economics; he began promoting events on behalf of several companies and decided to become self-employed by setting up a company to promote cultural events dedicated to young people. Cosimo, aged 27, with a degree in Communication Sciences, opened a recording studio for young artists by using his skills as a sound technician acquired by attending several courses whilst he was still a university student. What characterizes the initiatives of these young people was being original and distinguishing themselves in the activity that they carried out. In this way, they could be successful by combining professionalism and entrepreneurial ability.

12.7 Family

In the timespan of just over a decade, the employment perspectives of young people have worsened, whereas the family situation shows some openness towards greater independence of young people from their family of origin. The housing and family circumstances, observed in the young participants interviewed 10 years later, is the element of greater difference between the two samples. Among the participants in 2003, only one young 31-year-old woman lived alone, and another two participants had tried moving out of the family of origin to then return to live with their parents. None of the participants were married nor had children. Conversely, among the participants interviewed in 2013, 27 had moved out of the parental home. More specifically, 11 lived alone, 3 shared a house, 10 lived with their partner and 3 were married. None of them had children.

Among those still living with their parents, the desire to leave home was widespread, and they expressed the intention to do so as soon, as their employment situation would allow them to do so. Conversely, the young people interviewed in 2003 had imagined that they would leave home once they had achieved a certain level of stability in their personal and financial situation. Therefore, cohabitation with a partner (if not marriage) or a job opportunity in another city would have been the main reasons to achieve independent living.

> There are many difficulties to face… without a job and without money, I would bite off more than I could chew… the problem would be finding a regular job that would enable me to be financially independent and start living together… (Claudio, aged 20, accountant with a fixed-term contract, interviewed in 2003)

> I don't know if I'll leave my parents' house, I just don't like the thought of living alone… Unless something special occurs, like finding a job somewhere

> far away, I'm not going to live on my own. Perhaps I would go and live with a partner, so that I wouldn't be alone. (Roberto, aged 29, university degree, working under a fixed-term contract, interviewed in 2003)

The projections of a future family refer to a linear transition pattern where housing choices are subordinated to affective choices. Ten years later, the young participants appeared to be eager to leave the family of origin, and this was regardless of their employment or family situation:

> Even if I'm at ease at home, with Mum who does everything... I repeat, being independent is something I really like. Living alone is great. Perhaps I'll be little homesick... but I think I can cope. (Francesco, aged 20, apprentice hairdresser, interviewed in 2013)

> I've been living alone for four months, with a female roommate... After having lived in London, there you are independent, can do whatever you want... it triggered that desire to move out and live alone, and so as soon as the chance came up... thanks to the two jobs and anyhow finding a house I liked close to work. (Giovanna, aged 27, university degree, office worker, interviewed in 2013)

> About 6 months ago, due to me wanting to move into my own place, I moved to the suburbs, slightly outside Milan where the rent costs less. With my job I can get by, it's fixed-term, but up until now I've always had an income. (Ginevra, aged 30, university degree, interviewed in 2013)

As can be surmised from these accounts, being employed under a fixed-term contract did not necessarily enable participants to achieve independent living. For example, some participants were doing odd-jobs in the evenings or at the weekends, in addition to their day job, just so that they could manage to pay the rent.

The greater propensity towards achieving independent living could indicate a shift in the process of becoming adults. In general, leaving home could be perceived as an important step in becoming and feeling independent. However, Cicchelli and Merico (2007) have stressed that in the Italian case prolonging the stay with the family does not compromise the achievement of independence for young people, which also explains the high percentage of young people living with their parents. Although marriage and life as a couple retain their importance as a phase in the transition to adulthood, these stages are no longer portrayed as marking the transition to independent living. An emerging trend of new housing strategies has been observed, such as living with a roommate, living alone or with a partner, all of which were, until quite recently, a rarity among young Italians (Santoro, 2012). On the other hand, this multiplication of living arrangements can also be seen as a response to the difficulties faced by the younger generations in the labour market.

Up until a short time ago, postponing moving out of the parental home was tolerated because occupational instability was limited to the initial phases of entry into the labour market; the recent recession has rendered the route to full financial independence rather obstacle prone. Therefore, young people circumvent the obstacles represented by employment instability by opting for temporary and experimental living arrangements. Frequently, young Italians are also spurred towards these types of living arrangements due to the declining financial conditions of their parents, who can no longer manage to provide financial support to their children in purchasing a property, as was often the case in Italy (Santoro, 2015). To further illustrate this, it should be noted that among the interviewees who were employed, some declared that they gave a part of their salary (and in one case, in full) to their parents. In 2013, this custom was particularly widespread among young people from the lower social classes, although this was unheard of among the young participants from 2003, regardless of their social class of origin.

12.8 Conclusions

Over the course of the last 15 years in Italy, significant reforms in education and training have been implemented in Italy. They were intended to improve the educational levels of young generations and thus facilitate their entry into the labour market, implying that it was the lack of proper educational level if they were unemployed or underemployed. Indeed, the educational level of young Italians has improved during this period, just as the percentage of university graduates has increased. However, the labour market did not seem able to value and exploit this qualified human capital.

Young people with qualifications or a vocational degree who enter employment are often employed in lower-ranking roles, with scarce opportunities to improve their career prospects. Reflecting on the two pieces of research examined in this chapter, one can see how, despite the increase in training opportunities, the current young generations have lost faith in the usefulness of education, particularly in university education. Inversely, even if the increasingly widespread fixed-term employment contracts and lack of employment stability were perceived to be problematic, participants in the 2003 study still believed that university qualifications were important to be able to successfully deal with these uncertainties. This is an important orientation, which suggests a certain relation to wider society. A decade later, uncertainty is widely acknowledged to be the common situation in which all young people find themselves, regardless of the educational level attained, a situation that they can adapt to and within which they pursue their projects.

The young participants in 2003 appeared to be anchored to the concept of a linear and traditional transition, to be completed through marriage and parenthood. Even the participants in 2013 appeared inclined to this same route, or at least were not rejecting it. However, even though forming a family or entering a stable romantic relationship preserves its importance as a key milestone in life plans, young Italians interviewed in 2013 showed a marked propensity to undergo these events through a cohabitation period, seen as a temporary experiment. This also explains why, as mentioned before, the increase of this family form among young Italians has occurred in recent years (ISTAT, 2015; Santoro, 2015).

In this scenario, what kinds of pathways to transition then emerge after these socio-economic changes? The social class of origin and educational levels continue to be significant in determining the transition processes, above all in the period in which young people's conditions have worsened. Not only do the young participants coming from families in a high social class manage to achieve higher educational qualifications, but compared to the past, they also manage to complete the final stages of the transition in a shorter time frame. The prolongation of the educational phase is partially compensated by achieving independent living at an earlier stage, not necessarily accompanied by entry into their first union. Prior to the recession, young people with lower educational levels were able to complete a linear and swift transition due to their early entry into employment and, once they had achieved financial independence, to leave the parental home. Conversely, among the most-recent participants, those young people from working-class backgrounds and the lowest educational qualifications had the most tortuous trajectories and had to necessarily prolong their permanence in the family home. The occupational condition of the dropouts – early school-leavers who took training courses and were inserted in low-paid apprenticeships – were particularly vulnerable, and they did not always have the certainty of obtaining a stable job once their training ended.

The ways that the transition to adulthood is achieved depends to a great degree on the ability to adapt to environmental uncertainty. The adaptation process comprises putting into effect various strategies, one of which infers curbing expectations. This is an adaptive process that can also lead to putting ones' expectations aside to embrace or exploit opportunities unrelated to the educational level attained. For example, some graduates had accepted or were prepared to accept low skilled, low-paid jobs, which were unrelated to the university qualifications achieved in order to proceed with their transition. Others took on more than one job, as this seemed the only viable way to achieve financial independence. This curbing of expectations may have also contributed to many looking for opportunities abroad, following the example of friends and acquaintances who had emigrated. Emigration is seen as a viable solution for young people, as shown in a recent research on how 18-year-old young people imagined their future (Cuzzocrea, 2018). In the space of 5 years, the number of Italians who emigrated steadily grew, reaching the figure of 100,000 in 2015 (compared to 80,000 in 2013) (ISTAT, 2014c, 2016d), mainly concentrated in the 20–45 age span (Santoro, 2020). To conclude, some young people managed to modify their trajectories by means of innovative solutions. More specifically, they sidestepped the employment crisis by investing their skills in original and successful initiatives. The opportunity to fulfil these types of initiatives was often subordinated to the availability of family resources, channelled into the start-up of these business ventures. One participant, Virginia, was a prime example of such behaviour; thanks to being able to make use of family property, she was able to open her own dressmaking business.

The recession has accentuated the individualized approach to the transition to adulthood. If before the crisis young people still showed an adherence to a traditional transition model and the various phases were assumed to follow each other sequentially (finishing education, entering into the labour market, forming a first union, leaving the parental home), after the crisis not only has it become increasingly difficult to follow such a trajectory, but young people themselves have abandoned a *life plan* based on this model, signalling a shift in their aspirations. In this sense, it appears that young Italians are aware of the high improbability that they will benefit from the same (favourable) circumstances of previous generations, which led this model to prosper. For this very reason, they are forced to plan their lives within a context of greater constraints and fewer opportunities.

Note

1 The Italian educational and training system is organized in accordance to the principles of subsidiarity and autonomy of educational institutions. The State has exclusive legislative power for the 'general rules for education', while the Regions have exclusive legislative powers over vocational education and training. Law n. 53/2003 lays down the obligation for education and training for at least 12 years or until the achievement of at least a 3-year vocational qualification by the age of 18. This obligation can be fulfilled in three ways: in the 5-year secondary-school system (lyceums, vocational institutes and technical institutes) aimed at obtaining a diploma that allows access to university; in the 3- or 4-year regional educational and vocational training system aimed at obtaining a vocational qualification (level EQF3) or a vocational diploma (EQF4). Finally, usually the educational path also foresees the possibility to obtain an apprenticeship contract for youths aged between 15 and 19.

References

Billari, F.C. and Liefbroer, A.C. (2010). Towards a new pattern of transition to adulthood? *Advances in Life Course Research*, 15(2–3), 59–75.

Billari, F.C. and Wilson, C. (2001). Convergence towards diversity? Cohort dynamics in the transition to adulthood in contemporary, Western Europe. MPIDR Working Paper WP 2001-039, Max Planck Institute for Demographic Research, Rostock. Available at: http://www.demogr.mpg.de/papers/working/wp-2001-039.pdf.

Cavalli, A. and Galland, O. (eds) (1995). *Youth in Europe*. London: Pinter.

Cerea, S., Maestripieri, L. and Ranci, C. (2015). *Le azioni di social investment a Milano: Un'analisi del mismatch fra offerta qualificata e domanda del mercato e un bilancio delle misure per contrastarlo*. Milano: Camera di Commercio, Paper, available at: http://www.milomb.camcom.it/documents/10157/26557655/rapporto-Ranci-2015.pdf.

Cherlin, A.J., Scabini, E., and Rossi, G. (1997). Still in the nest: Delayed home leaving in Europe and the United States. *Journal of Family Issues*, 18(6), 572–575.

Cicchelli, V. and Merico, M. (2007). Le passage tardif à l'âge adulte des Italiens entre maintien du modèle traditionnel et individualisation des trajectoires biographiques. *Horizons stratégiques*, 4(2), 70–87.

Cuzzocrea, V. (2018). 'Rooted mobilities' in young people's narratives of the future: A peripheral case. *Current Sociology*, 66(7), 1106–1123.

Cuzzocrea, V. and Magaraggia, S. (2013). Challenging the inevitability of the threshold approach: Experiences of work and parenthood among young adults in Italy. In: Nicolas, A., Flaherty, I. and Crouch, M. (eds) *Trajectories in Time: Chronology, Age, and Visions of the Life-Course*. Oxford: Inter-Disciplinary Press.

Elzinga, C.H. and Liefbroer, A.C. (2007). De-standardization of family-life trajectories of young adults: A cross-national comparison using sequence analysis. *European Journal of Population*, 23(3–4), 225–250.

Eurofound. (2016). *Exploring the diversity of NEETs*. Luxembourg: Office for Official Publications of the European Communities.

European Commission. (2007). *Families and Transitions in Europe: FATE Final Report*. Luxembourg: Office for Official Publications of the European Communities.

European Commission. (2012). *EU Youth Report: 2012*. Luxembourg: Office for Official Publications of the European Communities.

Eurostat. (2010). 51 Million Young EU Adults Lived with their Parent(s) in 2008. *Statistics in Focus*, n. 50, Luxembourg: European Commission.

Eurostat. (2016a). *Eurostat Regional Yearbook 2016 Edition*. Luxembourg: Office for Official Publications of the European Communities.

Eurostat. (2016b). Education, employment, both or neither? What are young people doing in the EU? Patterns substantially change by age and over time. *Newsrelease*, n. 155, 11 August.

Fondazione Res. (2016). *Università in declino: Un'indagine sugli atenei da Nord a Sud*. Rome: Donzelli.

Furstenberg, F.F. (2008). Generational inheritance of children and youth in a changing world, ESF-LiU Conference: *The Transfer of Resources across Generations: Family, Income, Human Capital and Children's Wellbeing*, Vadstena, Sweden, 9–13 June.

Furstenberg, F.F. Jr. (2010). On a new schedule: Transitions to adulthood and family change. *The Future of Children*, 20(1), 67–87.

Holdsworth, C. and Morgan, D. (2005). *Transitions in Context: Leaving Home, Independence and Adulthood*. Maidenhead: Open University Press.

ISTAT. (2009). *Famiglia e soggetti sociali*. Rome: ISTAT.

ISTAT. (2014a). *Generazioni a confronto: come cambiano i percorsi verso la vita adulta*. Rome: ISTAT.

ISTAT. (2014b). *Rapporto annuale 2014: la situazione del Paese*. Rome: ISTAT.

ISTAT. (2014c). *Migrazioni internazionali e interne della popolazione residente. Anno 2013*. Statistiche report, Rome: ISTAT.

ISTAT. (2015). *Aspetti della vita quotidiana*. Rome: ISTAT.

ISTAT. (2016a). *Studenti e bacini universitari*. Rome: ISTAT.

ISTAT. (2016b). *I percorsi di studio e di lavoro dei diplomati e dei laureati*. Statistiche Report, 29 September, Rome: ISTAT.

ISTAT. (2016c). *Natalità e fecondità della popolazione residente: anno 2015*. Statistiche Report, 28 November, Rome: ISTAT.

ISTAT. (2016d). *Migrazioni internazionali e interne della popolazione residente. Anno 2015*. Statistiche report, Rome: ISTAT.

Kohli, M. (2007). The institutionalization of the life course: Looking back to look ahead. *Research in Human Development*, 4(3–4), 253–271.

Leccardi, C., Santoro, M. and Rusmini, G. (2004). *Families and Transitions in Europe – Italy National Report*. Working paper, Coleraine: University of Ulster.

Mauceri, S. and Valentini, A. (2010). The European delay in transition to parenthood: The Italian case. *International Review of Sociology*, 20(1), 111–142.

Modell, J., Furstenberg, F.F. Jr. and Hershberg, T. (1976). Social change and transitions to adulthood in historical perspective. *Journal of Family History*, 1(1), 7–32.

Murgia, A. and Poggio, B. (2014). At risk of deskilling and trapped by passion: A picture of precarious highly educated young workers in Italy, Spain and the United Kingdom. In: Antonucci, L., Hamilton, M. and Roberts, S. (eds) *Young People and Social Policy in Europe: Work and Welfare in Europe*. London: Palgrave Macmillan.

OECD. (2004). *Education at a Glance*. Paris: OECD.

OECD. (2018). *Education at a Glance*, Paris: OECD.

Santoro, M. (2012). *Le libere unioni in Italia*. Rome: Carocci.

Santoro, M. (2015). The meanings of cohabitation in 'low cohabitation land': The case of Italy. *Families, Relationships and Societies*, 4(1), 117–130.

Santoro, M. (2020). Italian youth and the experience of highly qualified migration to the United Kingdom. In: Cairns, D. (ed.) *The Palgrave Handbook of Youth Mobility*, London: Palgrave Macmillan (forthcoming).

Settersten, R.A. Jr. and Ray, B. (2010). What's going on with young people today? The long and twisting path to adulthood. *The Future of Children*, 20(1), 19–41.

Shanahan, M.J. (2000). Pathways to adulthood in changing societies: Variability and mechanisms in life course perspective. *Annual Review of Sociology*, 26(1), 667–692.

Afterword

Alessandro Cavalli

When I started studying Italian youth in the early 1960s, the question politicians, journalists and lay older people asked the researchers was: 'Why is it that so many young people do not care about politics and public life in general and are so deeply focused on the private sphere?' Still dependent upon their parents, but also looking to create their own family, they were willing to acquire first a television set and later, as soon as possible, a small Fiat 500. Apathy was the key word. Of course, young people were seen in contrast with the previous generation, who had been engaged in the individual and collective effort of rebuilding the country after the war. Somebody called the new male generation 'The three M generation': Mamma (mother), Macchina (car) and Moglie (wife). It was the generation of the so-called 'economic miracle', the first in the history of the nation state to enjoy (modest) well-being on a mass level.

The next generation was quite different. The experience of rapid and intense social change was grounds for the emergence of a new generation of young people who thought they could change society from the bottom up through collective action. Students and young workers were the main agents of a new season of social movements, which lasted at least until the late 1970s, when some fringes of these movements turned to terrorism and others were dispersed in the diaspora. A new wave of research accompanied the rise and fall of youth movements. Of course, only a minority of young people were active participants in the activities of such movements. However, even those who were not directly involved and only witnessed what was going on in schools and universities, but also in factories and on the streets, were somehow touched by the 'spirit' of the age, in which the significant transformation that was going on in society allowed one to think that radical change was possible and was just waiting around the corner.

If social movements fail to institutionalize, they are doomed soon or later to disappear; their success is not measured by the capacity to last but by the responses they evoke in the institutions they are attempting to change. In fact, their impact on higher educational institutions and on industrial relations has been quite substantial. However, in Italy this has been less so than elsewhere, such as France or Germany.

It was around the late 1970s and early 1980s that I started doing extensive research on the younger population, together with a bunch of colleagues, in which we undertook both quantitative surveys and qualitative inquiries. This also coincided with a rather long period during which young people no longer appeared to be active agents of change, and researchers spoke of rolling back to the private sphere. It was around this time that young people succeeded in negotiating larger spaces of autonomy, and parental authority declined. Though still economically dependent on their family, they no longer felt the need to leave home in order to acquire more freedom and experiment with new lifestyles. Experimentation was based on the feelings of security provided by a modernized and less autocratic family. One in three young adults still lived with his/her parents at the age of 30. The family could absorb and sustain prolonged education and delayed entry into the labour market. No political measures were taken to facilitate the transition to adulthood, and the traditional Italian (and largely South European) culture easily supported the prolonged presence of young males and (to a lesser extent) females in the family of origin. In fact, the size of the younger population was already slowly reducing because of the decline in birth rates, which had started in the mid-1960s.

This situation lasted until the second half of the first decade of the new millennium, when the financial and economic crisis broke out (when I reached retirement age and the IARD institute, which supported youth research for a quarter of a century, closed doors due to lack of financial resources). This book reports more recent research, which clearly documents how and why young people's situation in Italy during the last 10 to 15 years has worsened substantially. Unemployment's rates are almost the double for young people under 30 than for the adult population; young females' unemployment ranks still higher; young people are often employed in precarious jobs and more likely in the underground economy, without regular contracts and trade union's protection. Employment problems are much more dramatic in the southern regions, causing intensive waves of migrations to the north of the country, and to Northern Europe. Migrants are no longer poor illiterate peasants escaping hunger as in the past but highly educated men and women looking for better chances elsewhere. Poorer regions lose human capital, a crucial resource if you wish to initiate and support social and economic growth. Investment into education and research has been severely cut in the last 20 years due to budgetary difficulties, whereas cuts in retirement allowances encounter stronger political opposition, since the numbers of elderly voters increase whilst that of youngsters diminishes. To add a new element to this picture, it is young people who will eventually have to repay an enormous public debt accumulated through the financial system by the previous and present adult population. It is no wonder that young people are turning towards right-wing (but also left-wing) populist political movements. In the struggle between generations, young people are quite often on the losing side.

These are the themes present-day youth research investigates. The Italian panorama can be taken consciously as an example also for other countries in

Southern Europe. Not only does the distance from Northern Europe grow but will grow even more in the future, unless a new political awareness arises. In any case, there are enough good reasons to be preoccupied when asking the embarrassing question: 'What kind of adults will the present-day youths become, whose ideal and materials interests are so conspicuously ignored by the adult ruling classes of the present?'

Ken Roberts

Throughout the twentieth century and into the twenty-first century, Europe's youth researchers routinely contrasted the life stage in northern and southern countries (e.g. Couppie and Mansuy, 1998; Galland, 1995; Covizzi, 2008). The south remained economically backward throughout the north's '30 glorious years' that followed the Second World War. In Greece, Italy, Spain and Portugal, substantial proportions of the populations lived in rural villages. Early school-leaving (in early teens and sometimes before) remained common. Industrialization had arrived late in the south, and had been confined to specific regions of the countries, in Italy in the north and central regions. The countries did not develop strong and broad apprenticeship and other systems of vocational education and training. However, the southern countries had some of the continent's highest participation rates in higher education. This was explained in terms of the inherent prestige of university education, and secondary-school graduates having nowhere else to go. An outcome, which persists to the present day, has been high unemployment rates among university graduates (see Bernadi, 2003). This is a very old problem in Italy. Since the late-nineteenth century, there has been a balance between the labour market demand and the supply of university graduates only between 1951 and 1963 (Barbagli, 1982). The growth of strong welfare states in northern countries following the Second World War was not replicated in the south. Thus, in Italy, state welfare has offered little to young single people. The family has remained their welfare institution of first resort. Hence, young people have continued to live with their parents and have delayed marriage and parenthood for longer than their North European counterparts. The support of families means that young people can accept non-standard, precarious, low-paid jobs, or otherwise tolerate long periods of unemployment. The different parts of this 'southern model' of youth transitions have intermeshed into a sustainable alternative to the life stage as performed in the north of the continent.

However, during the twenty-first century, there have been signs of north–south differences narrowing (Moreno and Mari-Klose, 2013), and researchers have offered more nuanced dissections of the remaining differences (Cuzzocrea, 2011). There is plentiful evidence in the preceding chapters of Italy's youth remaining distinctively southern, but also of convergences. All European countries have been affected by the multiple dimensions of globalization and the latest wave of digital technologies. Whether industrialization happened early or late, labour markets have undergone deindustrialization. Employment is now overwhelmingly in services where the occupations may be high-salary professional jobs, or low-paid precarious work in the new gig economies. All European economies were jolted by the banking crisis of 2007–2009 and experienced subsequent recessions. Young people were invariably hit hardest. Large proportions of labour-market entrants throughout Europe have found themselves stuck in precarious work with no clear routes upwards (Standing, 2011). Young people's welfare rights have been reduced in most countries. Housing costs have risen throughout Europe. Thus, where relatively early independent living was most common, more young people are now remaining in their parents' homes until their late twenties and beyond.

Yet throughout Europe there has also been a countertrend towards young people moving away from their home places. Italy draws migrants from Albania and other poorer countries to its east, and also from North Africa. Young Italians continue to move from the south into their country's central and northern regions. There is another flow, further towards and into North Europe. Some intra-Europe youth migration is supported by *Erasmus* and other European Union (EU) programmes. As a result, previous chapters have been able to present examples of young Italians leaving their parents' homes in their late teens or early twenties, living singly or in shared housing, sometimes cohabiting with a sexually intimate partner with no immediate plans to marry. Young people who move abroad become part of a new generation of cosmopolitan young Europeans (Beck, 2000). Those who feel 'left behind' may express their frustrations in support for revived nationalist politics.

Its southern states are no longer the EU's poorest countries. These states are now part of a new majority of peripheral (economically) member states in an enlarged EU. Monetary union, to be followed inevitably by fiscal union, may ameliorate or could consolidate existing inequalities. Italy is now economically handicapped *vis-à-vis* some newer EU member states, regions of which have become integrated economically into an outer-Germany. Despite being a founder member of what is now the EU, and despite benefitting from decades of 'solidarity' measures, Italy's south still lags behind the north, and Italy lags behind other founder member states economically. Hence, the persistent differences, alongside the convergences, in the life chances of young Italians compared with their northern counterparts.

The convergences mean that many chapters in this book could be about young people in any European country. This applies to the contributions on individualization and reflexivity, and their compatibility with the reproduction of social-class divisions. It also applies to the chapters on youth and politics. Everywhere Europe's young people have disengaged from older political parties, and they are not becoming loyal members or voters on which new parties can rely. Young people are participating in new ways, specifically online. They can be mobilized in outbursts of corporeal activity, sometimes in elections, but more often in demonstrations, buycotts and boycotts, around specific issues. These outbursts surge, then fade away as rapidly.

It will be of wider interest that youthful political orientations in Italy now embrace all age groups up to 45. Similarly, young Italians are spending longer in non-standard jobs. They may be an extreme case, or Europe's trailblazers. We learn that the average age of Italian academics gaining their first tenured posts is now 40, and applications are received from individuals aged up to 50. In the EU labour force data, youth is now defined as ages 20–34. It is possible that hitherto youthful features of working lives and political participation will prove to be cohort effects, carried by today's youth into older age groups. Italy and the rest of Europe should be worried.

In one way, this book is a welcome throwback (another example is Checchi and Lucifora, 2004). International conferences once had scholars explaining their own countries to one another. Then the European Commission began to fund multi-partner, multi-country projects, usually based primarily on quantitative data. Researchers have sometimes pooled their data sets, then generalized about all the countries, or they have divided the countries into types. This book is by Italians, and it is about Italian youth, but the authors are addressing an international audience. Despite globalization and even more intense Europeanization, the single country remains the ideal unit for sociological examination, and a country's own scholars are always uniquely equipped to interpret quantitative and qualitative evidence from their own people. This Italian book will assist researchers from elsewhere in understanding how and why their own countries are similar to Italy in some respects, and otherwise different.

References

Barbagli, M. (1982). *Educating for Unemployment*. New York: Columbia University Press.

Beck, U. (2000). The cosmopolitan perspective: Sociology of the second age of modernity. *British Journal of Sociology*, 51, 79–106.

Bernadi, F. (2003). Returns to educational performance at entry into the Italian labour market. *European Sociological Review*, 19, 25–40.

Checchi, D. and Lucifora, C. (eds) (2004). *Education, Training and Labour Market Outcomes in Europe*. Basingstoke: Palgrave Macmillan.

Couppie, T. and Mansuy, M. (1998). *The Characteristics of Youth Employment in Europe: A Typology Based on Labour Force Surveys*, paper presented to Annual Workshop of the European Network on Transitions in Youth, Edinburgh.

Covizzi, H. (2008). First-time job seekers versus unemployed with previous work experience: Impact of individual, familial and institutional factors on unemployment durations in Italy. *European Societies*, 10, 711–735.

Cuzzocrea, V. (2011). Squeezing or blurring: Young adulthood in the career strategies of professionals based in Italy and England. *Journal of Youth Studies*, 14, 657–674.

Galland, O. (1995). Introduction: What is youth? In: Cavalli, A. and Galland, O. (eds) *Youth in Europe*, London: Pinter, 1–16.

Moreno, L. and Mari-Klose, P. (2013). Youth, family change and welfare arrangements: Is the South still different? *European Societies*, 15, 493–513.

Standing, G. (2011). *The Precariat: The New Dangerous Class*. London: Bloomsbury Academic.

Index